The Man Who Thought He Was Napoleon

The Man Who Thought He Was Napoleon

Toward a Political History of Madness

LAURE MURAT

TRANSLATED BY DEKE DUSINBERRE

WITH A FOREWORD BY DAVID A. BELL

The University of Chicago Press Chicago and London

LAURE MURAT is professor of French and Francophone studies at the University of California, Los Angeles.
DEKE DUSINBERRE is a freelance writer and translator.

The University of Chicago Press, Chicago 60637
The University of Chicago Press, Ltd., London

Printed in the United States of America

23 22 21 20 19 18 17 16 15 14   1 2 3 4 5

ISBN-13: 978-0-226-02573-5 (cloth)
ISBN-13: 978-0-226-02587-2 (e-book)
DOI: 10.7208/chicago/9780226025872.001.0001

Avec le soutien du

This work, published as part of a program providing publication assistance, received financial support from the French Ministry of Foreign Affairs, the Cultural Services of the French Embassy in the United States, and FACE (French American Cultural Exchange).
French Voices logo designed by Serge Bloch.

Cet ouvrage a bénéficié du soutien des Programmes d'aide à la publication de l'Institut Français. This work, published as part of a program of aid for publication, received support from the Institut Français.

Library of Congress Cataloging-in-Publication Data
Murat, Laure, author.
[Homme qui se prenait pour Napoléon. [English]
The man who thought he was Napoleon : toward a political history of madness / Laure Murat ; translated by Deke Dusinberre ; with a foreword by David A. Bell.
pages cm
"Originally published as L'homme que se prenait pour Napoléon : pour une histoire politique de la folie. © Copyright Éditions Gallimard, 2011"—Title page verso.
Includes bibliographical references and index.
ISBN 978-0-226-02573-5 (cloth : alkaline paper)— ISBN 978-0-226-02587-2 (e-book)
1. Projective identification—France—History. 2. Mentally ill—France—History. 3. Mental illness—France—History. I. Dusinberre, Deke, translator. II. Bell, David Avrom, writer of preface. III. Title.
RC455.4.P76M8713 2014
616.8900944—dc23

2014006514

⊗ This paper meets the requirements of ANSI/NISO Z39.48-1992 (Permanence of Paper).

To Amédée Germain Grêslon, a fourteen-year-old lover of travel books who was admitted to the asylum of Charenton on August 9, 1826. "In his ravings he wants to buy a horse and leave immediately to defend the Greeks. If it is objected that he is too young, incompetent, etc., he replies that he feels capable of such great things that all other minds will side with him. He wants to go discover unknown lands."

Those who hide their mad, die unspoken.

HENRI MICHAUX, *Face aux verrous*

Contents

Foreword

DAVID A. BELL

A man who claimed that after he had been guillotined, the wrong head had been attached to his body. A woman who claimed the poet Lamartine was a messenger from God. Many men, and even a stray woman, who all claimed to be the emperor Napoleon. What, it might be asked, could these deluded souls, inmates of nineteenth-century French insane asylums, possibly tell us about the great political events of modern French history?

As Laure Murat explains in the pages that follow, the answer is quite a lot. This remarkable study of the historical relation between madness and politics reminds us that the two have much more to do with each other than we would like to admit. History overflows with political figures who probably deserved clinical diagnoses (including, quite possibly, the emperor Napoleon). Alexis de Tocqueville once confessed to having "thought that in revolutions, especially democratic revolutions . . . genuine madmen have played a very considerable part." It is all too easy to confuse the borders of one's own particular political beliefs with the borders of sanity, as the leaders of the Soviet Union so horribly illustrated by imprisoning political dissidents in insane asylums.

At the same time, the form madness takes—and the ways society deals with it—reveals a great deal about prevailing ideas, anxieties, and preoccupations. Murat found that during the "July Monarchy" (1830–48), when a favorite pastime of French writers was to lament lost national glory, 25 percent of patients admitted to asylums were diagnosed with "delusions of grandeur." In the turbulent decades that followed the revolutions of 1848, psychiatrists across Europe composed learned treatises on the *morbus democraticus*—the "democratic disease." Already in 1818, the psychiatrist Jean-Étienne-Dominique

Esquirol wrote the following remarkable lines: "I could give the history of our revolution . . . from that of certain insane persons whose insanity connects itself with the events which have [so marked] this long period of our history." He never followed through on the speculation, but Laure Murat has taken up the challenge. "What," she asks, "does madness make of history?"

As Murat recognizes, following Michel Foucault, a history of madness is also necessarily a history of psychiatry. In France, the shifting relation between madness and politics reflected at every step the transformations of psychiatric medicine, especially during the period of the French Revolution. It was the Revolution in 1790 that put an end to the practice by which families could request royal arrest warrants (*lettres de cachet*) to incarcerate allegedly insane relatives. Three years later the psychiatrist Philippe Pinel, a pioneer of "humane" methods for treating insanity, took over what he envisaged as the first modern mental hospital: Bicêtre, just south of Paris. Yet even as he did so, the Reign of Terror was beginning, and over the next months and years he himself would list "events connected to the Revolution" as a leading cause of his patients' disorders. Murat nicely comments: "The French Revolution invented modern madness—or at least laid the foundations for its administrative organization and medical treatment—and simultaneously acknowledged itself to be the very source of that scourge."

Murat takes her story from this revolutionary moment, through the merry-go-round of regimes that succeeded each other in France during the nineteenth century, down to the foundation of the Third Republic in the 1870s, following the horrors of the Paris Commune. Even as she learnedly traces the way the sources of madness seemed to reflect the shifting political conditions, she also shows how politics shaped doctors' approaches to patients. In the era of Robespierre, doctors hoping to curb their patients' willfulness tried to subject them to what Pinel chillingly called "a formidable show of terror." Decades later, a disciple of Esquirol remarked that since madness had its origins in extremes of individualism, proper treatment required "the very principles of communism."

Laure Murat's book emerged out of a long, patient immersion in the archives. She spent years reading through the voluminous, dry registers of the principal Parisian mental hospitals, hunting the telling details that reveal how the institutions functioned, how their doctors and patients interacted, and how the foaming waves of political change crashed against their forbidding walls—and sometimes poured through their doors. It was a labor of love, and indeed Murat casts the archives themselves as an object of desire. The research left her exquisitely sensitive to the plight of the men and women who found themselves institutionalized—including, for many years at the asylum of Charenton, no less illustrious a "madman" than the marquis de Sade. It left her critical of the psychiatrists, but nonetheless more appreciative of their efforts and intentions than Foucault, who famously stigmatized them as agents of modern forms of repression. In a heartfelt and deeply dispiriting coda to this book, Murat speculates that the "antipsychiatry" closely associated with Foucault has, in practice, combined insidiously with free-market ideology and the move toward purely pharmaceutical treatment of mental illness to leave the patients worse off than ever.

Finally, Murat's research has left her brilliantly aware of the ironies that course through her story. On the nineteenth century's most common form of delusion, she writes: "A man who thought he was Napoleon was . . . usurping the identity of a usurper, not to mention that, as a monomaniac, he imitated a monarch who was himself said to suffer from delusions of grandeur."

Simon Leys, in his 1986 novella *The Death of Napoleon*, imagined that after Napoleon's defeat at Waterloo the emperor of the French escaped from his British captors and made his way back to Paris, where he was unable to convince anyone of his identity. At one point the character even visits an asylum and comes face to face with several self-proclaimed Napoleons who seem even more Napoleonic than he is. A woman he becomes close to treats him as a sweetly delusional lunatic. But how to determine who is truly mad and who is truly sane? The answer is not always obvious. In 1812, even as Napoleon's most grandiose adventure was coming to grief in the snows of Russia, a general named Claude-François de Malet attempted a coup d'état in Paris. It failed, and Malet, whom the regime had previously confined in a medical facility, was widely condemned as a madman. Yet at his trial Malet responded with what Murat rightly calls a "superb retort" when asked to name his fellow conspirators: "You yourself, Sir, and all of France—had I but succeeded."

Translator's Preface

Translating Laure Murat's *L'homme qui se prenait pour Napoléon* proved to be a delight and a challenge. Her exploration of madness and society, inspired by the work of Michel Foucault, is recounted in clear prose accessible to general readers as well as academic specialists. Murat's personal, sometimes playful approach to language also surfaces here and there: her stroll through the archives is preceded by a preamble and followed by a "postamble," her scholarly tone is periodically leavened by comments in the first person, and her occasionally inventive syntax lends relief to the text even as it keeps this translator on his toes.

Perhaps the trickiest challenge involved the strange question she poses at the outset: Comment délire-t-on l'Histoire? It might be rendered rather literally as "How do people rave about history?" or, more poetically, as "How is history deluded?" Yet in a nod to Foucault and in consultation with the author, I ultimately opted for a bolder formulation of the underlying idea: "What does madness make of history?"

Deke Dusinberre

Preamble

Every essay begins with a question that encapsulates it, serving as both beacon and thread, as frame of reference and guiding principle. As vague and absurd as it may initially sound, my query was, What does madness make of history?[1] This question arose from the time I spent in psychiatric archives and libraries, where one day I came across the case of a young man who thought he was Napoleon's son. Dr. Guillaume Ferrus, a physician with Napoleon's army who later worked at the Bicêtre asylum, cured the young man by pretending to enter into his madness. It is said that every madman thinks he's Napoleon—or Napoleon's son, it would seem. But is this Napoleonic delusion verified by asylum records? And if so, what might that tell us about the relationship between history and mental disorders? Very soon my initial question broadened into other issues. How might historical events affect madness? To what extent and in what forms does politics provide material for insanity? Can the role of revolution or regime change be assessed by studying the development of the discourse on madness? What social and political anxieties are embodied by delusions?

To answer—or at least shed light on—these questions, I had to go back to original sources. I had to analyze hospital admission records and diagnoses, taking up medical files one by one, examining clinical practice. For three years I explored the archives. *The Man Who Thought He Was Napoleon* is the product of that investigation.

"The influence of our political misfortunes has been so great," wrote Dr. Étienne Esquirol in 1816, "that I could give the history of our revolution from the taking of the Bastille to the last appearance of Bonaparte from that of certain insane persons whose insanity connects itself with the events which have [so marked] this long period of our history."[2] Esquirol never carried out his fine plan to write a history of France deduced—or traced—from delusions, establishing an "other scene" that would recraft the national narrative in its own way. Perhaps it was never really feasible. Whatever the case, it is worth mentioning another project conducted a century later by Charlotte Beradt, who collected some three hundred accounts of dreams by men and women in Berlin between 1933 and 1939, producing a veritable "seismograph" of the ravages of Nazism and its "abuse of souls" even in their sleep. Beradt's book, *The Third Reich of Dreams*, was conceived as an act of resistance and represents the first and most literal illustration of what is usually described metaphorically as the "nightmare of history."[3]

Madness has perhaps as much to teach us as dreams, to which it is secretly related. Frantz Fanon's analyses of the "reactive" psychoses of patients who were victims of colonial violence in Algeria,[4] like accounts by Françoise Davoine and Jean-Max Gaudillère of "the madness of wars," provide practitioners' detailed responses to this issue.[5] Cathy Caruth's development of a "theory of trauma" from a rereading of Freud and Lacan has also powerfully contributed to the previously overlooked field of the verbalization of suffering, whose mysteries have long been explored in literature ranging from Balzac's short story "Adieu" to Orwell's *1984* via Kafka.[6] Although the causes of madness can never be reduced to an isolated event, including political trauma, history clearly plays a role in the etiology of delusions. But which role?

"What is delirium?" asked Gilles Deleuze and Félix Guattari in *Anti-Oedipus*. "It is the unconscious occupation of a historical and social field. Out of delusions come races, continents, and cultures."[7] One might argue that such delusion is the most widely shared thing in the world, more than common sense. What, indeed, is delirium if not the unconscious grip on individuals of war, massacres, violence, and economic horror? Where did delusion lie in 1851 when Dr. Samuel A. Cartwright coined "drapetomania," a term forged from the Greek *drapetes* (runaway) and *mania* (madness) to stigmatize the "illness" of black slaves in the southern United States who fled servitude? And where was delusion when Soviet doctors replaced the word "dissidence" with "chronic paranoia"?[8] Not coincidentally, the Argentine junta gave the nickname "madwomen of Plaza de Mayo" to the mothers who gathered each week in that Buenos Aires plaza to protest the kidnapping and dis-

appearance of their children, devoured by dictatorship. Can the history of madness seriously avoid taking into account the madness of history?

In 1820 Esquirol indirectly returned to the idea of his unfulfilled project when he explained, "At that epoch, when [Napoleon] peopled Europe with new kings, there were in France many monomaniacs who thought themselves emperors or kings, empresses or queens. The Spanish war, conscription, and our conquests and reverses also produced their mental maladies. How many persons, stricken with terror at the time of the two invasions, remained monomaniacs! Indeed, we now find in madhouses many persons who consider themselves dauphins of France, and destined to the throne."[9] What could be less surprising, in the end, than to discover a concomitance between the upheavals of a changing society and people's minds, indeed a homothetic relationship between events and delusions? It is easy to see that the spectacle of the guillotine, for example, made people lose their heads in many respects, momentarily driving Terror-gripped minds insane. Philippe Pinel himself, a pioneer of French psychiatry who was open to new ideas, identified the leading cause of mental illness as "events connected with the Revolution," which allegedly provoked a veritable epidemic of madness.[10] Similarly, when Napoleon's remains were brought back to France, an event orchestrated during the reign of Louis-Philippe, the head physician at Bicêtre noted the arrival in his asylum of fourteen new "emperors." But what are the stages of an intellectual construction of madness and its relation to political history, from an analysis of the triggering event to the elaboration of a "revolutionary neurosis" or a new "monomania" called "delusions of grandeur," applied to people who take themselves for monarchs? How were these highly varied convergences experienced, analyzed, and then—above all—interpreted? Indeed, beyond the simple observation of history's impact on its players, witnesses, and victims, the real issue resides in the resulting discourse and the nineteenth century's constantly swelling commentaries on the relationship between political opinion and mental disorder. The line is often fine between the enemy of Bonapartism and the monomaniac who dreams of an imperial destiny (hand in his vest and eyes fixed on the horizon), between the rebel and the madman whose anarchist fury must be constrained by a straitjacket, between the Commune's female arsonists and women who are hysterical. Are the insane essentially dissenters? Or is it the dissenter who is always

considered insane? Since the situation is obviously not so simple, my quest became complicated: What does madness *make* of history, and how, in turn, were nosologies contrived or discarded as a function of change in regime? Where did psychiatrists, and consequently a society that listened to these new *experts*, draw the line between political passion and its morbid exaggeration, between personal convictions and maniacal excesses? And how should we interpret the shifting, variable nature of that line over time? In other words, how was the discourse between ideology and pathology elaborated and articulated in the nineteenth century?

Deconstructing the scientific and mental logos at work means first of all weighing its exact terms and structure in light of a corpus of theory that became increasingly dense as psychiatry established itself as an autonomous field. It also means studying discrepancies, manipulations, and oversimplifications—for example, the feminist Anne-Josèphe Théroigne de Méricourt, who was treated by a famous liberal Catholic doctor who hastened, after the fact, to ascribe her very real melancholy *to* her revolutionary commitment. And it also means identifying abuses and offshoots—for example, a new mental illness described with great earnestness after the revolutionary events of 1848 as *morbus democraticus* ("democratic disease"), which Charles Maurras would invoke in the early twentieth century in his counterrevolutionary movement, Action Française.

This overlapping tale of the evolution of psychiatry and political history, linked to what ethnopsychiatry eloquently labels the "theory of political emotions," inevitably triggers renewed debate over the *healthy* limits of freedom of expression, whether public or private, communitarian or individual, just as it occasionally sheds light on the notion of the collective unconscious. Whether they were dissidents reduced to silence or, on the contrary, individuals who carved out their own realm of expression, mad people—or rather the allegorical figure they incarnated—perhaps ultimately served as a focus of the anxieties and setbacks of the revolutionary nineteenth century.

* * *

On their own, these questions indicate the scope of a subject whose history and geography—both being theoretically borderless—need first of all to be circumscribed. The decision to take Paris as the epicenter,

and 1789 to 1871 as the period, reflected obvious historical considerations. Between the Revolution and the Commune, France underwent at least four revolutions; yet each one was usurped, reflecting the long death throes of the monarchy alongside the painful birth and constantly postponed emergence of a republic. Now, in a nation as centralized as France, it was in the capital city that the main political decisions were taken, where the most influential events occurred, and where, too, there were three specialized institutions to which most mental patients were sent: Charenton, Bicêtre, and La Salpêtrière, joined, after 1867, by the hospital of Sainte-Anne.[11]

It was during this period punctuated by insurrections and returns to order that psychiatry enjoyed its golden age and extended its power. Its official birth coincided with the Revolution and the abolition of arbitrary imprisonment (*lettres de cachet*), leading to a medicalization of mental illness; the collapse of the Second Empire marked the apogee of the great period of asylums just before their approaching decline. Between those two dates a strange chapter in the history of psychiatry was written. This new science, which struggled vigorously to assert itself, notably with respect to the legislative, judicial, and religious authorities, was simultaneously stigmatized by a kind of clinical impotence. Indeed, what treatment could it offer for the ills of people of the day? Neither hellebore, nor showers, nor bloodletting or other purgatives ever brought anyone back to reason. Doctors themselves steadily recognized this sad fact, obliged as they were to study the ridiculous number of cures over a century when the number of ill patients grew tenfold, from five thousand to fifty thousand. Psychoanalysis did not yet exist, nor did penicillin, which would have emptied asylums of the many patients struck in the final stages of venereal disease with general paresis (meningoencephalitis); nor did neuroleptics, electroencephalograms, or magnetic resonance imaging exist. Deprived of all that, psychiatry could only institutionalize, categorize, compartmentalize, theorize, prescribe. It isolated symptoms and patients; it administered, managed, and elaborated a health policy. How did this policy, which had to walk the thin line of powerful rhetoric, confront and deal with history? What impact did it have on clinical practice?

No one has better revealed and analyzed the development and stakes behind the terrific nineteenth-century expansion of the French psychiatric corporation than Jan Goldstein in *Console and Classify*.[12] The field

FIGURE 1. French school, *Gyrators*. Engraving from Joseph Guislain's *Traité sur l'aliénation mentale et sur les hospices des aliénés*, vol. 1, pl. V (1826). The spinning motion of "circulating swings" and "gyrators" was supposed to trigger a "vago-tonic" shock, employing one form of mental instability to cure another. Primarily used in Belgium and Germany, this "therapeutic" technique was abandoned in the latter half of the nineteenth century. Photograph © BIU Santé, Paris.

was young, and to impose itself as a specialty in the social landscape it had to do battle on all fronts: overtake the competition of religion (by taking over the monopoly of madness formerly entrusted to the confessor and the charitable orders); win recognition of its judicial necessity (by creating the "scientific" concept of "monomaniacal homicide," which only psychiatric specialists could diagnose, thereby justifying their role); and confirm the superiority of its "philosophical camp," that is to say, a physiological materialism that located madness in bodily organs, thereby promoting anatomical pathology over mind-based psychology. This victorious campaign culminated in a notorious 1838 law on mental illness that would remain in force in France until 1990.[13] The new law embodied the entire issue of madness and its relation to government. It required that each administrative *département* establish its own specialized asylum, withdrawing madness from general hospitals; it defined how placement would be made; it also required that every admission be accompanied by a medical certificate; and it placed all establishments—public, private, and religious—under the authority of the Ministry of the Interior. Asylums, henceforth perceived as a means of controlling the dangerous classes, were based on a doctrine of isolation that "gave ringing medical-scientific support to the government's concern with police."[14]

One man was at the heart of this battle, this system: Étienne Esquirol, a doctor who was part of the liberal trend. He was himself a favorite student of Philippe Pinel, the legendary liberator of the mentally ill who embraced the new thinking and was appointed to the Bicêtre asylum during the Terror. None of these details are gratuitous—few jobs were as politicized as psychiatric posts. Some physicians occupied multiple posts, for example, Étienne Pariset, who was the official newspaper censor during the Bourbon restoration as well as a doctor at La Salpêtrière, and Ulysse Trélat, who succeeded Pariset at La Salpêtrière (subsequent to membership in the anti-Bourbon "La Charbonnerie" movement) and was briefly minister of public works during the Second Republic. Following the Orléanist overthrow of the Bourbon monarchy in 1830, the director of the insane asylum in Rouen, who had followed Louis XVIII into exile in Ghent in 1815, was sacked. He was replaced by Lucien Debouteville, whose file—now in the Archives Nationales—explicitly mentions that he participated, with his mother, in the July 31 march on Paris that toppled the Bourbons.[15] At Esquirol's

FIGURE 2. Auguste Pichon, *Portrait of Étienne Esquirol* (nineteenth century). Oil on canvas. Étienne Esquirol, a pioneer of clinical psychiatry who became the director of the Charenton asylum, posed for Pichon beneath a bust of his mentor, Philippe Pinel. Esquirol largely inspired the 1838 French law on mental illness that would govern conditions of internment up to 1990. Photograph © Bibliothèque de l'Académie Nationale de Médecine, Paris.

death in 1840, the directorship of Charenton, highly coveted by the very conservative Alexandre Brierre de Boismont, ultimately went to the Orléanist supporter Achille Foville—who lost his job in 1848 when Louis-Philippe d'Orléans was forced to abdicate. And so it went.

Psychiatry was a machine—including a political machine. Mental illness, that barometer of nations, was used as a tool of measurement by the incumbent authorities. "This malady associates the physician in some manner with the public administration," wrote Esquirol. "The physician enlightens the government about mental tendencies (*la tendence des esprits*); his familiarity with the cause and character

of regnant madnesses furnishes [the government] with the most certain (*positifs*) elements of a moral statistics of the population."[16] This illuminating insight is a useful reminder that psychiatry incorporated what Robert Castel calls "the state apparatus."

How do lunatics fit into this framework? And what do they have to say? Is it possible to detect, in the joint murmur of patient and doctor, or rather beneath the official discourse of psychiatrists—those scribes of insanity—the potential political discourse of the mad? We know that psychiatry is a political field, but what does madness have to say about politics?

* * *

Those are the questions this book seeks to address, if not to answer. It has been constructed—indeed, conceived—from a vast, fragile, shifting source that has been my unremitting passion for the past twenty years: archives. I have handled all kinds of archives in those two decades. From contracts stored in the Minutier Central des Notaires to letters by the likes of Alexandre Dumas, André Gide, and Gertrude Stein, to bookstore ledgers, police files on seditious pederasts and reports on prostitutes, to political correspondence, prison registers, private diaries, telegrams, charters, and administrative reports. Archives have brought me immense joys as well as trivial ones; they have convinced me I'd acquired hard-won trophies when, incredulous, I discovered documents such as the diagnosis of Guy de Maupassant during his final months or the report by a police commissioner who encountered, in a bordello for homosexuals, a hapless "Proust, Marcel, aged 46, of independent means, residing at 102 Boulevard Haussmann."[17]

Within this endlessly varied and vibrant museum I have a notable weakness for medical archives, especially psychiatric archives. They are the driest and the least appealing—curt and mechanical, they open up only after laborious decipherment. The documents slumbering in often empty libraries—registers of asylums and clinics (pointedly called "law books," or *livres de la loi* in French),[18] files of medical observations, and mandatory two-week assessments—add up to a considerable mass of histories as fragile as they are crucial. Such documents are often daunting, since they are hard to read not just because of the handwriting but also because of technical or ambiguous meanings. But they all relate to a timeless enigma—mental illness—and

the daily lives of people conventionally known as the "insane." It is a world of its own, one very difficult to decipher, in which two sorts of rhetorical delusion clash: that of a person who raves—the madman—and that of another who records—the psychiatrist.

Several years ago a new literary review featured a column devoted to various archive collections around the world. The column was wittily titled "Aux Fonds."[19] This clever pun on the expression *au fond* (in fact, basically, "at bottom") and the term for archive collections, *fonds*, suggests that archives indeed allow us to get to the bottom of things. But there is a paradox: the tenuous, laconic nature of the information in this case (date, name, diagnosis), in all its dryness, prompts endless speculation and limitless reverie, opening onto a multitude of possibilities and situations. In the fibers of these dead, forgotten papers, inside the sticky folders and damp-infested ledgers that are slowly but surely crumbling and decomposing, there proliferates endless life; under the dust teem tragedies, funny incidents, entire lives, summed up in a handful of words scribbled in the performance of a function—psychiatry—thought not to concern itself with literature. Yet every comma, every crossed-out word counts. The blanks are surprisingly eloquent, the margins are chatty. This emaciated landscape is in fact a teeming tableau. An archive reads just like its alleged antithesis, a novel.

There is a "hysterical" tradition when it comes to archives, dating back to the moment when historian Jules Michelet first entered the realm of bundled documents. There he saw a world resurrected before his eyes as armies arose and men and women crawled out of the folders; in his moonstruck vision, Michelet was gripped by "the galvanic dance of archives."[20] This hysteria continued, in a way, with the Annales school of history, which asked archives to transcend their preferential claim to "constructive information" to become "poems, paintings, plays—our own records, our witnesses of living history, replete with ideas and latent action."[21] The Annales school agreed with Michelet that archives could contribute to "the complete resurrection of life."[22] This hysteria culminated with Michel Foucault, whose distinct talent for "dramatizing archives"[23] and whose Hugo-like prose were linked—stylistically at least—to the nineteenth century, that most lyrical and "most retrospective of centuries."[24] This use of archives in a poetic vein is a very French tradition, inextricably linked

to "literature" or, if you prefer, to the simultaneously hypnotic and revealing power of language, which imprisons and liberates historical meaning in the same gesture, as a loom weaves its fabric, by crossing the warp of documents with the weft of words, in which selection and arrangement—in other words, style—determine the transfer of knowledge, the transmission of a sensibility.

If I stress the poetic aspect of archives, that is because it dictated the methodology of this study along with, perhaps, its limitations. That methodology can be summed up succinctly: start with the archives alone, then hew from the mass an outline dictated solely by the documents. Armed with a single question—What does madness make of history?—lacking any preestablished plan or gloss, I went through hundreds of ledgers and folders. One might object that starting with the archive as a source that is not unique but *primal*, coming to it with fresh eyes (eyes almost untainted by written commentaries) meant taking things backward, depriving myself of the introductory, hermeneutic lessons of printed sources designed to stake out the terrain. And it also meant running the serious risk of discovering things that were already known, already published. Well versed in the problematics of inversion, however, I fully acknowledge and defend my decision.

Nothing, indeed, can replace the immediate grasp of *primary* information, whose sensual power, however dangerous it may be, imparts an overall perception and direction to the brain. When I read, with no prior baggage or filter, comments such as "she saw the sun fall at her feet"[25] or "I ask him if he's unwell, he says, 'from love,'"[26] I acquire a sharp, unique, irreplaceable awareness along with an imago of life in the asylum. Faced with a raw document, only the effect experienced on reading it—unease, puzzlement, jubilation—guided my selection of quotations (a selection of sounds, in short), for the necessary and sufficient reason that they struck me as significant (assuming I can explain why, of course). That the psychiatrist used direct description ("she saw the sun fall at her feet") rather than "she *thought or imagined* that the sun had fallen at her feet" (which would have been more logical), suggests to me that the doctor, in using this convenient shortcut, is *also* accrediting the delusion and, in a way, legitimizing the hallucination within his own discourse (a hypothesis I will support by many subsequent examples). The idea that being "unwell from love" can lead uncritically to institutionalization provides me with a better measure of the relationship between psychiatry and the theory of passion than any textbook could.

In what way would my parsed, poetic analysis have suffered from a preliminary reading of published material, whether contemporary or later? This question calls for an explanation. Twelve years ago I wrote a book called *La maison du docteur Blanche*, which plunged me deep into psychiatric literature. I have obviously retained a foundation and a few basic concepts from that reading, partially reused in a more recent work, *La loi du genre: Une histoire culturelle du "troisième sexe."* Yet at the moment I began *The Man Who Thought He Was Napoleon*, I favored "ingenuous"[27] discovery and decided against returning—if just for an initial period—to this corpus whose powerful influence should not be ignored. On the one hand, psychiatrists gripped by the demon of classification establish a nosology, lay down definitions, and strip and immobilize delirium in order to pin down mental illness. On the other hand, ever since Michel Foucault published his theses, historians of psychiatry have been clashing in a courtroom where everyone is summoned to takes sides for or against, caught in the grip of a groundless suit that pits—to caricature a little—psychiatry's accusers against the defenders of a philanthropic practice, depending on whether you consider an asylum to be a site of ostracism or a "machine for socializing people," whether you view mental therapy as an act of silencing or as the first stage of a person's insertion back into democratic society.[28] Which goes to show that the history of insanity is, first and foremost, the history of psychiatry.

Is a history of madness possible? To grasp the stakes behind the issue we must return to Foucault's *Madness and Civilization: A History of Insanity in the Age of Reason*, first published in 1961. His book rested on the hypothesis that ever since the Middle Ages the exclusion associated with madness was elaborated through its progressive capture by reason. Madness, formerly left to wander on a medieval "ship of fools," then forced outside the gates of the city, found its horizon constantly reduced, until in the seventeenth century the insane were confined to former leprosariums, along with criminals and those with venereal disease. This conflation of mental illness with contagious disease and of hospital with prison, through an incestuous alliance of charity and repression, culminated in 1656 with Louis XIV's founding of the *hôpital général*, a government authority designed to deal with delinquents, vagabonds, the poor, and the mad. Thus began the "total confinement" system that permanently exiled madness by enclosing it within the walls that would become asylums.

Reason not only immobilized madness, it ended its own dialogue with it. Madness, formerly the embodiment of obscure truths and a fertile wildness, was gradually deprived of its sacred status and its tragic dimension as celebrated by Shakespeare and Cervantes; it evolved from a relationship of reciprocity with reason to a kind of remoteness, followed by exclusion, in which madness found itself slowly cast out of the world of the living, who could no longer stand to hear its voice. Reason's purportedly "strange coup," according to Foucault, was the way it reduced madness to silence, which dates back to a "specific decision" taken by René Descartes in the first essay of his *Méditations métaphyiques* (1647). Foucault argued that Descartes's text, which sought to distinguish the tangible basis of knowledge from a mental basis, ascribed madness a different status from mistaken impressions. During wakefulness (subject to illusion) and sleep (dense with unreal imagery), there always remains a "residue of truth," such that madness is purportedly "excluded by the doubting subject."[29] People who are misled or asleep inevitably "wake up," whereas the insane are irrevocably imprisoned by their madness—which translated into physical incarceration during the age of reason.

Descartes purportedly provoked a crucial rupture in the history of ideas. "While *man* can still go mad, *thought*, as the sovereign exercise carried out by a subject seeking truth, can no longer be devoid of reason."[30] The constitution of the subject who thinks—and who therefore is—allegedly springs from this same dividing line between madness and reason triumphant. Madness is consigned to obscurity, beyond *cogito*.

Foucault stressed this inaugural rupture throughout his book, in patent and latent ways. It was the keystone of his project, as he emphasized in a preface that returned to this divorce between madness and reason, symbolized by suppressed speech:

> There is no common language: or rather, it no longer exists; the constitution of madness as mental illness, at the end of the eighteenth century, bears witness to a rupture in a dialogue, gives the separation as already enacted, and expels from the memory all those imperfect

> words, of no fixed syntax, spoken falteringly, in which the exchange between madness and reason was carried out. The language of psychiatry, which is a monologue by reason *about* madness, could only have come into existence in such a silence.
>
> My intention was not to write the history of that language, but rather draw up the archaeology of that silence.[31]

This admirable, often-quoted passage raises more than one problem, as Jacques Derrida demonstrated in an implacable text initially published in 1963, in which he mused about Foucault's "mad" project—"no pun intended," quipped Derrida—of writing not a history of psychiatry but an archaeology of madness, *madness itself*, "before its capture by knowledge" and consequently a history—or rather eulogy—of silence.[32] But how can one eulogize a silence, asked Derrida, except through logos, employing the very same weapon of reason with rational concepts of history and archaeology, using legal documents of exclusion? In what invariable but never revealed sense could Foucault speak of "madness"? Can madness even be conceived in univocal historicity? Fifty years later, these questions remain open.

Foucault's act of writing a structural history *around* a blank, delineating its outlines and constraints, constituted in turn a "strange coup" insofar as, for the first time, madness acquired the status of epistemological object. In so doing, Foucault not only staked out a field into which all his adversaries would be obliged to march, trapped in a sphere whose borders he defined, but he also forged—by revealing a new concept and adopting a commanding perspective on it—a global vision that immediately enjoyed unprecedented authority and permanence, becoming editio princeps.

Madness, elevated to a prime vantage point for observing the birth of the modern individual, henceforth assumed the value of a paradigm that could reveal the ambition of governments and the grand designs of authority. The fringes were drawn into the center of debate, and this debate was clearly nothing less than political; that is to say, it concerned affairs of state and the organization of society: Tell me what you do with your insane, and I'll tell you who you are. But Foucault ended his political and ideological history at the French Revolution, at the very moment when, within the structures of domination he brought to light (and which survived throughout the nineteenth century), there emerged an attempt to renew a dialogue with madness, as Gladys Swain's research has demonstrated. But whose dialogue? Here we return to a perfect impasse: the lunatic's side of the dialogue lodges in the discourse of the psychiatrist, who retranscribes it and delivers it to us in a tight mesh of rhetoric. We must avoid deciphering this rhetoric too hastily, because the "capture of knowledge" by the medical field, which perhaps freed the insane from their bonds the better to alienate them within the chain of discourse—thereby enjoining silence once again—is perhaps more porous than it initially appears.[33]

Any talk of asylums almost inevitably leads to caricature. Madness, whether romanticized or demonized, summons up exaggerated language and judgments, as though serenity and grayness had no place in the corseted world of frock coats and straitjackets, a world in black and white populated by visions, shouting, and wretchedness, where passion wrestles with terror and where good intentions justify coercion. But becoming a detractor or a defender means repeating the nineteenth century's moralizing stance of confidently separating the wheat from the chaff, playing the endless refrain of victim versus torturer. Perhaps we would do well, when speaking of madness and its relation to history, to follow Pantagruel when he advised Panurge to seek advice from a "fool," by which he meant a sage, the very type of person who, "departing from himself, rids all his senses of terrene affections, and clears his fancies of those plodding studies which harbor in the minds of thriving men," namely, a sense of abandon that is commonly "imputed to be folly."[34]

By working on archives alone, although never claiming to overlook these polemics or to escape the dichotomy they imply, I simply wanted to conduct an experiment in getting closer to that "sense of abandon." It is not more objective—on the contrary, I confess to a highly personal method of selection—but by being less systematic it is more attentive to the originality, nature, and transcription of the delusions at play.

It is no coincidence that Pinel referred to the case studies he recorded throughout his life as *historiettes* ("vignettes").[35] By choosing a term famously employed by Madame Marie de Sévigné in her letters, defined as "a written or spoken account, real or fictional, often amusing, of little importance,"[36] Pinel was not displaying disregard so much as expressing (and proving) his storytelling ambitions. Despite the deprecating connotation of the diminutive form, these vignettes imply a narrative—a strategy involving weaknesses, failures, and ruses ultimately vulnerable to interpretation, open to several readings. Psychiatric literature, with its blanks and hesitations, its axioms and stammerings, is an inexhaustible source of material for an exegete.

If the language of madness manages to be heard through the research—manages to rise to the surface of the psychiatric romance—what anxieties does it convey? What tragedies do "reforming paranoias," "religious monomanias," and "delusions of grandeur" reflect? The first thing that strikes the researcher is the constancy of the objects and themes that insanity seizes on: delusions of God, wealth, and love all employ the same words and display the same symptoms. Neither the nature of the *illness*—whether organic or not, whether real or imagined—nor the arbitrary nature of institutionalization alters the consistency of insane speech and acts. These little stories—the product of "domestic woes," "reversals of fortune," "war weariness," or "political disorder"—often merge with history itself and are the tangible trace of its bumblings.

The language of madness enters into conversation with these worn pages whose fading ink and deteriorating condition provide the historian with a concrete measure of that rawest of materials, time. The language itself is worn. To restore its original vigor, we must go back to the early days of psychiatry, to its forgotten vocabulary and to the ambivalence of a lexicon based on the great invention that stemmed from Pinel's revolution and broke the chains of restraint: the new approach of treating the mind. This approach focused on everything mental as opposed to physical, everything to do with the mind including good behavior and morality as distinct from immorality. Thus care must be taken when probing an expertise that the field itself jealously kept secret, where all words have a double meaning right from the start. Which ancient defect is the cause of "*depraved* conformations"? What is meant by a form of epilepsy "without insanity but complicated by *poor* instincts"? What impairment is suffered by hospitalized prostitutes who are "unaware of the *indignity* of their status"? And how can we assess "masturbatory habits" that are inevitably *deplorable*, or "*insidious* lunatics" who suffer from "*corrupted feelings*"? This double language extends into administrative vocabulary, as illustrated by the decision to label as "voluntary" all committal requests made by a third party (usually a family member) as distinct from compulsory committal orders issued by the regional administration. Where does normality end and deviance begin? For physicians of the soul, the healthy and unhealthy tread the same dividing line that separates good from evil, legitimate from illegitimate, respectable from indecent. Emphasizing the variable geometry of these routine expressions here does not represent tendentious insinuation; on the contrary, reviewing the choices and construction behind an instantly signifying terminology constitutes an attempt to understand the motivations, accomplishments, and setbacks of bourgeois society and the disciplinary order, as organized around an institution that itself contains a double meaning: asylum.

The never-ending issue at the heart of all archive research concerns borderlines, the infra-thin distinctions of "reading" and interpreting—Who is speaking, who is writing, who is reading? And what discourses arise from all these intersecting layers? Using, studying, and mulling over these materials automatically raises a personal issue that it is ethically impossible to sidestep: the subjectivity of the archive researcher toward her material. Inert paper remains speechless until it meets the eye of someone who yearns to read it, someone who had, in a way, an initial intuition. So one obvious point bears mentioning: it is the reading that makes the archive, which can be made to say whatever you wish (or almost).

Now, reading entails—among other things—imagination. For three years I saw how horizons were reduced to the scale of an asylum: I lived with the people there, the ones who talked, the ones who treated, and the ones who died there. I went to the shower room, I entered the cells. I saw convalescents leave without being able to follow them into their newfound freedom; I saw some of them reenter the walls of the hospital like old acquaintances. I listened to the psychiatrists, I weighed their discourse, and I sensed the great distress that often overcame them. I learned to read between the lines of their work. Such a journey leaves its marks.

This research required constant vigilance. Working an archive—like working a coal seam—is a *physical* exercise that calls for stamina. Stamina against fatigue, first of all, when handling ledgers that weigh over twenty pounds, gigantic folio volumes that can only be read standing up; and stamina against the dust, which invades everything with steely determination and winds up giving the researcher an illusion that, as in transubstantiation, she is becoming parchment herself. And stamina with respect to endless hesitations and misunderstandings caused by the handwriting—all those upstrokes and downstrokes of another era, those spellings that only slowly if steadily become standardized—until the intended meaning of a text could be determined through its details. Stamina, finally, to resist the tempting interpretations, the inevitable preconceptions built on personal history; in short, to resist haste. Woe to the impatient—a group to which I permanently belong. When in a hurry to discover, you have to be careful to wait, sometimes at length, recopying endlessly like a donkey until a coherent picture emerges, until statistics cohere, until a problematic emerges. It can be long and tough, yet gratifying.

This book is therefore the product of hundreds of hours spent with one main source: the nineteenth-century medical records of the major mental asylums in the Département de la Seine (the greater Paris area): Bicêtre (thirty-six volumes), La Salpêtrière (forty-six volumes), and Sainte-Anne (twenty-seven volumes), plus the records of Charenton (fifty-four volumes).[37] The exact time span ran from the Revolution of 1789 to the Paris Commune of 1871. These were the ledgers—literally and figuratively—of social wretchedness, the balance sheets of the fates of thousands of men and women, many of whom were working class and had often lost everything else before losing their minds. In the month of January 1818 alone, two women entered Charenton "entirely deranged" by the same cause: the increase in the price of bread, which made them fear they could no longer feed their children.[38] One was transferred, still unwell, to La Salpêtrière; the fate of the other remains unknown. There were countless examples of this kind throughout that long century of poverty. Descriptions by Victor Hugo and Émile Zola were not inventions, as everyone knew. In this respect these records—irrespective of their usefulness in exploring the issue of the articulation of ideological and pathological discourse—provide a direct, invaluable vantage point for understanding nineteenth-century living conditions and their tragic consequences.

I must make a few general comments about sifting through these archives. The first concerns a certain forbearance in every sense, because these records are lacking in more ways than one. The first volume of medical records at Bicêtre, for example, runs from 1795 to 1853 and is listed in the Archives de l'Assistance Publique as "incomplete."[39] These gaps are partly, if not completely, filled by Pinel's observations on his experiences at Bicêtre between 1793 and 1795 (published in his *Medico-philosophical Treatise on Mental Alienation*), by the Charenton archives from 1798 onward, and by the records of voluntary and compulsory committals that began in 1838. Similarly, the medical records at the asylums evacuated during the Franco-Prussian War of 1870, Bicêtre and La Salpêtrière, offer only blank pages for the period of the Paris Commune, yet the annotated records of Sainte-Anne function as a relay. Thus with a few geographical shifts it is possible to stitch together, year in and year out, all the chapters of the period 1793 to 1871.

The second significant feature of this mass of documents is their simultaneously homogeneous and disparate quality. Homogeneous because from a distance all the documents resemble one another: date of admission, date of release, name and profession, registration number, diagnosis, and, where appropriate, autopsy. The same vocabulary and the same criteria keep cropping up. Yet they are disparate because from close up they do not resemble one another at all. Some records are unbelievably eloquent, exploring the patient's past, describing his or her behavior with a lavishness in which both compassion and the pleasure of storytelling play a part; others are limited to curt comments from which nothing else can be drawn: "Insane. Incurable." This unevenness is largely due to the doctor in charge during any given period. Some worked with application, others with dispatch. Many doctors, in fact, perceived only their own specialty—Valentin Magnan, for example, the specialist in alcoholism whose work inspired Zola's novel *L'assomoir*, thought he saw patent or latent dipsomania in every mental patient. Vigilance, then, was required when researching a path strewn with such potholes and obstacles.

The inconsistencies across periods and material required more than diligence, however. They made any definitive conclusions—indeed, any reliable statistics—risky. It is hard to assess the proportion of delusions triggered by political events when certain hallucinations are fully described on one page while on the next page the doctor merely noted "visions and stupor," with the details lost forever. Asylum records are more conducive to literature than to math, so I generally preferred to probe specific, detailed periods rather than gathering necessarily specious and imprecise statistics. I nevertheless made an exception for the period of the Paris Commune—March 18 to May 28, 1871—attempting to draw up, over a longer and above all more homogeneous period than the three-day revolution of 1830 and the brief revolutionary outbursts in February and June of 1848, a quantitative diagram of diagnosis and social status, comparing the chart of women against that of men.

I cross-checked this initial source of documents with others, mainly stemming from the Archives Nationales, the Archives de Paris, and the Archives de la Préfecture de Police de Paris. Bureaucracy has the cold ability to redefine things. It provided the crucial administrative counterpoint required to understand mechanisms of control over souls that, if taken in their raw nakedness, inevitably lead toward the ever-present danger of a sentimental fascination with original, authentic documents that offer a live account of human distress, activating a world that seems more real than any other.

This return to the source also raised a crucial problem stemming mainly from the fact that the archives of madness can be read only from the standpoint of reason, just as a patient's speech is delivered solely through the doctor who reports it. How, then, can we grasp the mad person's discourse? Dispossessed of his or her own speech, reduced to a "summary" that is usually more revealing of the psychiatrist's own obsessions than the patient's sufferings, the expression of madness is fundamentally hijacked and corrupted. In other words, the history of madness can never be more than the history of psychiatry insofar as it depends on the sufferance of psychiatry to deliver the material for its analysis and evolution. The history of madness is thus like histories of illiterate, anonymous, marginal, "voiceless" people, where historians can reach their subjects only through the political discourses of authority and scholarship, resigning themselves to commenting on commentaries for want of access to the primary source. The relative paucity of first-person accounts, even when incoherent or unintelligible, makes this history also similar to the early history of homosexuality, in which researchers had to content themselves with academic and moralizing books of the late nineteenth century as they attempted to unravel a *certain* history of morals. More broadly, it is possible that the quest for this phantom discourse is like all vain attempts to pin down an abstract category: the discourse of "madness" can no more be circumscribed than can the discourses of "the people" or "homosexuality." Toward the end of his life Michelet wrote, "I was born of the people, I had the people at heart. . . . But their language, their tongue, remained beyond my reach. I could not manage to make it speak."[40]

Despite all these limitations, asylum archives contain something irreplaceable in their very fiber, something printed books of the day lack: a sense of urgency. When making his rounds, the head doctor had no time to lose—a euphemism quantified by Dr. François Leuret at Bicêtre, who calculated that he could devote no more than eighteen minutes to each patient *per year*.[41] One jest became a commonplace: "'The doctor's coming by, the doctor will be by'—and sure enough, he went by, because he didn't have time to stop."[42] A physician's spontaneity (inevitably tempered in scholarly publications) and the need to note certain details in vivo while overlooking others thus provide intrinsically invaluable information on a doctor's priorities, whose immediacy is guaranteed by the tyrannically ticking clock. The mere fact, for example, that the column reserved for *traitement moral*—mental therapy[43]—is inevitably blank in Bicêtre's records says much more than a long discourse on theoretical claims that this therapy is literally *untranscribable*. Similarly, a telling attachment to certain specific cases, the periodic return of the same symptoms, and the persistence of attitudes and patterns provide valuable clues toward an understanding of mental illness, allowing us to read these records like a palimpsest in which several voices overlap.

Finally, so much time spent listening to the language of madness, noting its repetitions and refrains, scrutinizing documents—not only through records, but also through plans of asylums, engravings of the shower rooms, portraits of psychiatrists and lunatics alike—creates the impression of being steeped, as if by slow infusion, in a theoretically very alien world. This immersion in the archives creates an intimacy with the subject that no other source will ever have the power to convey. It is this power of evocation that I want to capture in this book; it is the pleasure of awakening these slumbering archives that I would like to share.

Taken together, these scattered documents compose a picture that will long remain fragile, necessarily partial, and highly incomplete. Yet it is one that I hope will unravel a few of the intricacies and elucidate some of the patterns of a *particular* political history of madness.

ONE * Revolutionary Terror, or Losing Head and Mind

Here, as promised, is the exact truth of what happened. On getting down from the carriage for his execution, he was told that he had to remove his coat; he made some objection, saying that he could be executed just as he was. On being told that this was impossible, he himself helped to remove his coat. He made the same objections when it came to tying his hands, which he then held out himself once the person accompanying him said it was one last sacrifice. Then he asked if the drums would roll throughout; the answer was that they did not know. Which was the truth. He climbed onto the scaffold and sought to move to the front as though wishing to speak. But it was pointed out to him that this, too, was impossible. So he allowed himself to be led to the place where he was bound, and where he shouted very loudly, *People, I die innocent*. Then, turning toward us, he said: *Gentlemen, I am innocent of every charge laid against me. I hope that my blood may seal the happiness of the French people*. Those, citizen, were his true and final words.

This extraordinary account of the death of Louis XVI was written by Charles-Henri Sanson, his executioner. It was sent to the *Thermomètre du Jour* to refute the account of a journalist who claimed he was told by Sanson himself that the condemned man, showing cowardice in his final moments, tried three times to cry "I'm doomed!" On the contrary, Sanson added, "And, to honor the truth, he bore all that with a calmness and steadfastness that amazed us. I remain most convinced that he drew this steadfastness from the principles of the religion in which no one seemed more imbued nor certain than he."[1] This correction was corroborated by some of the reports of the day, such as a similar story published in *Révolutions de Paris*, which added details that

Sanson's sense of propriety censored. "At ten minutes past ten, his head was separated from his body, and then displayed to the people."[2] The burial took place in the nearby cemetery of the church of La Madeleine. Witnesses who signed the official report declared that corpse had "no cravat, coat, or shoes" but was "dressed in a shirt, a stitched vestlike jacket, gray broadcloth breeches, and a pair of gray silk stockings." The corpse "was seen to be whole in all its limbs, the head having been separated from the trunk."[3] His head was placed between his legs in an open coffin that was lowered into the common grave and covered with quicklime and earth.

"A USEFUL INVENTION OF A LETHAL KIND"

On that Monday, January 21, 1793, the last king of France died. Kings, as we know, were viewed as having two bodies.[4] The mortal, secular body was twinned by a sacred body, the dynastic symbol of a monarchy of divine right. As Louis XIV had put it, "The nation is not a body in France, it resides entirely in the person of the king,"[5] an idea summed up by the more famous—if apocryphal—"L'état, c'est moi" (I *am* the state). The king was an individual endowed with a function that transcended him yet was incarnated in a body considered inviolable and inalienable (a principle that was moreover accepted by France's revolutionary constitution of 1791). An attack on the king was an attack on France, which is why regicides always deserved the worst torture (the 1757 dismemberment of Robert-François Damiens, who had attempted to assassinate Louis XV, was still on everyone's mind).

Yet this inviolable principle was delivered a lethal blow by the guillotine that severed the head of state along with the head of Louis XVI. The blade that fell on that day overstepped its usual role and flaunted its metaphorical powers. In an instantaneous image—a picture of gushing blood—it showed an age-old political regime tumbling into a wicker basket. Real body, symbolic body, one and the same: the guillotine hypostatized the king's two bodies through this dismemberment on the public stage of the scaffold, putting a final end to tyranny. The crowd—which upon the death of a king usually shouted, "The king is dead! Long live the king!"—greeted the decapitation of Louis the Last with cries of "Long live the Republic! Long live the Nation!" Some people dipped a handkerchief, the blade of a sword, or the tip of a bayo-

FIGURE 3. German school, *The Tragic End of Louis XVI, Executed on January 21, 1793, on Place Louis XV.* This highly popular color print depicts a critical moment in the ritual of the guillotine: exhibiting the decapitated head to the public like a trophy. Musée de la Ville de Paris, Musée Carnavalet, Paris. Photograph: Agence Bulloz. Photograph © RMN-Grand Palais/Art Resource, New York.

net in the royal blood, supposed to regenerate the nation and consecrate the birth of the Republic, henceforth confirmed by the literally staggering sight of a supernatural body suddenly split asunder.

The death of Louis XVI also confirmed and consecrated another obvious fact: the theater of political power, once restricted to Versailles, had shifted to Paris. The revolution was a drama being performed outdoors, in public. Right from the early days of 1789, François-René de Chateaubriand noted the effervescence of salons, cafés, and streets where everything became part of the spectacle of this "celebration of destruction."[6] From 1792 onward, the scaffold became a leading stage. "The theater of the guillotine," added contemporary commentator Louis Sébastien Mercier, "was always ringed by an audience."[7] The executioner Sanson was the great coordinator of these "red masses" that drew daily crowds curious to see "the new play that could never have more than one performance," as Camille Desmoulins ferociously quipped only months before his own head fell.[8] Artists took up their places at the foot of the scaffold to capture the expressions on faces faced with death, whose public staging offered the hope that skilled pencils might decipher its mystery. A plethora of engravings were published, endlessly showing the executioner brandishing a bloody head by the hair. Final words were noted down, poses were recorded.

Those sentenced to death, meanwhile, prepared to perform their final role. Imprisoned in Sainte-Pélagie, monarchist actress Louise Contat promised to sing a song of her own composing when she climbed the scaffold—a fate she was ultimately spared—which began with the lines, "On the scaffold shall I appear / for 'tis just another stage."[9] The distance between street and stage vanished. *Révolutions de Paris* indicated as much in a strikingly metaphorical comment designed to suggest that life was returning to normal the very afternoon of that most exceptional January 21, 1793. "The show carried on without interruption; everyone joined in, people danced on the edge of the former Louis XVI Bridge."[10]

The guillotine became an everyday reality during the Terror. It was depicted, recounted, and bandied about by popular songs with their series of refrains on "the widow," "the national razor," "the patriotic haircut," "the sword of equality," and "the altar of the nation." People no longer referred to "being guillotined" but spoke of "sticking your head through the cat-flap," "poking through the window," or "sneezing into the basket." Pro-republican women keen to flaunt their colors would wear earrings shaped like miniature guillotines from which hung pendants of a crowned head.[11] Victor Hugo informs us that the artist Joseph Boze painted his teenage daughters "*en guillotinées*; that is to say with bare necks and red shifts."[12] Once the Terror had ended, notorious "victims' balls" were held in Paris where relatives of the guillotined gathered in mourning dress, each wearing a red thread around the neck with hair pulled up or even shaved, the better to exorcise, in a cathartic *danse macabre*, the tragic escalation that the Thermidorian reaction finally brought to a halt.[13]

In the meantime, the machine did its job rigorously, oblivious to propaganda, fantasies, and black humor. Figures vary depending on source, but it has been estimated that 2,600 to 3,000 people were guil-

FIGURE 4. Guillotine earrings (ca. 1793). Gold and gilded metal, 5.7 cm. During the Terror, there was a spate of products such as these gold and gilt-metal earrings of a guillotine topped by the revolutionary Phrygian cap, with a dangling crowned head as a pendant. Musée Carnavalet, Paris. Photograph © Michel Toumazet/Musée Carnavalet/Roger-Viollet/The Image Works.

lotined in Paris between March 1793 and August 1794 (executions throughout the entire country during that same period totaled some 17,000). During the Terror, then, an average of five heads were lost in Paris every day—an average that should nevertheless be tempered by the fact, for example, that sixty-eight executions took place on July 7, 1794, just two days before Maximilien de Robespierre fell.[14]

It is hardly surprising that the guillotine became what Dr. Georges Cabanis called "the standard" of the Revolution, indeed was an emblem synonymous with the Terror. The Revolution severed the past, amputating diseased limbs from the body of the state, accomplishing an inevitable separation. The guillotine superbly exemplified and epitomized the vital need for rupture, which constituted the condi-

FIGURE 5. Poirier de Dunckerque, *Cutting Manners* [*Les formes acerbes*] (1796), 34 cm × 38 cm. This print shows Joseph Le Bon, who sent hundreds of suspects in the region of Arras to the guillotine. The picture provides a powerful synthesis of the horror provoked by decapitation, the mutilation of bodies, and the bloodthirsty "Terrorists." Musée de la Ville de Paris, Musée Carnavalet, Paris. Photograph: Agence Bulloz. Photograph © RMN-Grand Palais/Art Resource, New York.

tion—and promise—for remaking the world. As a modern machine derived from the laws of geometry and gravity, it promised an egalitarian, democratic death. It put a permanent end to the hierarchy of punishments under the ancien régime, which sentenced witches and arsonists to be burned at the stake, regicides to be tortured, and thieves and criminals to be hanged, reserving decapitation by the sword for the nobility. It was to do away with this inequality—even in death—that on October 9, 1789, Dr. Joseph-Ignace Guillotin, an elected representative to the Constituent Assembly, suggested a new form of capital punishment that would be identical for all. Article 6 of the statute adopted on December 1 read, "Criminals will be decapitated, through the action of a simple mechanism." But three years passed before the decision was implemented. The revolutionaries spent less time in 1789 debating the potential abolition of the death penalty—an abolition stoutly defended by Robespierre—than on discussing the modalities and implementation of the dreadful machine, which saw the light only in 1792.

France did not invent this method of execution, but it altered the scale of operations, bringing death into the era of technical mass production. Other beheading devices had proved their worth in the past, such as the *Diele* in medieval Germany, the *mannaia* in sixteenth-century Italy, the "maiden" in Scotland, and the "Halifax gibbet" in England. The French guillotine was nevertheless more efficient than its predecessors, thanks to the development of a swivel board on which the condemned person was bound, the design of a lunette (double-sided yoke) that held the head steady, and finally the use of a diagonal rather than a crescent-shaped blade, which meant that the instrument "never failed," according to a report submitted on March 7, 1792, by Antoine Louis, its true inventor. Indeed, the machine was briefly nicknamed the Petite Louison or Louisette. Louis, like Guillotin, was a

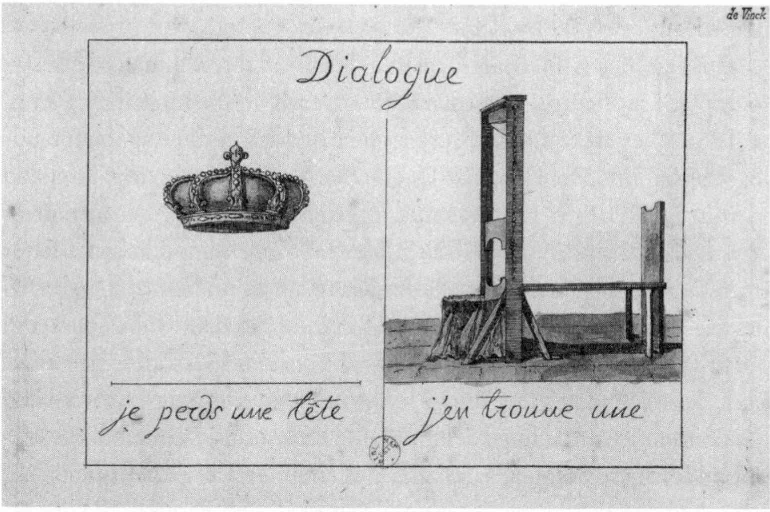

FIGURE 6. French school, *Dialogue: I've Lost a Head* [says the crown]; *I've Found One* [replies the guillotine] (1793). Colored etching, 11.2 cm × 16.2 cm. The guillotine introduced impersonal, assembly-line executions. Even the king was reduced to just one head among many in this chilling "dialogue" of 1793. Bibliothèque Nationale de France, Paris. Photograph © BNF.

doctor. In fact, he was a famous surgeon who served as the permanent secretary of the Académie de Chirurgie, making him the ideal person to accurately assess the conditions required for a swift, flawless severing of the head.[15]

Once Louis's report was accepted, the machine could be built. The joiner at the royal household having submitted an estimate judged too steep (5,660 livres), the choice fell on a Prussian piano maker, Tobias Schmidt, whose bid was far more reasonable (960 livres). But the Ministry of the Interior refused to grant Schmidt the patent he had requested. "It is humanly distasteful to grant a patent for an invention of this kind; we have not yet reached such a level of barbarity. While Monsieur Schmidt has produced a useful invention of a lethal kind, since it can be used only for carrying out legal sentences he must offer it to the government."[16] There was a double meaning being expressed here: while the government was not adopting the guillotine with a joyful heart, it truly intended to make it a "machine of government" (as writings of the day refer to it, in fact). So it was a political machine designed to implement a death alleged to be painless and also impersonal, because a pulley, a diagonal blade, and two uprights—the product of talented French engineering—would replace the hands of the accredited executioner.

The first successful trials—on live sheep and three human corpses—took place in Bicêtre, just outside Paris, early in the morning of April 17, 1792. They were done in the presence of doctors once again, including the famous Dr. Cabanis. Decidedly, the medical corps attended upon the guillotine. Nor was that all. In the fall of 1795—once press censorship had been lifted—*Le Moniteur Universel* published a letter from Dr. Samuel Thomas von Sömmering, an anatomist who had written his thesis on the arrangement of cranial nerves, which sparked a polemic over the potential survival of consciousness after decapitation. Based, among other things, on experiments by Luigi Galvani and the persistence of feelings of amputated limbs, this German doctor reported testimony of heads that gnashed their teeth after beheading. He remained convinced that "if air still regularly circulated in the organs of the voice, had they not been destroyed, these heads would speak."[17] Sömmering felt that the allegedly humanitarian guillotine was barbaric and a much poorer option than hanging, which led to death "via sleep."

That is all it took for a debate to flare up. The Franco-Prussian journalist Conrad Engelbert Ölsner—to whom Sömmering addressed his letter—went to bat in the *Magasin Encyclopédique*, followed in that same publication by Jean-Joseph Sue (father of novelist Eugène Sue). Ölsner then went on to publish his notes in a small book on the question.[18] The French notably referred to the death of Charlotte Corday, beheaded on July 17, 1793, whose cheeks purportedly reddened in indignation when her head was pulled from the basket and slapped by a revolutionary. Was this incident rumor, collective hallucination, or a conspiracy by enemies of Jean-Paul Marat? The posthumous outrage reportedly displayed by the "angel of murder"—as Alphonse de Lamartine dubbed Corday—fueled discussion in the press when Cabanis who, like Guillotin, was a member of the Ideologues group at the Nine Sisters Masonic lodge, decided to respond by publishing a *Note sur le supplice de la guillotine* (A note on execution by guillotine), which temporarily put an end to the dispute. Cabanis, who would later write a famous book on the relationship between human physical and mental faculties (*Rapports du physique et du moral de l'homme* [1802]), insisted that movement and feeling be dissociated: a headless chicken may continue to run around but feels nothing. A human being whose head has been severed through the spinal cord no longer has nerve sensations and can therefore in no case suffer. Corday's blush was to be dismissed as an absurdity. Potential movements of the face or body—convulsive or regular—"prove neither pain nor feeling; they result solely from the remnants of a vitality that the death of the individual, *the destruction of the self*, does not instantaneously extinguish in muscles and nerves."[19]

The guillotine thus served as the focus of highly lively and crucial debate on the mental, political, and metaphysical assessment of the individual: an individual, literally, is one who cannot be divided. Medicine, sister field of philosophy, not only took part by involving itself in the birth of the guillotine from conception to implementation, but appeared from one end of the process to the other as the instrumental, organizational, and rhetorical domain that acted as arbiter of life and death. Right from the start, medicine laid down the terms of debate: What is torture? What do convicts deserve? Should death be painless? Does consciousness outlive the flesh? What is a divided "self"? This, indeed, is the very site of the origin of the medical approach to madness: the invention of psychiatry.[20]

FIGURE 7. French school, *The Execution of Marie Antoinette* (between 1793 and 1799). Etching, 13.5 cm × 8.5 cm. This engraving, though archived under the title *The Execution of Marie-Antoinette*, has also been alleged to show the death of Charlotte Corday, whose cheek was seen to "redden in indignation" when her head was pulled from the basket and slapped by the executioner's assistant. This incident, apparently depicted here in the cloud, fueled debate over the survival of consciousness after beheading. Bibliothèque Nationale de France, Paris. Photograph © BNF.

A DOCTOR AT THE GOVERNMENT'S BEDSIDE

January 21, 1793. A citizen in uniform was present at the event, stationed at the foot of the scaffold. As an active member of the Place des Piques district (as were Robespierre and the marquis de Sade), he had been drafted to escort the carriage taking Louis Capet—formerly King Louis XVI—from the Temple prison to the Place de la Révolution (today Place de la Concorde). That same day, he wrote a letter to his brother: "To my great regret I was obliged to attend the execution, armed, alongside other citizens of my district. I write with a heart heavy with sorrow, in a stupor of profound consternation." After giving an account similar to Sanson's, the writer continued, "Louis was bound to the fatal plank of what is called the guillotine, and his head was cut off before he hardly had time to suffer, which is at least one advantage of this murderous machine that bears the name of the physician who invented it."[21] This citizen who espoused revolutionary ideals at an early date and claimed to be "far from royalist" was himself a physician. He was none other than Philippe Pinel, the founder of French psychiatry.

Pinel was fully familiar with the workings of the guillotine and "the physician who invented it." According to an account by the actor François-Joseph Talma, he was even present at Bicêtre, along with Cabanis, Louis, and Guillotin, in April 1792 when it was first tested on human corpses.[22] Guillotin would have been familiar to Pinel, at least by name, for in 1784 Pinel had published in his own medical periodical, *Le Journal de Santé*, a report by Jean Sylvain Bailly on the debate over animal magnetism, which cited Guillotin. Pinel had probably met Guillotin, along with Cabanis, at Madame Anne-Catherine Helvétius's salon in Auteuil, which he frequented along with other members of the Ideologues group.

This unexpected convergence between the legendary liberator of the mentally ill and the beheading of Louis XVI goes beyond mere anecdote. Similarly, the perfect coincidence of the birth of psychiatry with the invention of the guillotine stems not so much from chance as from historical correlations—including a semantic one, as suggested by the literal and figurative connection between "losing your head" and "losing your mind."[23] As far removed as treating the mentally ill may seem from beheading enemies of the Revolution—as distant as the development of a medical field is from the making of a death-dealing machine—psychiatry and the guillotine share an attachment to the link between head and body (whether joined or separated), to the integrity of self and consciousness. Both were conceived and delivered by the medical corps, both were part of a political project seeking to reform humankind and make society healthier.

But what date can be ascribed to the invention of French psychiatry, if such a birth could be pinpointed in time? One date is highly symbolic: March 16, 1790, the day a law was passed abolishing *lettres de cachet*, which allowed the government to arbitrarily intern any person upon petition by his or her family or by order of the king. Article 9 of the new law specified the status of alleged "lunatics."

> Persons detained for reasons of madness shall be questioned, within three months of the day of publication of this law and at the behest of government attorneys, by judges in the customary manner; by virtue of the judges' directives, they will be seen by doctors who, under the supervision of district directors, will discuss the patients' true condition so that, following a decision decreeing their status, they will be released or cared for in hospitals designated to that end.

"This decision by the first revolutionary Assembly," Robert Castel has rightly pointed out, "circumscribes the entire modern problematic of madness."[24] The abolition of royal arbitrariness, combined with transfers of authority to the justice system (local prosecutors and judges), the administration (district directors), and the medical profession, meant that yesterday's lunatic, locked up without any kind of due process, became a citizen in need of evaluation, a patient to be cured. This revolutionary act—which altered the status of madness without, however, liberating it—in fact reflected a trend that had begun under the ancien régime. As early as 1784, a government circular issued by the baron Louis de Breteuil, minister of the Royal Household, regulated and limited the use of *lettres de cachet*. The following year, Jean Colombier and François Doublet published *Instruction sur la manière de gouverner les insensés et de travailler à leur guérison dans les asyles qui leur sont destinés* (Instructions on the way to control lunatics and work toward curing them in asylums). They recommended the establishment of special facilities within each poorhouse, thereby laying the foundations of modern asylums. Their forty-five-page booklet constituted a warning about the situation of the mentally ill incarcerated in prisons, and it was distributed throughout the kingdom. Some of their arguments would reappear in Jacques Tenon's *Mémoires sur les hôpitaux de Paris* (Memoranda on the hospitals of Paris), published in 1788, in a chapter devoted to treating curable maniacs in the central Paris hospital known as Hôtel-Dieu (the incurable ones simply vegetated in prisons or charitable poorhouses), whose deplorable living conditions he exposed.[25] In addition to Hôtel-Dieu, there were roughly a dozen private institutions on the outskirts of the city that took in the insane—including the Belhomme mental home in the faubourg Saint-Antoine, where the medical consultant was none other than Philippe Pinel.

Paris had not been kind to Pinel, a provincial from Languedoc who received a degree in Toulouse in 1773 before going on to study medicine in Montpellier. In 1778 he decided to try his luck in the capital, where he encountered only "meanness and scheming" and realized his career would always be limited by his "lack of fortune."[26] Shorter than average height and austere in demeanor, the awkward and shy Pinel was too reserved to shine in society and furthermore suffered from a speech impediment he would never overcome: he had a weak voice, and his diction was labored and stumbling.[27] This man, who would devote his life to helping the mentally ill recover their "regular chain of ideas" (an expression that recurs throughout his writings)—that is, to restore their coherent thinking and fluid speech—was himself a stammerer. One of his students even reported that he "couldn't utter two words without gagging."[28]

Probably owing in part to his shyness and to this handicap, Pinel failed in his three attempts to obtain a grant for poor students at the Faculty of Medicine, and he was also refused the office of physician to Mesdames (the king's aunts) despite a recommendation from Louis XVI's doctor. He therefore resigned himself to making a living by giving private lessons in mathematics and publishing articles and translations. In 1784, after deciding against emigrating to America, he accepted two jobs: the editorship of the *Gazette de Santé* (a medical review to which he was already a contributor) and a consultancy at the Belhomme home, where he began to take an interest in mental illness and to develop a "mental regime" designed to cure patients.

Pinel's decision to devote himself to this new branch of medicine was largely inspired by the loss in 1783 of a friend who "went insane through excessive love of glory" and died because "all pharmaceutic remedies" failed to save him.[29] An eager reader of ancient authors and passionately interested in hygiene and nosology, Pinel further extended his great cultivation by translating the *Institutions of Medicine* by Scottish physician William Cullen. The Belhomme mental home, despite offering a good vantage point, was not the institution Pinel might have wished; the home's director, ever concerned to hang on to his rich clients as long as possible, was uninterested in—indeed, hindered—the treatment the doctor advocated.

When the Revolution came, Pinel was already forty-four. The ancien régime had ignored if not humiliated him; his second-rate career was blocked and stagnating. It is not hard to imagine the hope that stirred in him with the arrival of liberty. As an admirer of Montesquieu, a reader of Rousseau, and a friend of Condorcet, Pinel adhered to the new ideas with unadulterated enthusiasm.

Research has revealed that the French medical corps remained largely aloof from public affairs until 1789. For example, no doctor was included either in the Assembly of Notables convened in 1787 or in the provincial assemblies. In contrast, there were seventeen doctors (including Guillotin) in the Constituent Assembly (1789–91), twenty-two in the National Legislative Assembly (1791–92), and thirty-nine in the Convention (1792–95). The modern rise of the medical corps is indissociably linked to the revolutionary upheaval.[30] Pinel never became an elected representative, but he publicly committed himself. With a strong sense of his social role, the psychiatrist called himself a natural philosopher and viewed himself as an Enlightenment figure who could combine medicine and politics, as demonstrated by, among other things, an article he published in the *Journal de Paris* on January 18, 1790, which forthrightly linked the metaphor of "body politic" to "the body of the individual." In brief, Pinel argued that politics has a direct influence on health, observable in his daily meeting with patients. But not all "regimes" were good for the human organism, and he claimed that the ancien régime provoked serious dysfunctions among a population plunged into morbid lethargy: "The body was languishing in inactivity owing to the spread of laxness and luxury, and the unquiet activity of the human mind could no longer be sustained, leading to the unprecedented frequency of what are called diseases of the nerves and all spasmodic ailments." The masses of chronic and catarrhal ailments he diagnosed were thus to be imputed to "arbitrary government" that disturbed the functioning of bodies and minds, rendered ill by the monarchic system. But with the arrival of the Revolution, Pinel argued, the course of history had changed: "Scarcely one year has gone by, and everything has taken on a new countenance." The revolutionary "shock" had been beneficial, and Pinel the clinician was the first to recognize the "salutary effects of the progress of liberty." New energy was stimulating human character and giving the "animal economy" the spur it needed. "'I feel better since the revolution,' has been said by several persons honored by that sentiment; and indeed, how could the enjoyment of rights derived from well-ordered nature and which seem to enlarge and brighten the soul, do anything other than revive the organic function of the viscera and penetrate, as though by some electric virtue, the system of nerves and muscles of a new life?" Pinel was saying that politics indeed influenced the mind, which acted explicitly on the body, a conclusion whose impact on the future psychiatrist would be significant. When it came to the causes of madness, Pinel always favored "mental causes" whose effect on the epigastric region impinged on the brain.

After such an enthusiastic start, Pinel's article then pursued this line of reasoning, even as it nuanced it. The awakening of liberty, inevitably accompanied by acts of violence, also admittedly provoked a few "harmful effects"—convulsions and anguish occasionally leading to suicide—on "hearts that are pusillanimous and often self-tormenting." Women, because of their extreme sensibility, were reputedly the first to suffer from breathlessness and headaches accompanied by spasms and trembling, triggered by "consternation and alarm." Pinel prudently added that he was "not referring to the profound seizures that are generally produced by various bloody and atrocious scenes." Yet there could be no mistake that the "varied effects of human passions" were related "to the disposition of the heart, the sphere of understanding, and the clash of interests." Madness exacerbated noble or contemptible feelings that were there from the start, rather than creating from whole cloth some sort of exogenous delirium. Pinel thus distinguished two kinds of madness, in fact corresponding to maniacal insanity and melancholia, which, along with dementia and imbecility, represented the four main categories of mental illness:

> The first involves a certain ecstasy of public prosperity and love of country carried to the point of delirium, such as the visions of the madman who presented himself to the National Assembly as the representative of the Eternal Father, in order to relieve that assembly of its functions and to give new laws to France; what constitutes the other kind of madness, or rather the final degree of melancholia, is a dark despondency of the soul alternating with terror or rage accompanied by violent curses against the enemies of the state. The author of a booklet that has just appeared has assured me, based on research in the parishes, that Paris currently counts a greater number of madmen than usual.[31]

So were people really healthier after the Revolution? Pinel's conclusion seems to contradict his enthusiastic initial suggestion. Whatever the case, the additional energy injected into the "animal economy" by the new situation was accompanied by manifest disorders of mind and behavior, ranging from mania to depression.

In theory, the idea seems to make sense. What mind could remain unmoved by the overthrow of every institution and the insurrection of people determined to free themselves from tyranny? How could anyone remain unaffected by the terrific spectacle of the end of a world being played out in the street and in government? In the five months between July 1789 and January 1790, the French witnessed the birth of a Constituent Assembly, the abolition of the feudal regime and all aristocratic privileges, the nationalizing of church property, the adoption of a Declaration of the Rights of Man, and the division of the country into administrative *départements* and districts. France was still a monarchy, but sovereignty henceforth rested in the hands of the nation, in a land where all men were born free and equal in rights, a country being totally reshaped. In the provinces, panic was sparked by peasant uprisings known as the *grande peur* (great fright), by riots in Le Mans, Rennes, Lille, Strasbourg, Cherbourg, Colmar, Lyon, Rouen, Bayeux, Besançon, Marseille, Orléans, Versailles, Ajaccio, and Martinique, not to mention the peasant revolts (*jacqueries*) in Brittany, Perigord, and Guercy. Parisians, meanwhile, witnessed the burning down of forty of the fifty-four tax collection gates along the notorious tax wall ringing the capital, the fall of the Bastille (and the decapitation of its governor, whose head was paraded on the end of the pike), and the encirclement of the capital by the king's troops. The people cheered Louis XVI when he appeared on the balcony of city hall wearing a tricolor cockade, yet less than three months later the royal family—"the baker, baker's wife, and baker's boy"—was obliged to move from Versailles to Paris to the jeers of the crowd. The king's brothers emigrated, while the king himself was kept under surveillance in the Tuileries Palace. Once desanctified, an entire system collapsed; a whole society was reinvented.

So it is easy to imagine the tempest raging in people's minds. But what evidence do we have of it? None, obviously. The administrative organization of mental illness in France, leading to the famous legislative act of 1838, had not yet begun. And at the time, the Revolution had more pressing business than making a count of its lunatics. Furthermore, the far from ordinary nature of the events would probably draw undue attention, especially in the absence of statistics showing the surreptitious, hidden ravages of governance that is iniquitous yet without observable upheavals during periods of political calm.

Whatever the case, Pinel's allusion to an increase in madness during the Revolution was just the first in a long series that snaked throughout the nineteenth century up to the revolutionary Commune of 1870, itself accused of all the ills of the upheavals of 1793, 1830, and 1848. In 1790 Pinel merely reported the results of one study, with no further detail or judgment. For that matter, in general Pinel always remained cautious about establishing any *direct* correlation between insurrection and mental disorder, for reasons that related both to scientific circumspection and to political opportunism.

In that same year of 1790 Pinel published another article of the same patriotic stripe in the *Journal Gratuit*.[32] Titled "Medical Reflections on the Monastic Condition," it was prompted by the legislature's abolition of monastic orders and religious vows on February 13, 1790, followed on July 12 by a law on the civil constitution of the clergy, a reform that established a government-controlled Catholic Church whose "ecclesiastical civil servants" were required to take an oath of loyalty to the new constitution. Given the context of sharp tension and religious turmoil, Pinel's unambiguous goal was to lend his professional backing to a political decision, which he framed as a question of public health.

Humans were made to live in human society, he argued, and it was the job of doctors to release monks and nuns from the baleful influence of their stubborn superiors who tried to force them to respect their vows despite the new law. "Madness often brings mental disorder to a peak," he declared, "and there is no monastery that fails to offer an unfortunate example of it every day." A monastery (or convent), described as a "grim tomb" where "apathetic cenobites" wasted away, was ostensibly the site of "ills" that were "countless" yet needed to be named. The appeal of Pinel's demonstration thus lies in its efficiency at *translating* the demands of a mystical life into clinical terms. First he focused on meditation and the "various degrees of *inner life*," or rather the "true symptoms of religious melancholia." Following the "mystical effusion" and serenity procured by "silent prayer," the contemplative soul passes to a third stage—"of delirium or holy intoxication," in which it is assailed by "supernatural-like illusions or visions" (in other words, hallucinations)—and then on to a state of "ecstasy," which is "a kind of catalepsy."

> The faces of ecstatics at first have an attentive, stunned air; their eyes stare, motionless; their limbs resist an external impulse, as is the case in catalepsy; they feel almost no pain when struck; their pulse is strong, broad, and steady; their breathing slow and irregular, like a man who is out of breath; they can be heard to mutter a few muddled words; toward the end of an attack of this sort, their faces become red and florid, as though they were awaking from a deep sleep, and they harbor a small smile; but the mind remains in a kind of imbecility during which they speak only of marvels and miracles; the vigils, the fasts, the fervent prayers, the reading of ascetic books, and the sight of people struck by the same illnesses steadily lead ardent minds toward this state of exaltation.

It is easy to recognize here what Jean-Martin Charcot, a century later, would precisely label the "cataleptic" phase of hysteria. Pinel, for that matter, carefully graded the various mystic states observed in analogous situations: the exhilaration experienced by creative artists, the aloof inwardness of great thinkers, ravings sparked by drugs or intense fevers, and the "state of rapture provoked by some fits of vapors or bouts of hysteria."[33]

Once it was described in medical detail, and subsequently compared with other states of ordinary secular life—including organic conditions such as fever—the religious experience seemed stripped of its aura of mystery. Pinel rationalized, banalized, and desanctified, forging a "modern" perspective that countered the obscurantism of the ancien régime. In the Middle Ages people had been possessed by the devil, but the Revolution no longer believed in miracles and thus foiled divine ecstatics.

The two other points of monastic existence that drew Pinel's attention were the sedentary aspect of cloistered life and vows of sexual abstinence, constituting the materialist and structural side of his demonstration. In 1788 he had already published in the *Gazette de Santé* his "Observations on the Baleful Effects of a Sedentary Life and an Overly Strong and Long Mental Containment."[34] It was a subject dear to his heart. By not allowing the body the physical exertion it required, and by prohibiting the exercise of emotions that nourish the mind, the rules of monastic life provoked—especially among nuns—"the most inveterate diseases of the viscera, attacks of hysteria, pale complexion, lymphatic engorgement, scirrhous growths [hard tumors] of the womb," and "breathlessness." Furthermore, the better to resist temptation, convents blithely employed "all those little recipes, mysterious drugs and multiple refreshments" that impair the stomachs and health of "young, healthy and robust neophytes." Part magic, part charlatanism, neither convents nor monasteries had their place in the century of reason.

Pinel concluded these observations, based on experience, with the example of a young monk he had treated, which also allowed him to provide a glimpse of his methods. The "young cenobite" was hounded by "the most seductive images of voluptuousness" and was a victim of sperm discharges, having struggled unsuccessfully for many years against his ardent temperament. Tonics, calmatives, and "other frivolities to which the physician is always reduced when there is no resort other than pharmacy" all failed, one after another. "I ask every man who has not abandoned his gift of reason," exclaimed Pinel at this point, "is not marriage the sole remedy indicated by the voice of nature? But that voice had been stifled by a foolhardy engagement, and one was obliged to prescribe other methods." Those methods were precisely the foundation of Pinel's approach, based on a return to nature, a regulated mode of life, and an insistence on physical labor. He would never waver in this approach: console the patient by adopting a benevolent tone, monitor hygiene, and prescribe a balanced diet, long walks, and above all sustained work in the field every day. Those simple rules would bring sleep and health to the monk even as they warded off his demons and melancholy. And yet treatment to help "those wretched recluses" had henceforth become pointless "since the true remedy [had] already been prescribed by the National Assembly" when it voted to abolish religious vows.[35] In other words, laws were like prescriptions, and the role of the state—to monitor the health of society—merged with that of physicians, whose duty was to stand up on occasion, as here, to legitimize the political authorities.

Pinel was earnestly committed to the Revolution. And yet this article might seem surprising. Hadn't he himself donned a cassock at age eighteen? As a seminarian with the Fathers of Christian Doctrine, he had joined the Blue Penitents, where he was listed as a "tonsured cleric," a title that he added to his signature at the time.[36] And between 1767 and 1770, when studying for his doctorate in theology at the University of Toulouse, he faithfully attended the courses given by Father Jacques Bourges (the priest who exhorted Jean Calas to abjure his Protestant faith when Calas was publicly tortured in 1762). It was not until he was twenty-five that Pinel finally abandoned this path in favor of medicine. After this late but crucial decision he apparently lost his faith, according to his biographer, Dora B. Weiner. It is nevertheless impossible to read his "Medical Reflections on the Monastic Condition" without taking into account that long period of his youth, and recollections of it perhaps supplied this enthusiastic convert to the Revolution with his arguments.

Pinel's political opinions would nevertheless evolve, and his ardor would cool. The invasion of the Tuileries Palace by the Paris mob on June 20, 1792, worried him. "If the hereditary representative of the nation is no longer respected," he wrote to his brother Louis, "then there will be no more government, no more society, and we will wind up slaughtering one another."[37] The massacres that took place in September appalled him. In November he nevertheless advised his brother, a priest, to counsel the country folk "to avoid periodic excesses in drink and to direct their activity elsewhere, in patriotic celebrations and civic gatherings."[38] The execution of Louis XVI, which he attended as an armed guard, provided an occasion to draw up an initial assessment.

> You know that in the early days of the revolution I, too, had ambitions [to go into politics]; but my life, like those of my colleagues, was in such danger even though I was merely seeking justice and the good of the people, and I devised so profound a dread of the clubs and popular gatherings that ever since that time I have remained aloof from all public positions that have nothing to do with my medical profession. . . . As a physician and philosopher, accustomed to meditating on governments ancient and modern, and on human nature, I can foresee only anarchy, factions, and wars that will be disastrous even for the victors, now that I truly know [Paris] and the full worth of so many pygmies making so much noise.[39]

Citizen Pinel cherished democratic values. But the escalating violence disgusted the moderate Enlightenment thinker in him. Why, then, was he still a member of the national guard for the Piques district in 1793? And wasn't the decree appointing him to the post of physician at Bicêtre on August 6, 1793, issued during the Terror? Historians have often suggested that Pinel was a political opportunist during this period. But all these contradictions and ideological paradoxes may shed light on the motives of the famous inventor of "mental therapy," a socially conscious, fraternal method—as he sufficiently stressed—that straddled the medical and the political. It is worth adopting this dialectical perspective, which makes it possible to recognize a mirror relationship between Pinel's political opinions and his therapeutic method, when reading his "Observations on Mania at the Service of the Natural History of Mankind," delivered in December 1974 and now considered to be the founding document of French psychiatry. Indeed, the keen promoter of new ideas, the heavyhearted witness to the king's execution, and the former tonsured cleric celebrating the abolition of monastic vows were all the same man who would advocate both consolation and domination, benevolence and intimidation when treating the insane.

Thanks to his experience at the Belhomme home and especially to his first year at Bicêtre—which had such a major impact on him—Pinel decided to describe, for the first time in any depth, what madness is: in short, it is a disease of human sensitivity, whose causes were to be found in the torments of life—mourning, despair, jealously, desire for fame, excessive bookishness or religion. He observed two categories of maniacal insanity: one was constant, or chronic, whereas the other was intermittent, occurring in fits. Only two specific forms were considered curable, namely inflated pride and religious fanaticism, two passions that perhaps function as symbols of the aristocracy and the clergy.

Under Pinel's nuanced pen, madness—an ailment arising from the passions, but usually momentary and curable—was liable to appear in all healthy people but was no longer inevitable, a curse that thoroughly corrupted the mind. In this respect Pinel represented the key shift from a Kantian conception of madness as the Other of reason to a Hegelian vision of madness as a "mental derangement," a mere "contradiction in a still subsisting reason."[40] Madness was henceforth like a physical illness that weakened health but did not totally overwhelm it to the point of death.

> The idea of madness should by no means imply a total abolition of the mental faculties. On the contrary, the disorder usually attacks only one partial faculty such as the perception of ideas, judgment, reasoning, imagination, memory, or psychologic sensitivity. A madman who died this year and who thought that he was Louis XVI was a living example of the nonconformity of ideas with the objects that occasioned them, since he saw in all persons who entered the hospice so many Pages or Guardsmen come to receive his orders.[41]

The mentally ill do not rave all the time, or about everything, but retain a substrate of reason, which the doctor should try to reawaken. But how? The second part of Pinel's paper mentioned his own method—influenced by English psychiatry—treating the mind. Yet he only mentioned it, because Pinel never waxed theoretical about his famous therapy, which he always preferred to illustrate by concrete example. He often repeated the basic rules: listen, comfort, reassure, and distract the patient from the exclusive focus on his or her delusion; always favor gentleness and benevolence over harshness; avoid repression; prohibit physical violence in all but an ultimate extremity. These are in fact excellent principles, which no one would consider criticizing. One year after Pinel began working at Bicêtre, thanks to his efforts and the attention paid to food and hygiene, the death rate—which in 1788 had been over 60 percent—apparently fell to 14 percent, according to his own report. This figure alone demonstrates the progress made in asylums by the Revolution—and simultaneously underscores the barbaric methods of the ancien régime.

"Treating the mind" meant first protecting patients, then earning their trust, a preliminary phase in a therapy that included another key technique: intimidation. Indeed, madness had to be suppressed—although without raising a hand against it—by adopting "a thundering voice," a "most firm and imposing tone," and employing, if necessary, dissuasive force (for example, by sending several nurses at once in order to awe the patient). Pinel's conclusion was no less than spectacular: "One of the major principles of the psychological management of the insane is to break their will in a suitably timed manner, [to tame them] without causing wounds or imposing hard labor. Rather, *a formidable show of terror* should convince them that they are not free to pursue their impetuous willfulness and that their only choice is to submit."[42] The approach was unambiguous: break, tame, submit. And it was to be based on *a formidable show of terror*—an astonishing turn of phrase.

The date, remember, was late 1794. The Terror had fallen only in July, along with the head of Robespierre. And the Terror meant an emergency government, the disease of suspicion, and the triumph of the guillotine. How could Pinel, a critic of revolutionary excesses and a careful crafter of prose, have based the heart of his philanthropic method of treatment on such an inflammatory word? It might be argued that there is something specious in singling out and dwelling on a word or phrase in this way, that the expression was part of the idiom of the day, a rhetoric that was fashionably martial. But that is precisely why Pinel's choice of words is significant—it owes nothing to historical coincidence. The semantic richness of the word "terror"[43] (the arbitrariness of violence as part of a policy of useful, necessary virtue, that is to say as all at once attribute, method, and system of government) in fact is perfectly suited to the ambivalence of the birth of psychiatry, of its structure and ideological options. Pinel belonged (symbolically speaking, of course), to an emergency revolutionary council charged with saving the republic of reason in its fight against insanity—the insanity of both tyrants and lunatics. But the fight Pinel was waging against the mentally ill, who were subject to a dominant passion that corrupted their good sense, had to be done alongside the reasonable man that he remained despite himself. How can we reconcile, within a program of treating the mind, a "formidable show of terror" with a stated desire to dialogue with the insane? This contradiction permeates the entire history of mental therapy, trapped between the demon of domination and the ambition of communication with the mad, leading to the failure we are familiar with. Perhaps this setback should be understood as the incompatibility between a collective ideological program and an individual encounter with the singularity of madness, apparently truly taken into account only by the psychoanalytic method, with its techniques of transfer, detached listening, and benevolent neutrality.

There is another article by Pinel from this period, titled "Observations on the Asylum for the Insane at Bicêtre." It is identical with the paper cited above on every point, apart from a few tiny variants. The most important change is that Pinel replaced the sentence "Men are most often led from the free use of reason to madness by overstepping the limits of their good qualities and of their generous and magnanimous inclinations" with "Every repercussion of the revolution brings madmen into the asylum; these *pure patriots* have been pushed in the opposite direction by the clash of parties, thus after 9 Thermidor [the day Robespierre fell] a commanding officer of the Paris artillery arrived at the asylum."[44] Pinel's patriotism, meanwhile, accords with an interpretation of the asylum as a model of centralized Jacobinism, in which patients are *governed* and order is maintained by an *internal police* headed by a single man who holds all the *power*.

The lone man who managed the insane and imposed a commanding tone on them was not, as has been often thought and written, the doctor. The ward supervisor (or superintendent) performed that task, under the intellectual guidance of the expert in the matter. Pinel was very clear on this point.

> One of the essential features in every well-run hospice is having a general center of authority who makes decisions with no appeal, aimed at keeping order among the staff, exercising correct restraint over turbulent or very agitated patients, and determining whether a patient is suitable for the interview requested by one of his friends or close relatives. This overall authority must lie with the superintendent, and there is general confusion if the doctor or any other employee is weak

> enough to give way to complaints made to them and set their wishes and instructions in opposition to those of the superintendent.[45]

In most of the case studies Pinel published, it was indeed the supervisor—the philosopher-physician's military adviser—who played the leading role, taking the initiative, intervening, reassuring, correcting, and containing the insane. At Bicêtre the supervisor was Jean-Baptiste Pussin. On several occasions Pinel acknowledged his debt to Pussin, a former scrofula patient who went from cared-for to carer and thus never again left the hospital grounds. Of imposing height and authoritarian temperament, this former tanner from Lons-le-Saulnier unwittingly pioneered the profession of psychiatric nurse. Pussin had very set ideas on the treatment to be imposed on the mad in the hospital ward allocated to them, called Saint-Prix, of which he was appointed superintendent in 1785. Pussin practiced what Pinel would later theorize—he subjugated and controlled patients nonviolently thanks to the iron rule of a strong voice with a clear unhesitating tone. It was Pussin who was responsible for famously "freeing" the mentally ill from their chains after Pinel left for La Salpêtrière hospital in 1795.[46]

On the eve of the French Revolution, the hospital at Bicêtre was a hellhole. Contemporary chronicler Louis Sébastien Mercier offered a striking description of it in his *Tableau de Paris*. "A dreadful ulcer on the body politic; a wide, deep, suppurating ulcer that can be viewed only by averting your eyes. Even the air of the place, which you can smell from eight hundred yards away, tells you that your are approaching a place of force, an asylum of wretchedness, degradation, and misfortune."[47] Forty years later the situation, as described by Victor Hugo, appeared unchanged.

> Seen from a distance, there is a certain majesty to the building. It unfolds on the horizon, on the edge of a hill, and from afar retains something of its former splendor, a royal chateau. But as you approach it, this palace becomes a hovel. The crumbling gables pain the eye. Something shameful and impoverished soils these royal facades—you would think the walls had leprosy. There are no more panes, no more glass, in the windows, but instead a grid of massive iron bars, to which there clings here and there the gaunt figure of a convict or madman.
>
> That is life viewed close up.[48]

Prison, hospital, and hospice (for the poor), this grim institution housed four thousand people in appalling conditions. Two hundred of them were insane, idiotic, imbecilic, demented, or epileptic, chained up and mixed with the vagabonds and the criminals, the scabious and the venereal. On arrival, the insane were issued a uniform they never changed: a tailcoat, gray breeches of linsey-woolsey, stockings, a cap, and wooden clogs. The most dangerous or recalcitrant were locked up, tied with ropes to planks fastened to the wall. Others slept straight on the floor or on a pallet in one of the 173 six-foot-square rooms on the ground floor, whose doors had a slot just wide enough to pass food. Cold and damp gnawed at walls and bones. The food was inedible, the air unbreathable, the ground strewn with detritus. Bicêtre was a garbage dump a league outside Paris, ignored by the world. The inmates fought at night to snatch a neighbor's blanket, amid cries and lamen-

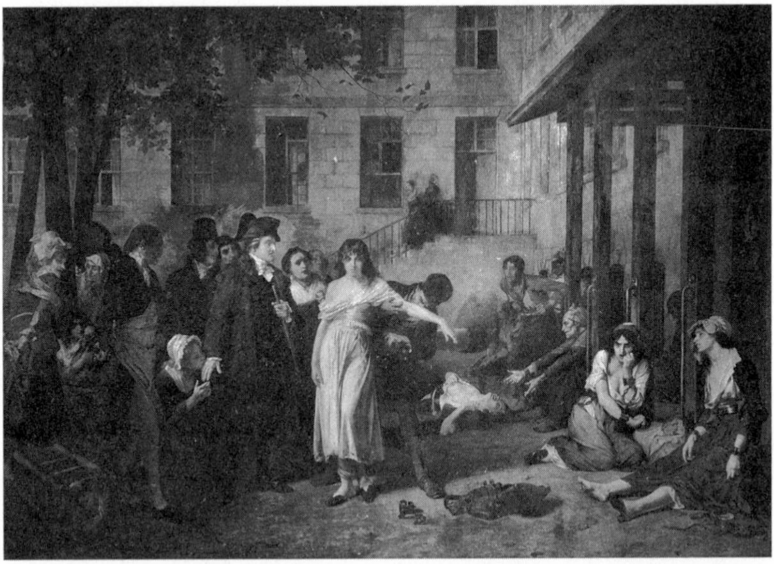

FIGURE 8. Tony Robert-Fleury, *Dr. Philippe Pinel Orders the Removal of the Chains from the Insane* (1876). Oil on canvas. Hôpital de La Salpêtrière, Paris. Although Robert-Fleury's painting shows Pinel freeing the insane from their chains at La Salpêtrière, the event probably occurred at Bicêtre several years earlier, at the initiative of the ward supervisor, Jean-Baptiste Pussin. This painting helped create the legend that this ceremonial gesture by the philanthropic Pinel represented the birth of French psychiatry. Photograph: Agence Bulloz. Photograph © RMN-Grand Palais/Art Resource, New York.

FIGURE 9. French school, *The Bicêtre Hospital* (1710). Colored engraving. In 1632, Louis XIII ordered that a military hospital be built on the ruins of the château de Bicêtre. Later transformed into a general hospital, prison, and madhouse, Bicêtre became the symbol of "total confinement." Pinel was appointed director there in 1793. Bibliothèque Nationale de France, Paris. Photograph © Charmet Archives/ The Bridgeman Art Library.

tations, while in daytime they vegetated on rotten straw pallets when not allowed to wander in the courtyard. The warders, who sold little items of straw made by the patients during their free time, enjoyed the circus of madness, spurring on the most excitable, the better to shower them with blows or deliver them to the voyeurism of the numerous visitors who came to watch, at the cost of few farthings, the spectacle of convulsives behind their grated windows.[49] A commission appointed in 1790 made a visit to the site and asked if there were "any method of cure used for madness." The steward answered, "No, all the madmen sent to Bicêtre remain *in statu quo* until it pleases nature to favor them."[50]

"EVENTS CONNECTED WITH THE REVOLUTION"

Once he arrived at Bicêtre in September 1793 to assume his functions, Pinel got down to work and drew up a chart of the two hundred mental patients in his care, based on information supplied by Pussin. For eighty of them, he managed to identify the "known occasional causes," divided into four main categories:

Domestic misfortunes
Financial troubles, jealously, forced divorce, or the loss of a beloved child are often the cause of insanity, and Bicêtre numbers twenty-seven madmen of this kind [33.75 percent].

Love
Eight patients [10 percent] went mad owing to excessive sentimental sensitivity and five owing to fiery temperament. The latter carry out indecent acts when they see women.

Religion or fanaticism
These number eighteen [22.5 percent], some of whom believe themselves to be gods or prophets, while others perform puerile acts of religion, sometimes exhausting themselves through abstinence and fasting.

Events connected with the Revolution
There are twenty-seven patients [33.75 percent] whose reason was deranged because of events connected with the Revolution, through either reversals of fortune, fear of requisition, or other incidents.[51]

Note that this classification, which is neither alphabetical nor numerical, lists in last place the category that, from a quantitative standpoint, should be placed first, especially since it overlaps with at least two other groups: "reversals of fortune" (usually attributable to revolutionary upheaval) and divorce (which, whether forced or not, was legalized only on September 20, 1792). Furthermore, how many people sank into extreme religiousness or fanaticism after the revolutionary laws on the civil constitution of the clergy and the outlawing of monastic vows? As difficult as they are to measure, these traumas stemming from legal and political upheavals could figure as the indirect consequence—indeed collateral damage—of the Revolution.

In the first edition of his *Medico-philosophical Treatise on Mental Alienation, or Mania*, published in Revolutionary Year IX (1800), Pinel refined his assessment, this time based on 113 cases. Imitating the first chart, the new breakdown gives:

Domestic misfortunes	34 cases [30% of the total]
Love	24 cases [21%]
Religion or fanaticism	25 cases [22%]
Events connected with the Revolution	30 cases [27%][52]

God, money, love: it is hardly surprising that we find here these key, ritual subjects of mental delusion, which run throughout the history of psychiatry. On the other hand, the confirmation of "revolutionary events" as one of the four major causes of mental illness is worth dwelling on. It represents the appearance, for the first time, of political turmoil as a *pertinent* category in the etiology of madness. And this new type of illness accounted, according to Pinel's estimates, for one-quarter (27 percent) to one-third (33.75 percent) of all identifiable causes of madness at Bicêtre. As he justifiably exclaimed, "What period could be more favorable than that of revolutionary storms, ever prompt to supply the passions with burning issues, or rather to trigger madness in all its forms!"[53] True enough, the origin of the illness still resided in the passions, but that those passions were henceforth associated with a specific, explicitly described political moment represented a watershed that carries a certain irony. The French Revolution invented modern madness—or at least laid the foundations for its administrative organization and medical treatment—and simultaneously acknowledged itself to be the very source of that scourge. The Revolution would therefore treat what it supposedly helped to cause, or at least to spread. Indeed, the corollary question was obviously whether the Revolution simply brought to light a particular group of mental patients or whether it triggered an actual increase in the number of lunatics.

According to figures supplied by Pussin, during the Revolution madness apparently decreased—at least at Bicêtre—in an almost continuous curve, admissions sliding from 142 in 1787 to 67 in 1797, representing a drop of over half in ten years. This spectacular decline is nevertheless skewed by the fact that from 1791 onward the seventh ward, headed by Pussin, received only those lunatics judged incurable—the calmer ones were sent to a rest home. Furthermore, food shortages dramatically increased the death rate, invalidating estimates that are impossible to verify.[54]

Whatever the case, we still need to understand the conditions under which "events connected with the Revolution" emerged as potential triggers of mental disorder and how those events translated into delusions and affected everyday life at the asylum. What can they tell us, if we read between the lines, about the relationship between ideology and pathology?

Raising this issue means returning to a period of preromantic sensibility when the modern individual and the political subject were emerging, as outlined by the Jean-Jacques Rousseau of *The New Heloise*, *The Confessions*, and of course *The Social Contract*. Rousseau's "new man"—who abandoned the encyclopedic project in order to grasp the world through his own subjectivity, who identified with the characters in psychological novels, and who based self-knowledge on introspection—was henceforth a citizen endowed with rights in a world where sovereignty was suddenly shifting from monarchical verticality (God, king, subjects) to democratic horizontality (people and nation). The tension between the birth of the modern "individual" and the sovereignty of "the people" marked the entire nineteenth century as politics invaded the private sphere just as men and women became increasingly involved in the affairs of the commonweal.

This political revolution of mores, although impossible to evaluate in terms of its impact on hearts and minds, can be observed in the social evolution of one particular act: suicide. An enlightening study by Dominique Godineau has recently shown that while it is materially impossible to assert that the number of suicides increased during the eighteenth century, suicide in Paris became—along with madness—a topic of public anxiety, one much evoked, described, and discussed. Although lacking hard figures, society "had the impression" that suicide was increasing—a peak seems to have been reached during the Revolutionary Years II and III (1793–95), linked to economic depression—and that the rise was related to the political situation, as witnessed by reports filed in police archives between 1789 and 1795. For example, social unrest "warped the mind" of a servant who threw himself into a well on July 17, 1789; a former soldier killed himself in Year II (1793–94) for fear of "being considered a suspect," while a woman threw herself into the water because, she said, she was the "wife of a [political] émigré." These examples of suicide by people in despair over revolutionary violence, or else swearing to die "republicans and democrats" while consigning their souls to the Supreme Being,[55] belonged to the same society as the patients locked up at Bicêtre. Former subjects of an abstract monarchy became citizens swept up in the turmoil—sometimes "kicking and screaming"—as politics became an object of concern or even dread, reflected every day in the street.

The suicides related to this new political awareness were mirrored by the self-inflicted deaths (attempted or accomplished) of many political leaders: Clavière, Roland, Condorcet, Barbaroux, Buzot, Pétion, Roux, Robespierre the Younger, and Lebas, not to mention the last Montagnards of 1795. Similarly, madness might well have two faces and be shared between victims and perpetrators. The ever-escalating horror, such as the massacres of September 1792 and the "freeing" of the princesse Maria-Thérèse de Lamballe, the better to slay her, was perhaps a symptom of collective madness. Didn't Michel-Mathieu Lecointre-Puyraveau request, during a session of the Convention on March 21, 1793, that Marat be declared in a "state of dementia"?[56] The accelerating Terror, which culminated in a paranoid frenzy and a series of summary executions, largely contributed to the now banal comparison of the French Revolution to a bout of madness.

There is no doubt that the unleashing of terrific energies during the Revolution led to agitated minds and troubling behavior. But to go from there to a glib diagnosis of "madness" proves, if proof were needed, the worrisome elasticity of a word quickly exploited for ideological propaganda by popular culture of every political stripe. For example, a monarchist tale published in May 1793, titled *Voyage du diable et de la folie, ou Causes des révolutions de France, Brabant, Liège et autres* (The voyage of the devil and Folly as causes of the revolutions in France, Brabant, Liège, and elsewhere), featured Lucifer and his dreadful female traveling companion named "Folly" (a minion of "His Majesty Insania"), who spurred people to all kinds of crime and wickedness.[57] Revolutionaries were not to be outdone: for example, once monastic vows were outlawed, they distributed educational prints showing a monk and a nun kissing on the altar of love, with the caption, "Foolishness and madness locked us in the cloister, but reason has returned us to this world." Another print showed a madman with donkey's ears, dubbed "atheism," breaking the zodiacal ring of wisdom and trampling the harvest.[58] Given the running series of capitalized struggles between the likes of Progress and Barbarity or Humanism and Tyranny, the times could hardly overlook the "natural" duel between Reason and Madness.

It is easy to appreciate the danger of seeing "madness" everywhere, even as allegory. It drains politics of meaning and goals, blurring motives by comparing policies to delusions that, once dismissed as insane, can no longer be conceptualized. Citing "madness" when judging the ancien régime or the Terror means abdicating any scrutiny of their methodical plans and refusing to examine the concerted violence of their actions, which is the very opposite of political analysis.

Given this situation, what was the reality of madness in 1793? What cries issued from the asylum, and what were they symptoms of? For answers we must once again turn to Pinel, that crucial interpreter of the sweeping revolutionary disorder. "I have always very greatly valued semeiology [*sic*]," he wrote.[59] This term, which once referred to the study of clinical symptoms, now means, in its modern spelling of semiology, the analysis of systems of signs and communication. Observing and transcribing: these two approaches are inseparable, and the psychiatrist Pinel paid particular attention to both, following in the footsteps of Hippocrates, whose accurate, concise, and pure writing he admired.[60] Pinel not only was a shrewd clinician but was a skilled writer with a real talent for storytelling. In just a few words he could sketch a portrait, describe a situation, or capture a psychological trait. Like everyone, he had his preferred vocabulary and his tics. The most recurrent terms in his *Treatise* include "chain of ideas," "order" (in the asylum, in the mind, in reasoning) and "disorder" (in senses, organs, and ideas as well as in "scenes of disorder," the "nature of their disorder," and "physical disorders"); those in his records at La Salpêtrière notably featured *révolution* in the sense of physiological "turmoil" (which included menstrual flow), sometimes employed in expressions such as "delusion subsequent to turmoil [*révolution*] from having seen a man hanged" and "she experienced turmoil on the death of her child."[61]

Pinel spent nineteen months at Bicêtre (1793–95), an asylum that accepted only men, and twenty-five years (1795–1820) at La Salpêtrière, a hospital reserved for women. Why, then, do men occupy such a preponderant place in his *Treatise* of 1800, republished in 1809? True enough, the first edition largely comprised earlier articles. But nine years later Pinel had already been treating the madwomen at La Salpêtrière for fourteen years. The new edition was expanded by two hundred pages, in which women were of course more often present, but usually only in general statements (proportion of unmarried patients, average length of treatment, rate of relapses, etc.). Individual cases very rarely made it into publications—there are no detailed portraits and only a few vignettes. Yet even by Pinel's admission madness affected twice as many women as men,[62] a circumstance related to poverty and

FIGURE 10. Adam Pérelle, *Plate 31: View of La Salpêtrière Hospital in Paris* (1680). Engraving, 20 cm × 29 cm. La Salpêtrière was the first establishment within the general hospital administration founded by Louis XIV in 1656. It was also the largest place of confinement for women who were beggars, prostitutes, or mentally ill. Ten thousand female inmates lived in this veritable city within a city on the eve of the French Revolution. Châteaux de Versailles et de Trianon, Versailles. Photograph: Gérard Blot. Photograph © RMN-Grand Palais/Art Resource, New York.

to the policing of the many prostitutes and "debauched women" in La Salpêtrière. These beggars, whores, and senile old women often could not read or write, and they had no social status apart from belonging to the anonymous mass of the poor. They did not belong, as individuals, to history.

Women therefore were the object of generalizations, statistics, and probabilities; to men belonged the specific, explicit tale. Pinel's penchant for narrative drew him primarily to his patients' personal tragedies, to their picturesque attitudes or their harangues inside the asylum, and to didactic descriptions of their treatment (even when it failed). His "vignettes" are not only psychological in inspiration, but also moral and political. For example, Citizen Pinel unhesitatingly opined that "derangement of the nobility" is "almost always incurable," on the grounds that the active, working life they despise represents the sovereign road to recovery.[63] The regular, mechanical life he advocated was furthermore always envisaged in a model family context that relegated libertines, single people, religious fanatics, and unworthy mothers to a dire diagnosis.

So what actually ailed victims of "events connected with the Revolution," those "fevered minds" and "lost souls"? Many of them, from whatever social class, had lost all their possessions—the fruit of an entire lifetime—as well as their reason. They had suffered shocks that, often aggravated by destitution, led to the asylum. Take the farmer's daughter who, during the civil war in Vendée, saw her family massacred and—abandoned, destitute, mad with sorrow—ended up in La Salpêtrière. Then there was a young soldier whose brother was killed right beside him and who was taken home stunned; a third brother, seeing him in that state, fell into a similar bewilderment—both men were then taken to the asylum. And then there was the fifteen-year-old who, witnessing his father's violent death, fell mute and lost his mind.

But lethal violence was not the only cause of trauma—far from it. Frustrated ambition could cause lasting damage. Take a grenadier who helped lead the attack on the Bastille but whose valor went unrecognized; he was overcome with maniacal delusions that cost him two years in Bicêtre. "He should have been given the rank of captain rather than all that bathing and hosing," commented Pinel in the common-sense tone he enjoyed adopting.[64] Conversely, recognition could have fateful consequences: "In Year II of the Republic, an artilleryman presented the Committee of Public Safety with a plan for a newly invented canon that would be terribly effective. It was decided to test it at Meudon on a given day, and Robespierre wrote such an encouraging letter to the inventor that on reading it the man was transfixed to the spot; not long afterward he was sent to Bicêtre in a state of total idiocy."[65]

Yet these emotional shocks, whose variety precludes any specific conclusion, cannot be *directly* imputed to the Revolution. It is tempting to agree with Esquirol that death, bankruptcy, and "bloated pride" would probably have caused the same damage in other historical circumstances. But the Terror produced in Paris a very specific climate of threat and fear, easily detectable in the causes of admissions to the asylum. According to the firsthand account of Louis Sébastien Mercier, the population of Paris was dazed by the confusion and swiftness with which events unfolded. Carried away by an indiscriminate power that was beyond them, the passive, mute people of Paris became automatons, remaining speechless before the violence of the tiny, bloodthirsty gangs silently condoned by political leaders. The senseless overheating of the political machine triggered a traumatic collapse among men and women who sincerely wanted freedom but fell into inertia and paralysis.[66] The people were *literally* stupefied. While historiography has made much of the evil joy of mobs celebrating beheadings and massacres with dreadful bacchanals, we should not overlook the petrifying, Medusa-like impact of the sight of a "decapitated head." And in the asylums a face could be put on this terror, one with an abstract geometric shape framed by the outlines of a very concrete device: the guillotine.

SPECTERS OF THE GUILLOTINE

"The scaffold," wrote Victor Hugo, "has something about it which produces hallucination. . . . The scaffold is a vision." He viewed it as a being with a life of its own, "possessed of I know not what somber initiative," throwing him into "frightful meditation."[67] The guillotine projected an image of unrivaled formal impact—a symbol as much as a method of execution, it would haunt minds and populate nightmares. In 1794 the marquis de Sade, incarcerated in the Coignard prison in the Picpus neighborhood, could see the Place du Trône Renversé (today Place de la Nation) where executions were being carried out. The corpses were then dumped into ditches dug on the very grounds of his prison. "My *republican* imprisonment," he would write, "*with the guillotine before my eyes*, did me a hundred times more harm than every imaginable Bastille."[68]

Familiarity with death during the Revolution in no way lessened the horror of decapitation. The new mechanical method of bisecting a living being triggered an anxiety similar to the obscurantist fear that had long accompanied the dissection of corpses. It violated the same taboo. What prisoners awaiting the carrying out of their sentences dreaded was not so much death itself as the public dismemberment, the end to the integrity of the body in a gush of blood. The death of the king had already produced acts of despair, as reported in the periodical *Révolutions de Paris*: "We have learned that a soldier, formerly decorated with the Cross of Saint Louis, died of sorrow on learning of the death of Louis XVI; that a bookseller named Ventre, formerly associated with the Revels, went mad; that a wigmaker on rue Culture-Sainte-Catherine, known for his royalist zeal, slit his throat with a razor out of despair" (thereby mimicking his king's fate).[69] A new law, adopted on September 17, 1793, expressly targeted "suspects" and thereby intensified the pressure on everyone.[70] Pinel had taken up his post at Bicêtre on September 11.

Now, if there is one trait that characterized victims of "events connected with the Revolution," it was indeed anguish at the idea of losing their heads. A specific feature of this particular theme of delusion was that it concerned all kinds of madness, from maniacal insanity to melancholia. It could be serious enough to lead to death. "An object of fear or terror," wrote Pinel, "can produce habitual consternation that leads to wasting away and death. I thus saw two Austrian soldiers, made prisoners of war, succumb in the infirmary at Bicêtre, convinced that they were about to perish on the guillotine."[71]

This conviction might be more or less justified, and given the climate of terror it is hard today to assess the element of reality versus that of fantasy. On one hand there was the steward of a great lord, ruined by the Revolution, imprisoned and fearing daily a summons to the scaffold, who lost his mind and wound up thinking he was the king of France; and on the other there was a young patient who grabbed a knife from the asylum's kitchen and threatened to cut off everyone's heads.[72] Both as a recurring hallucination and as a very real horror, decapitation crystallized all kinds of anguish and violence.

Two cases Pinel mentioned eloquently illustrate this point. The first concerned a worker who one day freely expressed his opinion of the sentence meted out to Louis XVI. His patriotism henceforth came under suspicion in his neighborhood: "Upon hearing some vague hints and a few threatening comments whose danger he exaggerated," the man "betook himself trembling and in dark consternation to his own house."[73] He lived in perpetual fear, losing the ability to eat and sleep until he lost his mind. He was sent to Hôtel-Dieu, where he was given the usual treatment based on bloodletting. Failing to improve, he was transferred to Bicêtre. When he arrived at the asylum "the idea of his death haunted him night and day, and he unceasingly repeated that he was prepared to submit to his impending fate." Pinel, applying his usual principles, encouraged the man to take up his trade of tailor within the asylum, making himself useful by repairing other patients' clothing. Improvement soon followed, lasting several months until hot summer weather arrived, when the patient had a relapse and spoke only of going through with his death sentence. Pinel then turned to a method he would often employ: ruse. He informed the ward supervisor that a supposed commission from the legislature would soon be arriving at Bicêtre to try the citizen-patient and would acquit him if his innocence was established. Pinel recruited three young doctors and "assigned the principal role to the eldest and gravest of them."

> These commissaries, who were dressed in black robes suitable to their pretended office, ranged themselves around a table and caused the melancholic to be brought before them. He was then questioned on his profession, former conduct, the journals he had been in the habit of reading, and other particulars respecting his patriotism. The defendant related all that he had said and done and insisted on a final judgment, as he did not think himself guilty of any crime. In order to make a deep impression on his imagination, the head of the small delegation pronounced in a loud voice the following sentence: "By virtue of the power which has been delegated to us by the National Assembly, we have entered proceedings in due form of law against Citizen ****, and having duly examined him . . . we declare that we have found the said Citizen **** a truly loyal patriot; and, pronouncing his acquittal, we forbid all further proceedings against him. We furthermore order that he be freed and returned to his family. But inasmuch as he has obstinately refused to work for the last twelve months, we order his detention at Bicêtre to be prolonged six months from this present time, which said six months he is to employ, with proper sentiments of gratitude, in the capacity of tailor to the house, and we hold the ward superintendent responsible for carrying out this sentence at the peril of said superintendent's life." The commissaries then withdrew in silence, and everything indicated that the impression produced on the patient's mind was most profound.

In the following days the stratagem seemed to have worked, at least according to Pinel's criteria, because the patient went back to work and asked that his child be brought to him—signs of progress. But this improvement did not last, and the patient lapsed back into inactivity, reviving "traces of his previous delusion, exacerbated by the imprudent disclosure to him that the final sentence pronounced in the name of the National Assembly was pure jest. I now consider his case as absolutely incurable."

This edifying tale sheds an alternative light on the causes of delusion and the methods of treatment. That the tailor, based on "vague" hints and "exaggerated" threats, believed himself—*wrongly*, as Pinel suggests—to be scheduled for the guillotine appears to be of secondary importance here. In an environment where beheading was a perfectly plausible punishment for speaking one's mind, it was not so much the authenticity of the facts and their origins as the realistic effects of the phantasm that should be treated. How? Not by trying to persuade the deluded character of his mistake in order to lead him back to his *right mind* but, on the contrary, by showing him he is *right*. This attempt to enter into patients' delusions and thereby to validate their distress opened another avenue to mental therapy by attempting to converse with madness or at least to find some common ground with it. Although such a dialogue is obviously skewed, involving manipulation, it nonetheless represents a dialogue, a mirror relation in which the lunatic's "deluded fiction" is reflected—flipped—by the psychiatrist's "healing fiction."[74] The symmetrical implementation of this tactic, designed to eradicate fear (of decapitation) through fear (of the trial) in no way runs counter to a strategy of intimidation. On the contrary, the "show of authority," the (phony) judges' "grave" air, and the responsibility assigned to the ward supervisor to carry out the sentence ("at the peril of his own life"!) on all points recall the "formidable show of terror" on which Pinel based his methods.

But the anticipated salutary effect did not last long, because even before learning that he had been duped, the patient lapsed into his earlier delusion. Pinel reprinted the first part of this case study word for word in the second edition of his *Treatise* but cut the part on the unsuccessful hoax.[75] The pioneer and storyteller of 1800 was replaced by the respected physician, professor, and statistician of 1809. I might add that in none of his writings did Pinel see fit to pay tribute to Joseph Daquin, a doctor from Chambéry who was the first to encourage physicians to "bend to the nature of the lunatic and to become, so to speak, one [themselves]" in order to heal insanity by not systematically denying the object of delusion.[76] He developed this idea as early as 1791 in a book titled *La philosophie de la folie* (The philosophy of madness), which set out the principles of a "humane" treatment of the mentally ill, whom he had freed from their chains in his own asylum. Unfortunately, Daquin burned all his clinical notes, which would surely have shed light on an important chapter in the birth of psychiatry.

Perhaps even more spectacular was the second case Pinel recounted, involving a famous Paris clockmaker. The man was driven by the idea of perpetual motion—a pipe dream that the Académie des Sciences had declared impossible and had even condemned in 1755 for fruitlessly wasting engineers' inventiveness. But the clockmaker nevertheless pursued this impossible quest, working with a zeal that deprived him of sleep and fired his imagination to the point of delirium, a delirium that the "revolutionary storms" helped to excite by riveting his attention on perpetual motion of another sort—that of the guillotine.

> His loss of reason was marked by a most striking feature. He fancied that he had lost his head on the scaffold; that it had been thrown indiscriminately among the heads of many other victims; that the judges, having repented of the cruel sentence, had ordered those heads to be restored to their respective owners and placed upon their respective shoulders; but that, in consequence of an unfortunate mistake, the gentlemen who had the management of that business had placed upon his shoulders the head of one of his companions in misfortune. This idea of this change of head occupied this thoughts night and day, which determined his relations to send him to Hôtel-Dieu. Thence he was transferred to the asylum at Bicêtre. Nothing could equal his outrageousness and noisy bursts of jovial humor. He sang, shouted, danced; and since his maniacal insanity entailed no act of violence, he was allowed to go about the hospital freely, in order to expend his tumultuous effervescence. "Look at these teeth," he would cry, "mine were exceedingly handsome, but these are rotten. My mouth was healthy; this one is diseased. What a difference between this hair and mine before my head was changed!"[77]

Shortly thereafter, however, the watchmaker became enraged and violent. He was confined to a separate cell, where he remained for several months. When he calmed down in winter, he was allowed out again. Still driven by the idea of perpetual motion, he was allowed to practice his craft. Pussin even permitted him to set up a workbench in his room, so that he could pursue his passion until the day when, convinced that he had solved the mystery yet was unable to prove it, he abandoned his quest. However, he still needed to be cured of his remaining obsession—his change of head.

> A witty, irrefutable jest seemed the best way to correct it. Another convalescent of a gay and facetious humor was instructed in the part he was to play; an interview with the watchmaker was arranged, and the other patient adroitly turned the conversation to the famous miracle of Saint Denis who carried his head in his hands [after being beheaded], kissing it as he walked along. The watchmaker strongly asserted the feasibility of the deed and sought to confirm it through his own case. The other set up a loud laugh, and replied with a tone of keen ridicule: "A madman you are, for how could Saint Denis kiss his own head? With his heel?" This unexpected and irrefutable retort struck the lunatic forcefully. He retired confused amid the peals of laughter all around him and never again spoke of his change of head. Close attention to his clockmaker's trade for some months completed the restoration of his reason. He returned to his family and has for more than five years now pursued his business without experiencing a relapse.

Different delusion, different tactic. Indeed, the clockmaker did not suffer from the same disorder as the previous patient, since he claimed that he *had lost his head* and therefore acknowledged, at least metaphorically, that he had *lost his mind*. What he wanted was the return of his healthy head, with its healthy teeth and mouth. Pinel's clever trick involved exploiting the logical dimension of his delusion, countering it with the myth of an allegedly true "miracle" recounted by a *madman* in the asylum. It is hardly surprising that the clockmaker sought to explain the possibility of kissing his own head; it might be supposed that, in his mind, the replacement head could well have kissed his original head. Nothing in this account, for that matter, indicates that he was convinced by the jest. It was apparently only the humiliation of the jeers that reduced him to silence.

While we may entertain doubts about this miraculous cure, or at least the efficacy of the method employed, the anecdote still shows how far the guillotine extended its empire over imaginations. Yet the most striking thing is the longevity of revolutionary trauma in psychiatric archives, the unprecedented persistence of the obsession with "losing your head." Decades after the event, in admission records at both La Salpêtrière and Charenton, the column devoted to the presumed causes

FIGURE 11. Villeneuve, *Louis Capet Being Welcomed to Hades* (1793). Aquatint, 26.8 cm × 36.7 cm. Louis XVI, having just stepped from Charon's boat with his head under his arm, is welcomed by Charles IX, described as "another murderer, like Louis, of the French people." Several other aristocrats brandish their decapitated heads. This imaginative realm of beheadings matches the delusions of many mental patients who were convinced that they had "lost their heads" and were obliged to live with a replacement head. Bibliothèque Nationale de France, Paris. Photograph © BNF.

of madness still mentioned revolutionary terror and the spectacle of the guillotine.

At La Salpêtrière, according to the register of patient transfers, fourteen cases were directly related to the Revolution, admitted between March 17, 1802, and August 1, 1804: "madwoman these past ten years, raving, caused by the Revolution"; "fears being guillotined"; "periodic madness since the Revolution began"; "first collapse at age thirteen, following grief at seeing her parents depart during the Revolution . . . on the 13th instant threw herself in the river to do away with herself."[78]

The litany continued at the Charenton asylum, which accepted both men and women but was mainly reserved for members of the military (and their families), civil servants, and other patients able to pay higher board. These higher social classes nevertheless had the same ailments. "She has been mad for fourteen years," wrote the doctor with regard to Madame Camus de Lam, who was admitted in 1807: "Her delusion dates from the Revolution, when she was imprisoned and suffered greatly . . . which appears to be the cause of her delirium; she raves, shouts, swears and is always ready to strike."[79] Memory of the Revolution's harmful effects seemed indelible. In 1819, when a sixty-four-year-old woman was brought to Charenton (where she would die two months later), it was noted that "she talks about the guillotine, she experiences panicky terror, she claims that orders have been issued, she feels persecuted."[80] Deportation, financial ruin, and the devastation of religious institutions left lasting marks. Thus one Sister of Charity was convinced that the Holy Spirit had come to her, yet in 1820 she still feared "being poisoned, led to the guillotine."[81]

It was the same story with men: Jean-Pierre Laujon, son of a famous popular songwriter, had gone to England when all the turmoil began. Placed on the list of counterrevolutionary émigrés, he joined the prince de Condé's army and fought against the revolutionary troops. Arrested on the Swiss border in 1796, he was taken to Paris and sentenced to death but went mad; he was interned at Petites Maisons and then at Hôtel-Dieu, being finally transferred to Charenton in 1802. On his arrival, Laujon displayed "an exalted opinion of his knowledge and talents" yet had fallen into "total dementia" and spent his time "drawing grotesque figures that all seemed to be based on the same model. He thinks they are masterpieces of art." The opinion of the doctor who established that diagnosis was apparently shared by Mademoiselle Flore, an actress who went to Charenton to see a performance of Molière's *Le dépit amoureux* (The love tiff) staged by the marquis de Sade, who had been incarcerated in the asylum since 1803. "The little scene with [the valet] Mascarille," she wrote, "was very gaily performed by another madman . . . [who] was the son of the witty Laujon, dean of the popular songwriters. The poor young man suffers the delusion of thinking himself to be a great artist. On a piece of paper he draws houses, trees, and little figures, then sends these pictures to Madame de Saint-Aubin with a request for 40,000 francs."[82] But Laujon's harmless madness could also focus on more critical objects. "He has the most bizarre ideas," continued the doctor's report; "he thinks

FIGURE 12. Georges-François-Marie Gabriel, *Laujon the Younger, Idiot* (ca. 1823). Drawing. Bibliothèque Nationale de France, Paris. Photograph © BNF.

that he has been beheaded and that his head is still in England, that someone has probably given him another in its place; to replace missing teeth, he constantly wears pieces of cork in his mouth." These details are reminiscent, many years down the line, of the psychosis of the clockmaker who lamented a change of head and rotten teeth. Head cut off, replaced, obsession with teeth: dread of the guillotine carried with it a dread of castration, of a dismembered, dislocated body. Yet the kit for a body with its replaceable parts was still alive—it seemed that the miracle of escaping death by the blade represented a definitive victory over mortality, a triumph of the imagination over the threat of dismemberment. "Monsieur Laujon now combines the bizarre ideas

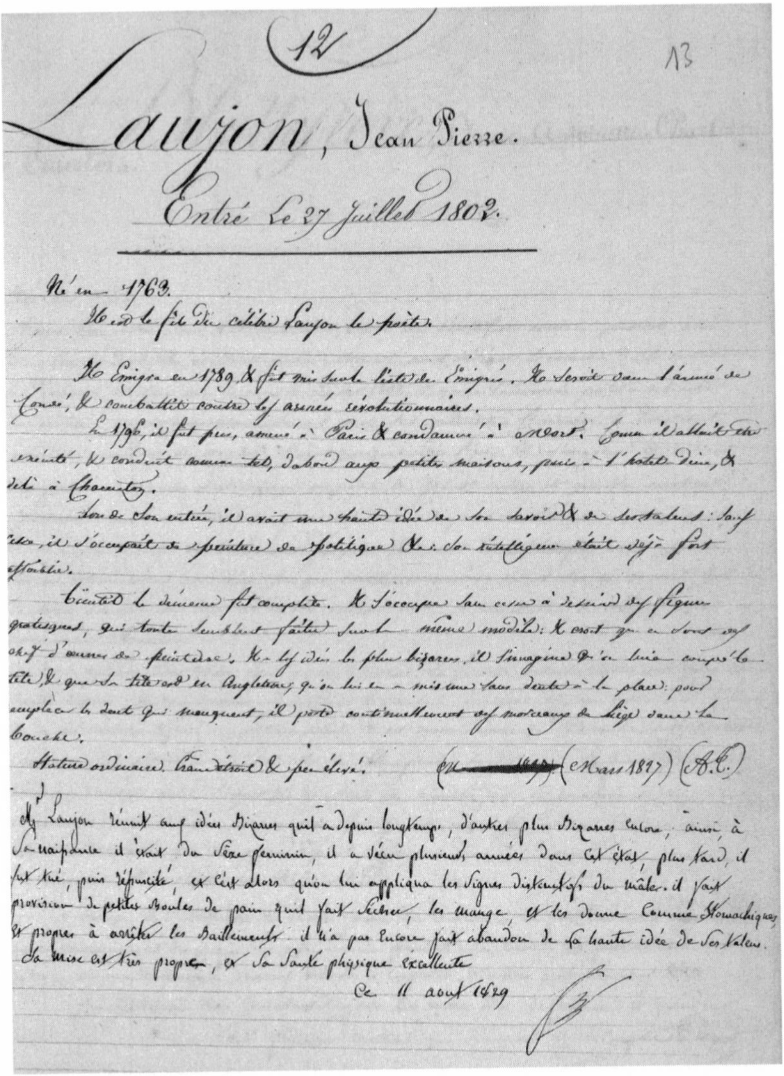

(12) 13

Laujon, Jean Pierre.

Entré le 27 juillet 1802.

Né en 1763.

Il est le fils du célèbre Laujon le poëte.

Il émigra en 1789 & fut mis sur la liste des émigrés. Il servit dans l'armée de Condé, & combattit contre les armées révolutionnaires.

En 1796, il fut pris, amené à Paris & condamné à mort. Comme il allait être exécuté, il [illegible] conduit comme tel, d'abord aux petites maisons, puis à l'hôtel Dieu, & delà à Charenton.

Lors de son entrée, il avait une haute idée de son savoir & de ses talens: sauf cela, il s'occupait de peinture, de politique &c. Son intelligence était déjà fort affaiblie.

Bientôt la démence fut complète. Il s'occupe sans cesse à dessiner des figures grotesques, qui toutes semblent faites sur le même modèle: il croit que ce sont des chef d'œuvres de peinture. Il a les idées les plus bizarres, il s'imagine qu'on lui a coupé la tête, & que sa tête est en Angleterre, qu'on lui en a mis une sans doute à la place: pour remplacer les dents qui manquent, il porte continuellement des morceaux de liège dans la bouche.

Stature ordinaire. Crâne étroit & peu élevé. ([illegible]) (Mars 1827) (A.C.)

M. Laujon réunit aux idées bizarres qu'il a depuis longtemps, d'autres plus bizarres encore; ainsi, à sa naissance il était du sexe féminin, il a vécu plusieurs années dans cet état, plus tard, il fut tué, puis ressuscité, et c'est alors qu'on lui appliqua les signes distinctifs du mâle. il fait provision de petites boules de pain qu'il fait sécher, les mange, et les donne comme stomachiques, et propres à arrêter les baillements. il n'a pas encore fait abandon de sa haute idée de ses talens. Sa mise est très propre, et sa santé physique excellente

Ce 11 aout 1829

FIGURE 13. Register of Medical Observations, Men and Women (Special Cases), Charenton (1827). Gabriel's portrait of Jean-Pierre Laujon (fig. 12, previous page) is accompanied by the page in the Charenton register devoted to his case. Having fled revolutionary France in 1789, Laujon was arrested on the Swiss border in 1796 and sentenced to death. He then went mad and was sent to Charenton, where he was obsessed with the idea that "he had been beheaded and his head was now in England." Laujon participated in the theatrical performances organized by fellow inmate the marquis de Sade. Photograph © Archives Départementales du Val-de-Marne.

he has long held with others still more bizarre," added the doctor in a later note. "For example, he was born a female and lived several years as that sex; later he was killed and then resuscitated, and that was when he was given the distinctive signs of a male."[83] This paragraph dates from 1829, forty years after the start of the French Revolution.

Many of Laujon's companions in misfortune in Charenton had had close brushes with death or some other dreadful danger. A former captain on duty when Louis XVI was sentenced to death—which "filled him with sorrow"—returned to France after a campaign in the mountains of Piedmont and "made several ill-considered comments." He "was arrested, tried twice" and "about to be sent to the scaffold. These various mental shocks seem to be the occasional causes of his illness, because he has constantly repeated from the start that he had been sentenced, that he would be executed, that he was leaving in order to restore the Bourbons." Admitted to Charenton in 1806, the captain was still vegetating in his cell in 1825, with no activity other than "unceasingly" taking the snuff rations allocated to all inmates. "His dementia seems to be total. Good physical health," concluded the report.[84]

The list goes on—and goes on for a surprisingly long time. In June 1855 Dr. Ernest Lasègue at Bicêtre could still write, "He has a mission to accomplish, his father died on the guillotine, he is related to Louis XVI and the emperor; he came to Paris to calm the factions."[85] The last such reference that I found in the archives dates from 1857. In a striking turn of phrase, it sums up the literal and figurative link between losing your head and losing your mind: "Raving dementia. Asked to be guillotined or placed in a straitjacket."[86]

It is most unlikely that these later patients, whose birth dates and ages are not mentioned in the ledger, actually lived through the Revolution (unless as infants). In contrast, they were part of the generation that lived through the political upheavals of 1830 and, not having experienced the Terror, appropriated a mental image of it and conceived an increasingly detailed picture. That picture was skewed and exaggerated by partisan attitudes, a mixture of history and phantasmagoria fueled by indirect rumors, recollections, and tales. Literature also played its part in the construction of a myth, beginning with "frenetic" romanticism in which the guillotine grew into an all-devouring monster that dug a ditch between the ideals of 1789 and the errors of 1793. Fantastic literature lapped up the dark blood of the guillotine in crazed visions of specters of Revolution all the way from Charles Nodier's 1821 psychological tale *Smarra, ou Les démons de la nuit* (Smarra, or The demons of the night) to Villiers de L'Isle-Adam's 1884 "Secret de l'échafaud" (Secret of the scaffold), in which the condemned man says he will blink one eye after he is beheaded to prove the will survives after death.

Victor Hugo's countless indictments of the death penalty, from *Le dernier jour d'un condamné* (Last day of a condemned man) in 1829 to *Quatrevingt-treize* (Ninety-three) in 1877, like Jules Janin's 1829 *L'âne mort et la femme guillotinée* (The dead donkey and the guillotined woman)—in which the heroine winds up on the medical school's dissection table—are all reminders of the barbarity of dismemberment, associated with a madness liable to derange any healthy mind. But the merit of having truly stressed the link between madness and revolution via the guillotine—with all the extravagance suited to the fantastic genre—goes to Alexandre Dumas. In 1849 the author of *The Three Musketeers* published *Les mille et un fantômes* (One thousand and one ghosts), a series of interlocked stories in which the narrator, back in 1831, found himself involved quite by chance in a strange event: a man killed his wife by cutting off her head with a sword, but her severed head retaliated by biting his right hand severely. This event serves as the point of departure for a series of chapters on the consequences of beheadings. "Charlotte Corday Is Slapped in the Face" recounts the notorious reddening of the royalist heroine's cheek after her decapitation, and "Solange" and "Albert," stories set in 1793, tell the story of a young woman who is beheaded but calls out to her lover from the basket where her head has fallen. These disembodied heads, which speak and act, are like the living dead of a period that has not yielded up its secrets, from which we await revelations from beyond the grave. They fueled the darker reveries of a people unable to eradicate the heritage of revolution.

Dumas lived through the events of 1830. *Les mille et un fantômes* was set soon after the overthrow of the reactionary Bourbon monarchy, but it was written just after the failure of the 1848 revolution dashed the hopes of an entire generation. Dumas's reinterpretation of the 1789 Revolution comes in the wake of this great disillusionment, as he explained in his introduction. "It is true that every day we take another step toward liberty, equality, and fraternity, those three great words that the Revolution of 1793—the other one, you know, the dowager revolution—tossed into the midst of modern society, as she would have done with a tiger, a lion, and a bear dressed in sheep's clothing; empty words, alas, that we read through the smoke of June [1848] on our bullet-riddled monuments."[87]

Dumas's despair was even more present in *La femme au collier de velours* (The woman with the velvet necklace), a novel published that same year of 1849, exploring the dividing line between history, madness, dream, and decapitation. The protagonist was none other the E. T. A. Hoffmann, that master of fantastic tales, who arrived in the nightmarish Paris of 1793. Harassed by French bureaucracy, "that endemic disease . . . being grafted upon terrorism" at the time,[88] the young German found himself simultaneously rebuffed (museums and libraries were closed) and exposed (to the obscene ballet of tumbrels taking the condemned to their deaths). To top it off, Hoffmann's first experience of Paris coincided with the execution of Madame Du Barry, the spectacle of a fall that he witnessed, traumatized. Since one spectacle followed another—as on the evening Louis XVI was guillotined—Hoffmann decided that same day to go the theater, where the beautiful Arsène, Danton's mistress, was performing. She wore around her neck a black velvet ribbon held by a diamond clasp in the shape of a guillotine. Hoffmann, fascinated, instantly fell in love. This love at first sight was accompanied by a prophetic vision: "He fancied that he saw Madame Du Barry's headless body dancing in Arsène's place, and sometimes that Arsène came dancing to the foot of the guillotine and into the executioner's hands."[89] Next to Hoffmann was a mysterious character who claimed to be a doctor, and whose snuffbox was decorated with a skull. Shortly afterward, Hoffmann managed to meet Arsène one night, at the foot of the scaffold. The lovers went to a hotel, but in the early morning he found her dead. The mysterious doctor arrived by magic, put his hand on the young woman's neck, and unfastened the diamond clasp closing the velvet ribbon. "Hoffmann uttered a terrible cry. No longer supported by the only bond that attached it to the shoulders, the head fell from the bed to the floor."[90] Arsène, who had been beheaded the night before, was merely a ghost. Hoffmann runs out shouting, "I am mad!"[91]

If Dumas is to be believed, the whims and speculations of an unwell imagination are no more absurd than history's own atrocities. The revolutionary government's crime was echoed by the symbolic murder of reason. The mirror relationship between losing one's head and losing one's mind nevertheless left a third character in the wings: the physician. Ageless and nameless, this disturbing, deathly cold figure was omniscient. He knew Voltaire and probably Sade, whose *Justine* he praised; he also hinted at a carnal relationship with Madame Du Barry. He seemed to be everywhere but believed in nothing. This disillusioned atheist understood human relationships and knew how the story would unravel (so to speak) and the key to the enigma: the relation of head to body, of ideas to flesh, of dream to history.

TWO * Asylum or Political Prison?

On August 6, 1793, the day Philippe Pinel was officially appointed to run Bicêtre, the Belhomme mental home where he had been a medical consultant since 1786 was turned into a prison by the authorities organizing the Terror.[1] The startling coincidence of dates meant that on the same day Pinel went from a rest home that became an official revolutionary jail to an asylum known above all during the ancien régime as a place of confinement.

Asylum and prison were already an old couple, wedded in France back in 1656 when Louis XIV founded the *hôpital général*, a multi-institutional authority responsible for incarcerating the city's madmen, venereal patients, beggars, delinquents, and criminals in shared premises. Both La Salpêtrière and Bicêtre came to symbolize such institutions. The law abolishing *lettres de cachet*, enacted on March 16, 1790, was supposed to eliminate the confusion between patients and prisoners and seemed to herald a new era by making madness a medical issue. But competent doctors were scarce, and institutions were poorly adapted. In fact, the situation barely changed—especially since in August 1790 a new decree "corrected" the legislators' original, laudable intention by granting the police "the responsibility to forestall or remedy unfortunate events that might be caused by madmen and lunatics left at large or by ferocious or harmful animals on the loose."[2] Hardly had the doors been opened than they shut once again on the insane, still being compared to beasts to be caged.

During the Terror, the authorities further consolidated the strange marriage of madness and law enforcement by requisitioning private health establishments—which offered the advantage of already being places of confinement—to turn them into jails. What might have

LA SALPÊTRIÈRE
37
Loges d'aliénées construites par Viel en 1789.

FIGURE 14. Georges Charles Guillain and P. Mathieu, *La Salpêtrière: The Cells for Madwomen Built by Viel in 1789* (1925). In the late eighteenth century, architect Charles-François Viel was commissioned to rebuild the cells for raving and dangerous madwomen. The building no longer exists, but this rare photo shows what Pinel found when he arrived at La Salpêtrière in 1795. Photograph: © Wellcome Library, London.

constituted a temporary, opportunistic solution to an unusual political emergency evolved, in fact, into an institution. Throughout the periods of the Empire, Restoration, and July monarchy, the association of mental asylum with political prison became unambiguous; it was an everyday reality that the government no longer took the trouble to disguise.

MENTAL HOMES OR PENITENTIARIES?

In the late eighteenth century *maisons de santé*, or "nursing homes," enjoyed a particular status, halfway between bourgeois lodging house and health clinic; they played on the ambivalence of a term that they seem to have adopted as their motto: discretion. As an expensive alternative to the public old people's hospices in Paris, they allowed affluent families to avoid the disgrace of public degeneration. A nursing home had private rooms instead of dormitories, pleasant gardens instead of grim courtyards, and above all attentive medical personnel. From this angle, the nursing homes were a godsend; but their hybrid status, outside all legislation, made them suspect. Usually established in the capital's outlying villages far from the center of Paris, they served to hide as well as to protect. Everyone knew that behind their high walls they occasionally served as a family dumping ground, reformatory, or penitentiary. The revolutionary terrorist Louis Antoine de Saint-Just had himself undergone such an experience, having been sent as a teenager by his mother to the establishment of a Madame Marie Sainte-Colombe in Picpus for having run away to Paris in 1786.[3]

In 1793, *maisons de santé* appeared to be perfect places for ad hoc detention. Some twenty in and around Paris were turned into jails, including La Folie-Régnault on the street of the same name, maison Escourbiac on rue du Chemin-Vert, maison Brunet on rue Buffon, and the Coignard home in Picpus. The most famous was precisely the one where Pinel got his start, the Belhomme mental home on rue de Charonne, which opened about 1770 when a former mirror dealer named Jacques-Étienne Belhomme agreed to take an aristocrat's idiot child as a paying boarder. The arrangement turned out to be profitable, and Belhomme decided to expand. More a businessman than a philanthropist, he recognized the gains to be made from wealthy families desiring to offload an inconvenient grandparent, a backward child, or a demented aunt, placed in the home either "willingly" or through legal writ of disability. The home's proprietor had little interest in curing his wealthy clientele, as Pinel would be the first to discover when trying to overcome obstacles to implementing his treatment. Pinel later commented that he had "little or no influence over [the establishment's] servants and domestic police; the head displayed a marked indifference to curing rich boarders, or rather an unequivocal desire to see all remedies fail; in other cases he placed sole trust in the use of baths or a few other petty, futile prescriptions."[4]

In 1791 Belhomme's nursing home had forty-seven patients—thirty men and seventeen women—whose average age was about forty. What ailed these middle-class clients (banker, goldsmith, surgeon, curate, priest, nun, merchant's wife), whose board was usually paid by their families? Three-quarters of them had mental problems: "insanity" or "madness" (38 percent), "dementia" (25.5 percent), and "imbecility"

(13 percent). The remaining quarter either stayed there "voluntarily" (12.7 percent) or were very aged or infirm (8.5 percent).[5] The records are silent when it comes to therapies employed; there are no pharmaceutical prescriptions or descriptions of the mental therapy that Pinel was then at great pains to test.

Belhomme was a moderate republican and commander of the local Popincourt militia, so in theory he was on good terms with the authorities at this time. Three years later, after his establishment was converted into a prison, the situation had deteriorated, as revealed by a report by the Comité de Sûreté Générale (Committee of General Security), which inspected the premises on 5 Pluviôse Year II (January 24, 1794) "in order to gather information on mandatory taxes . . . and above all on the physicians and surgeons . . . who are said to be highly ignorant and work for these homes at very modest cost." The police drew up an edifying report on the sight they encountered: around a table, thirty people fought over soup and eight apples; a Citizen Pelletier was paying one thousand livres per month for unfurnished lodging; Citizen Breteuil, a woman "known in this house by the name of Tonnelier," was found unconscious on her bed in a room "barely fit to live in"; two indigent, ailing citizens—"one lying on a pallet, the other on straw"—were without a fire in the middle of winter. The police asked Belhomme "why, if he made the rich pay so dear, he treated the sans-culottes so meanly." The average rent of 345 livres a month (roughly $2,225 in 2012 dollars), payable in advance, included neither food nor vital commodities (candles, wood, etc.) and was judged to be exorbitant, especially since "the home [was] in the poorest upkeep and the most unhealthful state." Some rooms were plagued by "highly dangerous sulfurous fumes." An arrest warrant was thus issued against Belhomme, guilty of "abuse of the rich and inhumanity toward the unfortunate." He was incarcerated first in Citizen Eugène Coignard's home (another nursing home converted into a jail), then in La Force Prison, while awaiting a trial that took place on 4 Floréal Year II (April 24, 1794). Belhomme was sentenced to six years in irons for misappropriation of public funds.[6]

What was Belhomme's real role in this affair? Was he, as alleged, colluding with the notorious public prosecutor Antoine Quentin Fouquier-Tinville to extort fortunes from people sentenced to the guillotine by delaying their execution? According to Jean-Charles Sournia's *La médecine révolutionnaire* (Revolutionary medicine), the system worked as follows: "When, after interrogation, an individual was placed under arrest, he could ask to be interned in a private home. This request presupposed awareness of this arrangement, and also that the arresting officer would agree to it in exchange for payment. A medical certificate of illness was a useful, but not an essential, document. If the home had room, the incarceration was decreed, and the police could then monitor the presence of the prisoner. The police paid the cost of lodging the prisoner to the managing warden, who assumed responsibility. The new lodgers, meanwhile, had to pay for their own board as well as any particular favor not part of everyday fare."[7] Belhomme could thus have profited at both ends, by receiving money from the government as well as from his boarders. This system involved four accomplices: the manager of the home, the corrupt police officer, the doctor, and the prisoner.

Did Belhomme abuse the system, or was he overwhelmed by the arrival of the 132 moderate politicians from Nantes, arrested on conspiracy charges, some of whom were lodged with him, perhaps obliging him to raise his rates to meet the considerable costs? This latter hypothesis, which does not exclude corruption, seems to carry the day. For how could Belhomme find himself behind bars if he were really in league with Fouquier-Tinville? Belhomme fought back, appealed his conviction, and won his appeal. He was freed on September 7, 1794, exonerated of all charges. Two days later he was once again running his home, where the likes of Gabriel de Talleyrand (uncle of the famous Talleyrand), the comte de Volney, and "Citizen Penthièvre" (otherwise known as the duchesse d'Orléans, widow of Philippe-Égalité) spent part of the Revolution.[8]

The links between the police and nursing homes, made official during the Terror, became even stronger after Napoleon's coup d'état on 18 Brumaire (November 9, 1799), thanks to Minister of Police Joseph Fouché. Fouché's ministry oversaw, among other things, jails, detention centers, prisons, and penitentiaries. During the Consulate period, the ministry also had a secret police division (*la haute police*) notably responsible for political affairs and conspiracies. It worked closely with the Paris Prefecture of Police, founded in 1800 as part of the Ministry of the Interior (transferred to the Ministry of Justice in 1802).

The police thus established a network of informers and spies that extended across Paris like a spiderweb. Napoleon—first as consul, then as emperor—had every reason to fear plots, both Jacobin and royalist. The watchwords of the day were suspicion, surveillance, arrest, and summary execution. Censorship muzzled the press, while torture, although outlawed, yielded information from accomplices of Chouan leader Georges Cadoudal, who was guillotined in 1804 following a failed plot.[9] The police combed the entire country, instructing regional prefects to infiltrate all establishments where people gathered—including spas. "I have carried out the most active surveillance," reported the prefect of Puy-de-Dôme in 1807, "of the baths at Mont d'Or. I have satisfied myself that nothing has arisen in conversations or activities that could cause concern to the government, and that people go there solely for reasons of health." The prefect appended a list of the spa's foreign clientele to his report.[10]

In Paris, the police maintained close control over medical establishments, all subject to regular checks of their ledgers. No nursing home could open in the capital without authorization from the prefect's office. Such monitoring extended to asylums. Between 1802 and 1805 the police took nearly three hundred women straight to La Salpêtrière, without passing via the admissions bureau that was supposed to diagnose them. Of those women, 107 were delivered back to the police once they were better.[11] The public hospital was thus one jail among others, a site of social control. Administrative detention and medical confinement, whether they succeeded one another or overlapped, were part of the same continuum, made possible by the legal vacuum in which mental illness found itself in the period between the abolition of *lettres de cachet* and the legislation passed in 1838.

Given this context, it is hardly surprising that the Belhomme home continued to perform a double role during the Empire period, as proved by the miraculous survival of one of its ledgers, basically covering the years 1808 to 1810. Patients and prisoners mingle from one page to another. In September 1808 a patient arrived from the Esquirol home, where he had been treated for melancholia; on November 10, a convict sentenced to two years in prison by a Paris criminal court was delivered to Belhomme, who was charged with keeping the man "*in detention and not otherwise* until his full sentence has elapsed"; and on the thirtieth of that same month the prefect of police sent him an individual, whose status was not specified, to remain "until further instruction."[12] This chilling comment represents a cold juxtaposition of clinic and prison under a government that reinstituted, mutatis mutandis, the old system of *lettres de cachet*.

Such detentions were primarily aimed at political prisoners who were given the privilege—especially if they were unwell—of serving their time in conditions less trying than a government prison. That was the case of Bénigne Louis Bertier de Sauvigny, who was transferred from La Force Prison to the Belhomme home on March 10, 1809. He was the third son of a former royal intendant of Paris who had harshly repressed the 1775 food riots known as the Flour War and who, being very unpopular at the start of the Revolution, was suspected of hoarding wheat in order to starve the people. Kidnapped by rioters, he was butchered in front of the Hôtel de Ville by having his heart ripped out and his head cut off. During the Empire his eldest son, Ferdinand, along with Bénigne, planned to unite royalist forces by creating a secret society. Since Bénigne was arrested in 1807, it was Ferdinand who alone founded the order of the Chevaliers de la Foi (Knights of Faith), an organization that campaigned for the restoration of the Bourbons, joined by the ultraroyalist faction that would come to the fore under Charles X, including Mathieu de Montmorency (future minister of foreign affairs), Jules de Polignac, Jean-Baptiste de Villèle, Guy de Delvau (named prefect of police in 1821) and, perhaps, François-René de Chateaubriand (whose membership in this secret society has never been formally established).

The police were well informed of Bénigne's activities, so it was based on charges of "scheming against national security" that he arrived at the Belhomme home. An order by the prefect, Louis Nicholas Dubois, stipulated that "Mr. Belhomme will have the prisoner under his responsibility. He is enjoined to keep close watch on the prisoner and to prohibit any kind of outing, even brief, without a formal order issued by ourselves or by H[is] E[xcellency] the Minister" (Fouché).[13] Bénigne remained there until May, when he was transferred to a nursing home on rue du Chemin-Vert run by Madame Reboul-Richebracques, and later to Dr. Claude-Henri Jacquelin Dubuisson's establishment on rue du Faubourg Saint-Antoine.[14]

Dubuisson's home seems a strange destination for Bénigne, for there he would come into contact with the staunchest opponents of Napoleon's regime. That is where the imperial government—which feared monarchists more than Jacobins—had sent several leading figures such as the Polignac brothers, who were sentenced to death in 1804 for their complicity with Cadoudal, but whose sentences had been commuted to life imprisonment. Also there was revolutionary general Claude François de Malet, an aristocrat who had been won over by the new ideas and became a staunch republican. In 1808 he organized a failed plot against Napoleon, and he spent his time in detention contemplating his next move. Although not all prisoners shared the same political opinions, they were united in their hatred of "the usurper." Thus Malet decided to form an objective alliance with the royalist prisoner Abbé Lafon, the better to pave the way for his famous coup d'état in 1812, when the emperor was beginning to retreat from Russia.

Having escaped from the nursing home that year, on the night of October 22/23, General Malet appeared at the Popincourt barracks to announce—with all the composure of a great actor—that Napoleon had been killed in battle outside Moscow and that a provisional government had been formed. The stunned commander of the barracks placed his men at the disposal of the general, who immediately headed to La Force Prison to free republican generals Guidal and Lahorie.[15] Lahorie then hurried to the Prefecture of Police, where he arrested the prefect, Pasquier, and then to the home of the minister of police (Savary, the duc de Rovigo), who was dragged out of bed and sent to La Force prison. Everything worked like magic for the plotters, whose staggering boldness had placed key strategic posts in their hands in a matter of hours. Their swift advance was halted, however, by the general staff of the first army division, where the head of security of Paris was not fooled for an instant by the news Malet delivered; he knew of the latter's past as a conspirator and had him arrested on the spot.

Malet's coup thus failed, but it revealed the extraordinary fragility of the regime and its police network, assumed to be infallible. Furthermore, in all the panic no one thought of Napoleon's infant son or shouted "Napoleon is dead, long live Napoleon!"—which shows that people's minds were not yet attuned to dynastic legitimacy. By October 28 Malet was put on trial. When the chief judge asked him to name his fellow conspirators, he made the superb retort: "You yourself, Sir, and all of France—had I but succeeded." Malet went before the firing squad the next day, along with thirteen of his confederates. The Empire was intact, but its image was tarnished. And since everything in Paris ends with a witty turn, the latest joke to make the rounds as people laughed at the arrest of Savary (redubbed the duc de La Force) went:

"Have you heard what's happening?"
"No, I haven't."
"Then you must be with the police."[16]

The resounding impact of the affair would also affect the image of psychiatry and madness with respect to government powers. Logically enough, the jailer-doctor Dubuisson was suspected of making it easy for the plotter to escape, but having already filed a report to the police concerning an earlier escape attempt by Malet, he managed to prove his good faith and was let off.[17] More serious, government propaganda exploited the figure of Malet to associate and belittle all conspiracy as a form of madness: "Although he was shot as a traitor, he was described everywhere as a madman, and his attempt was presented as an act of insanity."[18] That Malet was incarcerated in a mental home—of course, known to serve *also* as a detention center—encouraged this link, even subliminally, as reiterated by many contemporaries and historians. In her *Mémoires*, Laure Junot, the duchesse d'Abrantes, reported Abbé Lafon's confident assertion that Malet was insane, while Adolphe Thiers referred to Malet as a "bold maniac" and a "madman" driven by an obsession.[19] Dr. Max Billard was tempted to dub him a "monomaniac of conspiracy" but ultimately preferred "an athlete of coups d'état,"[20] whereas historian Henri Gaubert, a specialist on the Empire period, categorically sided with the diagnosis of madness, describing the "petty noble" as a "fanatic" who was "unhinged by his raving imagination."[21]

During the Bourbon restoration (1814–30) and the July monarchy (1830–48), people were incarcerated in mental homes simply for their political beliefs. Casimir Pinel, nephew of the "great Pinel," known for his liberal attitudes, hosted the cream of opposition journalists in his home on rue de Chaillot. They included Paul-François Dubois, founder of the *Globe* (the house organ of the Doctrinaires before the July revolution), sentenced to four months in prison in 1830 by Charles X's government; Charles Philippon, who founded *La Caricature* in 1832, joined at the end of the year by his famous cartoonist, Honoré Daumier, who sketched King Louis-Philippe as a devouring Gargantua; and finally Ferdinand Bascans, who ran the *Tribune des Départements* and was hounded by trials and lawsuits and hence pleased by his forced retirement. "This house is vast, has a divine exposition and superb grounds," he informed his mother, "and I spend my time delightfully between literature, the study of language, and good conversation."[22] In another letter he admitted, "As I told you, and repeat once more, I am better here than on rue de l'Oseille or at the newspaper office, even though I'm a prisoner. My only worry is that one fine morning the prefect of police will get it into his mind to transfer me to Sainte-Pélagie. Fortunately, my skeletal frame serves as a certificate of poor health, which reassures me."[23]

The pleasant retreat of the home on rue de Chaillot seemed more like house arrest, and not very closely watched at that. Riots triggered by the funeral on June 5, 1832, of General Jean-Maximilien Lamarque, whose body had been taken to the Pantheon by republicans, had placed Paris in a state of siege. The army, charged with rounding up political detainees, rushed over to Casimir Pinel's home to take Bascans—who had already fled through the grounds.[24] Had he been warned? What role did the doctor play in his disappearance? These questions remain unanswered, thus prompting another—entirely rhetorical—one: Why did the government place its opponents in these imitation jails, open on every side, if not to shield themselves from accusations of dictatorship by offering more "decent" conditions of house arrest instead of harsh state prisons?

A triple confusion thus prevailed from the Revolution of 1789 to the July monarchy of 1830–48, mingling psychiatry and politics: a confusion of *status* between health center and detention center (Belhomme and others); a confusion of *nature* between madness and political opposition to the government (Malet); and a confusion of *roles* among specialist physicians who cooperated with the government but also protected—indeed, aided the escape of—the detainees assigned to them (Dubuisson, Casimir Pinel). The institutionalizing of this widespread, well-known practice partly justifies—or at least explains—the suspicion weighing, throughout the nineteenth century, on the arbitrary nature of internment and the ambivalent complicity between psychiatrists and governments. It was ambivalent because the doctor's authority could act, inversely, *against* an arbitrary government, even in public asylums.

Pinel thus perhaps saved several political prisoners during the Terror by passing them off as madmen. In his *Treatise* he mentioned the case of a man who managed, through extravagant behavior, to get himself transferred from a prison cell to the ward for the insane. But the man's efforts to mimic madness did not fool the clinician's practiced eye.

> At every visit he exhibited some new antic. Sometimes he covered his head and refused to answer my questions; at other times he poured out incoherent, pointless babble; on other occasions he adopted the elevated tone and haughty air of some grandee. This variety of roles convinced me that he was not well read in the history of insanity, nor had he studied the character of people so affected. . . . I was no longer a dupe to his artifices, but as he had been sentenced to confinement on account of political matters, I postponed my report on him on the pretense of wishing to learn some new facts, and [the events of] 9 Thermidor a few months later put an end to the prosecution that had been leveled against him.[25]

Some historians have charged Pinel with seeking to distance himself from the Terror many years after the event, and to paper over the fact that he owed his appointment to radical members of the Convention, by presenting himself as a savior of victims of the Revolution. Yet not only did Pinel very concretely help to hide Nicolas de Condorcet after a warrant was issued for the philosopher's arrest by finding him a discreet boardinghouse, but correspondence from that same period between Pussin and the administration shows that the ward supervisor was probably employing a strategy similar to the physician's. At that point Pussin was acting as jailer, day and night, to at least seven detainees awaiting trial by the revolutionary court. Had these men, transferred from prison to the insanity ward, *really* lost their minds, or were they feigning madness to gain time, with the complicity of the people running Bicêtre? Pussin's clear reluctance to supply a precise list of names of the two hundred mental patients in his care was perhaps one of those acts of passive resistance to a police state. The ward supervisor's tone conveys the firmness of his position. One of the seven political prisoners, a thirty-seven-year-old woodcutter who went "raving mad in the space of roughly six weeks," was henceforth cured, and Pussin courageously petitioned the public prosecutor for dismissal of his case. On receiving no reply, he repeated the process with the Commission of Civil, Police, and Legal Administrations. "From the information he gave me, it appears that he fell ill only from despair, given that he was arrested late last Pluviôse as a suspect for want of a *carte de sûreté* (revolutionary identity card). He claims there is nothing else in his file. I think that it is only just to seek out information on this matter and that it should be included in the law that grants freedom to workers."[26]

Should Pinel and Pussin's initiatives be viewed as isolated acts? To what extent did psychiatrists back the authorities, and how far could they resist arbitrary decisions? How much maneuvering room were they allowed between the forced admission of a "prisoner" and the declaration of a bogus diagnosis that violated the Hippocratic oath?

DISSIDENCE OR DEMENTIA?

The ambiguity and variety of politically related "medical cases" in asylum registers call for an interpretation all the more circumspect in that nothing so resembles arbitrary internment as a psychiatric certificate drawn up in due form. This is partly the result of the terseness of such reports, which consign often poorly documented cases to the asylum and employ moral judgments framed in old-fashioned vocabulary—"royal fanatic, full of conceit," or "raving republican"—that can be hard to distinguish from medical diagnoses. Our modern eyes, accustomed to more "neutral" and, in short, more reassuring terms, have trouble dealing with such misplaced value judgments.

Yet we should not forget that science is always ideological, in every period, as amply demonstrated by the history of hysteria or of homosexuality, once viewed as degenerateness.[27] It is a safe bet that twenty-third-century historians who read today's studies of schizophrenia will be surprised by the work of contemporary psychiatrists, whose apparently objective and honest conclusions are inevitably biased.

Ever since the advent of antipsychiatry, interpreting nineteenth-century asylum archives has also had to deal with repeated invectives against psychiatry, which may sometimes be well founded but tend toward mindless generalizations. True, psychiatrists participated in a system of government surveillance and control, shaped by the authoritarian morality of their century. But no, they were not sadistic jailers of every delinquent on earth. So how can we try to understand this distinction, whose dividing line is harder to establish than it may appear? Not by seeking the hypothetical reality of a case of mental illness (almost impossible to establish after the fact), but by trying to shed light on the criteria of confinement and the complex system governing those criteria.

The dark legends associated with Napoleon purportedly include a "myth of interning opponents for insanity," to borrow from the title of an article by Michael Sibalis, who tracked down the relevant files in France's National Archives.[28] His conclusion can be read in the wording of his title. Broadly speaking, the police usually objected to the summary internment in public asylums of political dissidents falsely labeled mad. Notable exceptions, such as the case of Abbé Fournier, tended to prove that rule. On Pentecost in 1801, this priest referred to the death of Louis XVI in his sermon in the Paris church of Saint-Germain l'Auxerrois. In the margins of a police report on the incident, the government minister wrote: "If this is true, put him in Bicêtre as a madmen." Fournier's release from the asylum a few weeks later, based on medical opinion, pays tribute to the psychiatrists who were neither dupes nor accomplices of the government.

But what, on the other hand, do the medical archives tell us about those minds overly concerned with politics? The archives are often lacking: for example, psychiatric files contain no document on Théodore Desorgues, a poet and the author of a *Hymne à l'Être Suprême* (Hymn to the Supreme Being), who was interned at Charenton in 1805 for a song with a refrain that went: "Ah yes, the great Napoleon / is truly a great chameleon." Desorgues was also the alleged author of a witticism that hinged on Napoleon's Corsican background: when asked by a waiter whether he wanted lemon or orange ice cream, he said, "I don't like coarse skins [Corsicans]." In his *Notes historiques* Marc-Antoine Baudot, an elected member of the Convention, recalled, "I saw [Desorgues] a few days before his arrest; there was not the slightest air of mental illness about him, but he didn't hesitate to rail against the usurper of public liberty, and to anyone who would listen he read his anti-Corsican verses. Which could have been composed only by a sound mind."[29] Was Desorgues declared mad "*ex officio imperatoris*," as Baudot put it, or was his confinement justified by "the bizarre and incoherent nature" of the comments recorded by the police, leading the doctors at the central admissions office to confirm his loss of reason?[30] This question is impossible to answer, the two interpretations not necessarily being incompatible, especially if the suspect defended himself too energetically in an effort to create a scandal. At what point and according to what criteria does the expression of political opinion go beyond "reason"? At what point and according to what criteria can dissident behavior be described as "raving"? Yet infringements of basic liberties during the Empire period have been sufficiently well studied to leave no doubt about the government's intellectual dishonesty with respect to questionable prisoners. Take the case notes on a former navy surgeon, Victor Mariette, known as Wreight, who was admitted to Charenton on March 12, 1806:

> In the past seven years, [the patient has experienced] metaphysical and philosophical reveries on science, politics, morality, and religion, having traveled to the United States; statements against Napoleon, whom he called the Antichrist, for which he has been imprisoned for four years. Wrote a book on politics and legislation titled *Traité analytique de l'homme* (Analytic treatise on mankind). Not agitated, has a dreamy, musing air; obsessed with not being called his real name, Mariette, but *Wreight*, an assumed name. Taciturn. In the summer of 1806 suffered from insomnia, deep agitation, nervous movements, increased melancholia. Returned to his previous condition in the autumn, in which he remained until his release.[31]

What ailed a man guilty of "reveries" or remaining "taciturn," whose sole "obsession" was the desire to use an alias that suggests, at least phonetically, his conviction that he was in his *right* mind and within his *rights*? What is the dividing line between medical confinement and political internment for criticism of the emperor, factual mention of which becomes associated with etiological commentary? How can we interpret the date of his release—September 23, 1815, "in the same condition as he was admitted," specified the doctor—as anything other than a political liberation once we realize that Napoleon had been exiled to Saint Helena that August? All in all, Victor "Wreight," whose "melancholia" the physician neglected (or refused) to discuss apart from nonmedical comments, spent thirteen years in confinement, nine of them in Charenton.

On February 14, 1810, another character subject to dangerous "musings" joined Wreight in Charenton: the notorious Jacob Dupont, who had advocated atheism in a session of the Convention devoted to educational matters. On December 14, 1792, he proudly declared, "In all good faith I confess to this Convention that I am an atheist,"[32] to which Robespierre allegedly retorted, "Atheism is aristocratic." Dupont's medical file reads:

> Former Doctrinaire [i.e., former member of the Confraternity of Christian Doctrine], former representative in the Legislative Assembly and the Convention; withdrew to a small village near Loches, where he lived for eight years with a sister who died six months ago. Metaphysical and revolutionary reveries, notorious advocacy of atheism in the Convention; publicly gave a lecture on that subject on Place Louis XVI seven [nine?] years ago. Many writings full of the same madness. No violence, no delusions on other subjects.[33]

Here it is spelled out: atheism is madness. The assertion itself is not surprising in a society that largely shared Louis Sébastien Mercier's opinion that atheism was "the sum total of all the monstrosities of the human mind" and "a destructive mania . . . that is very close to dementia."[34] This time, however, the judgment served as a diagnosis penned by a physician who, even though he was using the term madness (*folies*) in a colloquial sense, admitted that Dupont had "no delusions on other subjects." This point is crucial, because it proves, black on white, that philosophical beliefs constituted a sufficient basis for confinement. This case is all the more remarkable in that the doctor, Antoine-Athanase Royer-Collard (about whom more later), was probably unaware that Dupont had been forced to resign his seat in the Convention 1794 owing to his mental state and was arrested the following year for raping a blind old woman.[35] Had he been aware of these details, they would of course have reinforced a diagnosis noteworthy for being based *solely* on the subversive aspect of openly declared atheism. Had Royer-Collard mentioned such facts in the medical register, Dupont would have been one of those ambiguous cases that the files blackened, whereas here the physician's stark frankness reveals not the mental health—something impossible to prove today—of a man unjustly sent to an asylum, but something much more important: the acknowledged arbitrariness of the criteria of internment.

Not only atheists wound up in Charenton. Alongside the infidels were many patients stricken by "religious monomania" of an equally dubious scientific validity, thereby swelling the statistics of insanity.

At Bicêtre, the head physician complained to the commission that oversaw hospitals about the presence of chaplains, whose religious ideas pushed the mental derangement of the inmates to an extreme. He therefore asked that the chaplains be removed. "Religion," wrote the doctor, "has been recognized by all physicians and everyone familiar with lunatics as one of the most frequent causes of madness." An employee apparently noticed that after every visit by the chaplain one patient, a former teacher, had a fit of epilepsy and then raved for two weeks. "Among the various kinds of mental illness, the one that stems from religion has always seemed the most difficult to cure, the one that most leads to frenzy and cruelty. In the Bicêtre asylum I saw a madman who had killed his wife because she arrived late for mass."[36]

At La Salpêtrière, Pinel drew equally alarming conclusions from his daily notes. Impoverished women who went to seek charity from their parish as a last resort were prime victims of priests who, once the Revolution was over, reproached women who had confessed to a constitutional clergyman, or had divorced, or had given a child a civil baptism. By refusing these women the succor of the church and threatening them with eternal hellfire, such priests pushed them toward an often incurable madness, fueled by hallucinations and infernal visions. Pinel even claimed to be able to "show the quarters of Paris where this melancholy devotion predominates, while in others compassionate and enlightened piety sometimes delays the development of derangement ready to reveal itself."[37]

In every case, it was at proselytes that physicians were pointing an accusing finger. In that respect psychiatry was emerging as a modern field, concerned to set itself apart from a religion that had long held a monopoly on madness and that had also burned at the stake witches and heretics whose very existence it had fabricated out of whole cloth. Religious feelings were not madness in themselves, since "compassionate piety" could, on the contrary, soothe troubled minds and set them back on the right path. It was fanatical zeal and mystical propaganda that, at the dawn of the nineteenth century, had to be clearly distinguished from rational, positivist science determined to triumph over obscurantism.

Atheism presented a different kind of threat, because it was synonymous with madness. "The fool says in his heart, 'There is no God,'" states the book of Psalms.[38] In the Middle Ages, the impious atheist was considered mad. But with the revolutionary promulgation of the Declaration of the Rights of Man, France guaranteed the right of religious freedom on condition that it did not disturb public order. In this respect Jacob Dupont's case was fairly clear: the troublemaker was considered mad, and sent to Charenton, for having advocated atheism in the public sphere, in speech and in writing. At that time Charenton was precisely where the most famous "prisoner" of that institution—and the most atheistic of philosophers—was languishing: the marquis de Sade.

SADE IN CHARENTON: "THIS MAN IS NOT INSANE"

Donatien Alphonse François, marquis de Sade, was a man whom everyone wanted to imprison but no prison wanted. The undesirable Sade was troublesome to every political regime and spent time in most of the major places of detention employed by royal, republican, and imperial administrations: Saumur, Pierre-Scise, For-l'Évêque, Miolans, Vincennes, the Bastille, Charenton, Les Carmes, Saint-Lazare, Picpus, Saint-Pélagie, Bicêtre. Subsequent to complaints, *lettres de cachet*, and police orders, he was arrested, sequestered, and transferred from prison to asylum. No one, including his jailers—ashamed of hosting such an infamous character—wanted to have this tirelessly rebellious blackguard. "Literally and in every sense," Sade was someone nobody knew what do with. Louis-Nicolas Dubois, the prefect of police during the Consulate and Empire periods, decided to commit the scandalous author of *Justine* to solitary confinement first at Sainte-Pélagie in 1801 and then at Bicêtre. Sade's family ultimately had him admitted to Charenton on April 27, 1803, where he died on December 2, 1814, after eleven years of imprisonment, without ever losing hope of being released one day.

The story of Sade's stay at Charenton is well known,[39] for it served as the stage of a strange play with three main characters—the marquis, the cleric, and the physician. The setting was an asylum founded by the Hospitaller Brothers of St. John of God in 1641 in a small town of several hundred souls where the Seine and Marne Rivers met just outside Paris. Country fields surrounded the neoclassical asylum buildings of dressed stone.

Sade was on familiar ground when he arrived at Charenton in 1803—

FIGURE 15. French school, *The Former Madhouse at Charenton-Saint-Maurice* (ca. 1910). This engraving, reproduced as postcard, depicts Charenton in the days of the marquis de Sade. Photograph © Archives Départementales du Val-de-Marne.

he had already spent nine months there between July 4, 1789, and April 2, 1790. Had he remained in the Bastille just a few days longer, he would have recovered his liberty when that "edifice of horror"—whose destruction he devoutly wished—was stormed by the people. Nevertheless, by abolishing the system of arbitrary *lettres de cachet*, the Revolution allowed him to leave Charenton, where he had spent nine months "among madmen and epileptics."[40] His jailers were not sorry to see him go. On January 12, 1790, Brother Eusèbe Boyer informed the Legislative Assembly of the status of people detained in the asylum. If the monk decided not to specify "the reasons for the [marquis de] Sade's detention, that is because the list would be too long and because he is widely known to the Legislative Assembly, which I beg to relieve me of such a person or at least authorize me to lock him away in order to protect this house from the evils with which it is threatened."[41]

By the time Sade was sent back there in 1803, Charenton had changed greatly. Confiscated from the religious order, the asylum was closed in the summer of 1795 and became national property; it reopened on June 15, 1797, under the Ministry of the Interior. It was run not by a physician, as the slow but steady medicalizing of madness would have had it, but by a worldly-wise philanthropist named François Simonnet de

Coulmier. This enlightened despot exercised absolute power, refusing to establish house regulations, to set up a board of directors, or even to specify names in administrative registers—from a concern for discretion, he claimed. Coulmier was sovereign within his realm of Charenton. He invested part of his personal fortune in renovating the buildings, and he supervised the work, oversaw the treatment of patients, and surrounded himself with a trusted team, forwarding to the bureaucrats accounts that were evasive to say the least. Dr. Jean-Baptiste Joseph Gastaldy, the former director of the mental asylum in Avignon, was Coulmier's assistant—and vassal. At a time when psychiatry was becoming a special field practiced by professionals under the sway of Pinel (who was running La Salpêtrière, while Dr. Jean Baptiste Pascal Lannefranque had taken over at Bicêtre), this surprising arrangement, based on personal fiat and "lay" therapeutic practice, turned Charenton into what Marcel Gauchet and Gladys Swain have called the ultimate bastion of an outmoded idea.[42] It helped to save the marquis de Sade's final years.

Sade and Coulmier had one thing in common that, like a magnet, both attracted and repelled them: Sade had dropped his title of marquis for that of citizen and headed the Place des Piques district, participating in the Revolution with determination; Coulmier was a former Premonstratensian cleric who was won over to the new ideas and became an elected representative to the Constituent Assembly. Yet these two eighteenth-century men, marked by the privileges of birth, retained from their earlier worlds an inner cosmic vision fed on personal fancy, itself hinging on two notions the Revolution had shelved: pleasure and sensuality. Born in a libertine age, they shared a rejection of convention and above all an enthusiasm for theater—as we shall see below.

The similarities ended there. Physically, the sixty-three-year-old Sade should be pictured as stately and obese yet retaining "a hint of grace and elegance whose traces could be found in his overall manner and language" and eyes that still had "an indefinable glow and refinement that lit up from time to time like a spark dying on a dead coal."[43] Against him picture a dwarf, or at least a very short man (contemporary accounts place Coulmier between three feet, four inches and four feet), age forty-one, deformed, with crooked legs and, apparently, a hunchback. Hardly Hollywood material—although it was the dashing Joaquin Phoenix who played Coulmier, ridiculously garbed in a cassock, in the film *Quills* (2000). More fundamentally, whereas Sade never wavered in his philosophical convictions and his "manner of thinking"[44] despite persecution, Coulmier was a model of political opportunism. After having served both ancien régime and Revolution, he even held a seat in the legislative body of the Empire until 1808.

As the story goes, Coulmier protected Sade from numerous affronts—which is true. It needs to be qualified, however. When Sade arrived at Charenton, he reproached Coulmier for countless things, suggesting that their initial encounter was stormy. He demanded consideration and care that Coulmier was not ready to grant him for financial reasons. Sade referred Coulmier to his family, which was paying his board, and assured the director that he wished "to be (as soon as possible) as far from Charenton as [he was] currently near to it," adding, "I am most pleased to have learned from you, Sir, a great truth contained in the letter you have just written to me, *that there are many people who do not think they are mad yet who are*. . . . How true that is, Sir!"[45] Sade would go so far as to file a complaint in court against Coulmier, a "very harsh, fierce" man who initially locked Sade up and allowed him out only two hours per day, "followed by the same guards who accompany the madmen."[46]

Who would ever be so silly as to include Sade among the lunatics he found himself lumped with? A lot of people, including the prefect of police who in 1804 continued to rant against "that incorrigible man" who was "in a perpetual state of libertine dementia."[47] But certainly not Coulmier, who housed Sade in the central building where free boarders lived and who tried to make his life more pleasant and his detention less harsh. Coulmier supplied paper and ink, let Sade wander freely in the asylum and its grounds, and allowed his most faithful companion, the actress Marie-Constance Quesnet (whom Sade nicknamed "Sensitive"), to have her own room at Charenton. There Quesnet stayed, through years of unflagging devotion, until Sade died. And yet the relationship between the two men vacillated between mutual annoyance and trust and hardly resembled the idyll that has sometimes been depicted. Coulmier alternated between benevolence and brusqueness, between discreet privileges and unbroken promises toward a patient whose lucidity and anger remained intact. One day the director would console Sade, the next day he would disparage him to his face, in the presence of his son; in the morning he would dangle the hope of imminent release, in the evening assure him that the government had sworn to keep him locked up forever. This back-and-forth pendulum, however, was typical of a basically capricious temperament and only superficially affected the very real liberalities and favors that Coulmier accorded Sade.

Hippolyte de Colins, a former cavalry officer, visited Charenton in 1812 and, despite the malevolence of his description, managed to grasp Coulmier's special connection to Sade. "The first thing to leap to the eye was his keen relationship with a monster doomed to public execration."[48] Keen, indeed, seemed to be the director's awareness of Sade's singular status and character. That is what emerges in the more concrete form of an anecdote recounted by a former prefect of the Eure region, Monsieur de Gaillion, who was one of the free inmates at Charenton.

> The first months went very well, I would come and go as I pleased. I was most astonished to learn that below me there lodged a Monsieur de Sade, the mere mention of whose name. . . . I could not master the impression made on me by the mere sight of him when I met him. I was then astonished to learn that such a man had a close relationship to Monsieur de Coulmier, a closeness that Monsieur de Coulmier would soon demonstrate. One day in his office he asked me why I did not associate with Monsieur de Sade—What had he done to me? I replied, highly astonished, that he had treated me civilly, which I reciprocated, but that it was impossible for me to associate with such a man. M. de Coulmier became angry and went so far as tell me that we see a mote in our neighbor's eye but not the beam in our own. As I left I told him that such comments reflected more poorly on him than on myself. A few days later, Sade insulted me in the garden, and after lodging a complaint with M. de Coulmier I was received by him very coldly. After that moment he made Charenton so unpleasant to me that I wrote to my family in order to leave, but I had some difficulty in succeeding because M. de Coulmier had managed to win their trust through fine but false words.[49]

Sade indeed had a "keen relationship" with Coulmier, who not only protected him from the authorities by allowing him to write and go about his business, but also staunchly defended a courteous inmate who, because of his reputation, was damned before he had even been met. This insignificant incident in the life of the asylum gives the measure of Coulmier's friendship with Sade, a tireless critic of social hypocrisy who would have unhesitatingly agreed with the parable of the mote and the beam. Coulmier even backed up his verbal support with deeds. When Gaillion, who managed to have himself transferred to the Belhomme home, was obliged to return to Charenton eighteen months later owing to lack of funds, the director had forgotten nothing and retaliated by housing him in the dreaded lunatic wing and denying him visits and outings.

It would probably be too facile to argue that Charenton was Coulmier's private little theater. Yet it is impossible not to recognize this spectacularly ugly and deformed man's penchant for manipulating and staging everything—including himself. This penchant was very concretely embodied in the plays that Coulmier put on in the asylum, plays he allowed Sade to direct, ultimately leading to the end of his own sovereignty at Charenton.

A play was performed every month. The theater, with terraced seating, boxes, and orchestra pit, was in the hall beneath the female mental patients' quarters. The plays were light comedies by the likes of Molière, Marivaux, and Louis Sébastien Mercier, preceded or followed by musical entertainment. The marquis de Sade was master of ceremonies, sometimes doubling as actor or even vocalist. On stage, mental patients performed alongside professional actors; in the audience, other patients mingled with guests from Paris. Indeed, according to Coulmier, theater was part of the mental treatment, although no document specifies his intentions regarding this therapeutic tool. At most it might be inferred that he intended to explore the cathartic power of theatrical performance (which, let me note in passing, institutional psychotherapy would pursue after World War II). Hippolyte de Colins, however, felt that this remedy was poisonous because it was based on illusion—it exacerbated the patients' delusions, muddied their relation to reality, and reputedly ruined any chance of a cure for the famous dancer Trénitz who, after performing in public, went into an uncontrollable rage at the idea of being shorn of his stage king's costume and returning to his cell. The true scandal for Colins, of course, was Sade's presence.

> How much confidence can one have in a director who often affords access and favor to a being to whom I cannot award the title of human; a director who agrees to take such a panegyrist, who allows a public performance in his theater of a play by him and to his glory, in which we find the crassest flattery, comparing him to the gods themselves, not to say allowing him to perform a part in another play—and what part would that be? The role of an evil character that he portrays with all the truth of the crimes he bears in his heart. I saw an entire audience shudder in horror at this spectacle, while the director reddened in anger on hearing no applause in the house.[50]

None of this struck a German doctor, August Friedrich Schweigger, who visited Charenton in 1808. Interested in the theatrical experiment, and probably unaware of the presence and identity of Sade, Schweigger nevertheless remained cautious, indeed skeptical, about the efficiency of the method, describing it in measured terms. On the other hand, when it came to therapies employed at the asylum, Schweigger, like Colins, confirmed the existence of harsh showers and "surprise baths" that entailed strapping patients to a chair and ducking them upside down in a vat of cold water. However, this barbaric technique, eschewed by Pinel and Esquirol, was "rarely used" at Charenton.[51] According to a contemporary booklet promoting the establishment, "These rooms [for baths] are sufficiently remote so that the shouts and ragings of the patients taken there can be heard only faintly by those whose serenity might be disturbed by any painful impressions they might create."[52]

It was Coulmier who decided everything—mental versus physical therapy, awarding of privileges or punishment—confident that he would be backed by the docile Dr. Gastaldy. But Gastaldy's death in December 1805 altered things. On January 23, 1806, Dr. Antoine-Athanase Royer-Collard, younger brother of the politician Pierre-Paul Royer-Collard, was appointed to the post of physician at Charenton, overriding Coulmier's view on the matter and ignoring Pinel's recommendation of Esquirol. The government's choice fell on Royer-Collard, a former Oratorian cleric become the head of a family, known for his strict morals; he came late to medicine, receiving his degree in 1802, and had no institutional experience of mental illness. Royer-

Collard thereby became the third actor in the drama played out between Sade and Coulmier, adopting the role of the physician who precipitated their fall.

In Lyon in 1791–92, Royer-Collard had published a political journal directed against the Jacobins of that city. Its title, *Le Surveillant* (The warder), is strangely suited to the role he would play at Charenton. Unable to impose his medical authority in an establishment where Coulmier constantly impeded his work, Royer-Collard piled up both frustration and evidence of the institution's dysfunction. In 1808 he wrote Joseph Fouché, the minister of police, a letter that merits a lengthy excerpt.

FIGURE 16. Ducarme, *Portrait of Antoine-Athanase Royer-Collard* (nineteenth century). Lithograph. The arrival in 1806 of a government-imposed physician, the austere Antoine-Athanase Royer-Collard, at Charenton would put an end to many of the freedoms Sade enjoyed since his arrival at Charenton in 1803. Photograph: © Bibliothèque de l'Académie Nationale de Médecine, Paris.

F. DE COULMIERS
Député de la Vicomté
ABBÉ REGUL.r D'ABBECOUR
et Prévôté de Paris.
Collection Générale des Portraits de M.M. les Députés à l'Assemblée Nationale
tenue a Versailles le 4 Mai 1789.

FIGURE 17. French school, *Portrait of F. de Coulmier, Abbé Regular of Abbecour, Representative of the Viscounty and Provostry of Paris* (1789). Etching, 23.5 cm × 18 cm. Coulmier encouraged the Marquis de Sade to put on shows in the asylum's theater. Bibliothèque Nationale de France, Paris. Photograph © BNF.

There exists at Charenton a man whose bold immorality has unfortunately made him overly famous, and whose presence in this hospice creates the most serious problems—I am referring to the author of the infamous *Justine*. This man is not insane. His rage is for vice, and it is not in a home devoted to the medical treatment of insanity that this particular frenzy can be curbed. The individual stricken by it must subjected to the strictest confinement, either to shelter others from his outbursts or to cut himself off from all objects that might excite or sustain his hideous passions. Now, the Charenton home, in this particular case, fulfills neither of those conditions. Monsieur de Sade's freedom is far too great. He can communicate with a fairly wide number of people of both sexes, receiving them at his quarters or visiting them in their respective rooms. He is allowed to stroll through the grounds, where he often meets patients with the same privilege. To some of them he preaches his dreadful doctrine; to others he lends books. Finally, there is a widespread rumor that he lives with a woman who passes for his daughter.[53] And that is not yet all: a theater company was unwisely established here under the pretext of having the patients perform plays, but without considering the dire effects that such a tumultuous organization would have on their imaginations. Monsieur de Sade is the director of this theater troupe.[54]

FIGURE 18. Man Ray, *Imaginary Portrait of D. A. F. de Sade* (1938). Oil on canvas and wood, 61.5 cm × 46.6 cm. Private collection. Copyright © Man Ray Trust/ADAGP, Paris/Artists Rights Society, New York. The Marquis de Sade, that "incorrigible man" in a "permanent state of libertine dementia," as characterized by François de Coulmier, is set here in Man Ray's painting against the Bastille in flames. Interned in Charenton in 1803, Sade benefited from the protection of the all-powerful director Coulmier until his successor Royer-Collard arrived in 1806. Photograph © Bridgeman-Giraudon/Art Resource, New York.

This valuable document should be read as a double indictment. On one hand, Royer-Collard the physician is exposing an error and a mistaken placement: Sade is not mad and should not be living in an asylum devoted to treating mental patients. This is the psychiatrist speaking, and we can be grateful for this crucial detail. Yet on the other hand—and this is the main object of his complaint—Royer-Collard becomes the prosecutor who objects to the presence of man who, having been tracked down, harassed, and regularly incarcerated over the past forty years, still enjoys a freedom that is "far too great." The impact of Royer-Collard's argument rests entirely on this shift from medical diagnosis to moral indictment, which remains subtle insofar as Sade is not "insane" (*aliéné*) yet is subject to a "frenzy" (*délire*) for "vice," which the physician, with all the authority of his profession, deemed should be "curbed" (*réprimé*). He was not only inserting a moral judgment between the lines of a professional one, he was illustrating a de facto amalgamation on which his own field was establishing itself: modern psychiatry was being authorized to set itself up as a judge of misdemeanors even when they very clearly had nothing to do with mental insanity—which had still not been defined. Sade was cast not as a *victim* of madness but as *guilty* of "hideous passions." His lucidity, far from absolving him, was precisely the issue and aggravated his case. In this surprising sleight of hand, a diagnosis that seems to play in Sade's favor ("this man is not insane") becomes the key piece of prosecution evidence (he must be "subjected to the strictest confinement").

What danger did Sade—rehabilitated on one hand by a school of medicine that condemned him all the more harshly on the other hand—really represent? Whence came the urgent need to deprive him, immediately, of chatting with others, strolling in the grounds, or indulging in what Coulmier felt was an "innocent" pastime—running a theater? Ultimately, a scandalous reputation and "widespread rumors" would theoretically be insufficient to justify such persecution. Like Gaillion, who refused to have any dealings with Sade *on principle*, despite the latter's "civilities," Royer-Collard based his rejection on the prisoner's reputation alone, being unable to report any putative affronts. The only palpable argument in his letter involved an allusion—lacking details—to the "dreadful doctrine" that the author of *Justine* was allegedly preaching in the asylum, where he lent "books" to other inmates (again, this eternal obsession with propaganda, the reason behind the internment at Charenton of the professional atheist, Jacob Dupont). Although we cannot know how familiar the physician actually was with Sade's writings and philosophical system, it is safe to assume that this devout believer—Royer-Collard came from a Jansenist family—saw in it only blasphemy and peril. Everything about Sade—his atheistic materialism, his call for a depraved imagination, his obstinate insistence on the preeminence of body over mind—could only disgust Royer-Collard as a spiritual Christian and a future follower of Pierre Maine de Biran's metaphysical theories. The intensity of his conclusions reveals the extent of his disgust.

> It is hardly necessary, I think, to apprise Your Excellency of the scandal of such an existence and to point out the various dangers associated with it. If these details became known to the public, what would it think of an establishment that tolerated such strange excesses? For that matter, how can they be reconciled with the moral aspect of the treatment of insanity? Do not the patients, who are in daily contact with this abominable man, constantly receive the imprint of his profound corruption, and is not the mere idea of his presence in the home sufficient to disturb the imaginations of even those who do not see him?

Sade's presence—indeed the mere idea of his disembodied presence—apparently sowed disorder and corruption, a sign of his extraordinary power; or, rather, it was a sign of an extraordinary phantasm on the part of Royer-Collard, who demanded an end to the very "existence" of the marquis de Sade, whose invisible ghost haunted him to the point of disturbing his work as a physician. Furthermore, Royer-Collard here exemplifies, better than any antipsychiatrist could ever hope to do, the perversely double meaning of the expression *traitement moral* ("mental" and "moral" therapy), a mental orthopedics in which reason is connected to virtue. Remaining perfectly consistent, the psychiatrist then pursued his prosecutorial logic and pleaded for life imprisonment. "I am not asking that he be sent back to Bicêtre, where he was previously confined, indeed, I cannot prevent myself from pointing out to Your Excellency that a prison or fort would be much more suitable than an establishment designed to treat the ill, which requires the most assiduous watch and most particular precautions."

An investigation was subsequently launched. Coulmier acknowledged Sade's role in running the theater at Charenton and "even said that he was much obliged [to Sade] in this respect," esteeming himself "happy to have in his asylum a man able to teach lunatics how to perform in the theater, whom [Coulmier] hoped to cure by this kind of remedy."[55] The minister of police, however, had made up his mind: Sade would be transferred to the fortress of Ham in northern France. But the transfer—postponed several times owing to petitions by Sade's family, to financial excuses made by Coulmier, and to medical certificates signed by the asylum's surgeon declaring Sade too unwell—never took place. On October 18, 1810, the minister of the interior issued instructions that were to be executed without delay. Sade was to be confined to separate premises and prohibited from any internal or external communication; he was also to be deprived of pen and paper. Coulmier courageously objected with a steadfastness that honors an otherwise guileful individual. "My birth and the various positions and ranks I have held credit me with being at the head of a humane institution; to become a jailer would be beneath me."[56] Coulmier's "birth" meant a sense of privilege, an ethic, and above all an awareness of belonging to an elite circle that linked him to Sade in a shared class attitude in which "some things are just not done." Such nobility—including noble sentiments—is something that Royer-Collard could not claim for himself.

Royer-Collard thus lost a battle, but not the war. His steady work of attrition slowly brought results. In 1811 Charenton's reputation declined further, partly because of the scandal provoked by the theatrical performances. Coulmier, rebuffed by the minister of the interior, decided to write directly to the emperor to justify his actions and to identify the source of all his misfortune.

> I had even thought of innocent entertainments, such as shows, balls, and music, that would awaken the minds of hapless people completely lost in the cruel illness of dementia.
>
> These innocent methods produced the most felicitous results and were even widely applauded by all friends of humanity.
>
> This mental treatment was devised with Monsieur Gastaldy, one of the most esteemed physicians in Europe. It was my misfortune not only that I lost him, but that he was replaced by Monsieur Royer-Collard.[57]

But Napoleon lent Coulmier his ear no more than the minister had. The emperor, who had limited the number of accredited theaters in

Paris to eight, while closely monitoring their repertoires, did not deign to reply to Coulmier, any more than he answered the pleas for release from the ailing, exhausted Sade.

According to L. J. Ramon, a young doctor who joined Charenton just a few weeks before Sade died, the asylum's manners were "quite indecorous and, it would appear, rather *loose*."[58] Royer-Collard was clearly aware of it but had difficulty assembling evidence since the director prevented him from coming to the asylum more than twice a week to monitor the health of some four hundred patients. If Royer-Collard's blinding and deafening anger against Sade had not prevented him from even approaching the abominable man, he would have discovered the erotic initiation that the seventy-two-year-old writer was conducting upon sixteen-year-old Magdeleine Leclerc, prostituted by her own mother, an employee at Charenton. A detailed account was recorded in Sade's coded diary. It was an "account" in every respect: Sade spent his time in calculations, adding and subtracting, not only counting the days of imprisonment but also in terrific musings on dates and symbolic numbers. Such accounts were coded, of course, from Sade's (justifiable) fear that the police, having already searched his premises, would take it from him and decipher his latest notes. Sade himself was "Moses," while Coulmier was simply "C" or an uncoded "M. de Coul." The symbol ø referred to sodomy, in which he indulged with young Magdeleine in exchange for a few "figures." This libertine education also included lessons in singing and reading, to which the young woman was amenable—in all, according to Sade's meticulous count, she paid him ninety-six visits.[59]

When it came to licentiousness, Coulmier was not to be outdone. According to the file of complaints now in the National Archives, the director of Charenton seems to have abused his authority to have his way with young female patients. In 1812 an incident involving one Fanny Hanowerth unleashed a series of allegations that make Ramon's comment appear highly euphemistic.

Hanowerth was about eighteen when she arrived at Charenton. She had been a chambermaid who watched from the third floor as her employer's child fell to its death. She immediately went into "convulsive periods . . . followed by delirium" and ultimately wound up in the asylum. Two weeks later, she recovered her senses. Coulmier, aware that she could not return to her former place of employment, suggested she stay at Charenton "to work with the female patients" in return for "considerable benefits," which she accepted. Soon, however, Hanowerth sought help from a protector to get her out of the asylum, alleging that the director had summoned her into his office to talk about her health, but he allegedly "threw himself upon her like a madman." She apparently fainted, and Coulmier's secretary, Chapron, intervened.[60] Faithful to his retaliatory methods, Coulmier then consigned Hanowerth to a remote room.

That, at any rate, was the first version of the report. On being questioned, the young woman shed a different light on the matter. The director indeed received her in his office, made comments "that she did not find agreeable," and then "ventured to open the kerchief at her neck." Upset by this inappropriate gesture, she suddenly felt unwell but retained "enough awareness to realize that *the director was more embarrassed than she was*." She even told Royer-Collard, who participated in the investigation, that she could not "prevent herself from smiling on seeing the director"—who, recall, was handicapped by his deformities—"try to climb on chairs in order to open the window" just as Chapron, who had been called in, came to the rescue.[61] The letter she allegedly sent to a protector to get her out of Charenton was written not by herself, but by another patient who had had a similar experience and was seeking revenge.

As news of the affair spread, tongues loosened. The prefect of police soon received a letter, signed "Julie," recollecting that Coulmier had thrown himself "like a satyr" upon a girl in the household (which, according to the girl's own testimony, was not true). The letter also asserted that the director was living "quite openly with a boarder named Émilie Cournand, as well as others in the establishment, in such manner that it resembles a harem more than a hospital." Chapron, on being questioned, confirmed Coulmier's official affair with Cournand. Chapron was well placed to answer such inquiries—his wife was a former boarder at the asylum whom the director had turned out, and Chapron was so moved by her situation that he offered her his protection and asked for her hand, even though he had never thought of "tying himself to any woman." According to Chapron, the director was carrying on with Mademoiselle Christophe (the daughter of a laundress at the house), Mademoiselle Montfort (a rich boarder), and an opera ballerina called Zélie. Apparently Coulmier had "a strong passion" not only for women but also for a nurse's daughter "who [was] seven or eight years old, with a very pretty face" and whom he "frequently [kept] close by him."

The director's pedophilia may have been pure conjecture, as the honest Chapron's scruples—or caution—induced him to point out. The same file nevertheless contains another anonymous letter, signed by "a poor soul from the Charenton hospital," which describes not only mistreatment and brutality by the nurses, but also the wretched conditions at the asylum. "As to the head, I only had the benefit of seeing him once. He had me come to his room, but I hardly got to talk to him because he was surrounded by five or six girls." Then there was another inmate—a disabled, alcoholic veteran—who in florid language accused Dumoustier, the former Oratorian priest who worked under Coulmier, of being a despot "a thousand times more absolute than an oriental potentate," "who wallowed in filth and mire." The letter concludes, "The only favor I request of you, Sir, is to have me transferred to Bicêtre, Brest, Rochefort, the Marguerite Isles, Missicipi [*sic*], or to the ends of the earth, even among the cannibals, so thoroughly do I wish to leave this den of vice."[62]

And there was more. About 1808, on his own initiative Coulmier had promoted a Dr. Bleynie to be "chief surgeon" at Charenton even though the doctor had neither solicited the job nor possessed the qualifications. Coulmier was probably seeking to acquire the goodwill of a man he thought he could turn against Royer-Collard. The maneuver failed, however, and over time discord between the two men grew into hatred. In 1812 Bleynie sent a letter of complaint to the minister of the interior. Coulmier punished him by denying him wood for heating and by disparaging him in front of staff and patients, subjecting him daily to public humiliation and harassment. The source of conflict, of course, was Royer-Collard, whom Bleynie supported.[63]

The sun finally began to set on Coulmier in 1813. Chapron, who had reportedly been fired, in fact quit his job so that he "no longer had to witness the director's misconduct."[64] On May 6 a ministerial decree put an end to the theatrical performances. Coulmier was removed from his post the following year, being replaced on May 30, 1814, by the administrator Simon Martin Grégoire de Roulhac Dumaupas, a lawyer who got on well with Royer-Collard, finally enabling the latter to assume full medical management and to launch his reform of the institution.

The two men swiftly got down to work, jointly drawing up a set of internal regulations for Charenton that would serve as a model for decades to come. But the rules would never apply to the marquis de Sade, who died on December 2. Contrary to his last wishes, Sade was given a religious burial. Coulmier died four years later, a forgotten man. An era had come to an end.

* * *

Charenton was the scene of a clash between men and mentalities, and more especially between two visions of the world. The battle pitted two libertines—two solitary, fearsome aristocrats—against the bourgeois morality of a new disciplinary order. Charenton, as a nineteenth-century asylum that came under the sway of an ancien régime director, represented a kind of historical anomaly. In the space of just a few years it presented the spectacle of a transition between two incompatible, mutually antagonistic eras. On one side there was Coulmier, the philanthropist of an earlier century, holding court and exercising insolent, arbitrary power over both staff and patients. On the other side was Royer-Collard, steeped in his mission for the public good, incarnating moral authority and peremptory virtue, the figure of an avenging Commendatore who tirelessly sought to bring down his rival even has he called for the head of an old man whose lucidity he found appalling. Between petty king and office manager, between good life and good intentions, the choice can be a hard one.

There is no doubt that asylums served as prisons for Sade and others. Yet if we take the idea of political prison in a broader sense, as a place of incarceration where politics is played out, then Charenton becomes a symbol—in light of the endless duel between Coulmier and Royer-Collard—of a transition between two ways of conceiving the world, one based on pleasure, the other on work.

It is no coincidence that theater was at the heart of the struggle, the key stakes in the battle. The government was aware that the stage was a site of subversion par excellence, where the keen complicity between Sade and Coulmier could blithely revive a bygone era with all its conventions. Imagination and playacting provided the mentally ill with a diversion from the wretchedness of lives devoid of the least happening. On the stage or in the audience, the mad were transported to an unanticipated elsewhere, free to play a role other than the fool, traveling across landscapes that at last enlivened the dull horizons of their cells. Coulmier was criticized for sparking their passions, for making a spectacle of them before mocking audiences; his use of illusion was attacked as dishonest and misleading. Yet we should not forget that Pinel indulged in "curing fictions" by staging phony trials and other fanciful vignettes in order to help people recover their minds. But the difference—a big one—is that Pinel's patients were unaware and unentertained, being the objects of a maneuver steeped in its own earnest, beneficial aims.

On a close look, Charenton under Coulmier paints a faithful picture—in theory, at least—of a Pinel-style asylum. The promotional booklet written in 1804 by Charles Giraudy, Dr. Gastaldy's assistant, roundly praised Pinel's treatise on insanity, taking up its principles one by one. Patients should submit to order and obedience, being the objects of their warders' benevolence and care. Furthermore, Coulmier himself wrote phrases that seem to come straight out of the philanthropic prose of Pinel or Daquin. "I must present myself to the patients only as a father who consoles them, listens to their complaints—whether founded or unfounded—and even talks nonsense with them in order to win their trust."[65] Charenton's great originality lay in its theater, to which the name of Sade gave a satanic dimension.

I am inclined to think that the real scandal over the theater at Charenton lay not so much in the therapeutic issues that prompted cries of alarm by psychiatrists (including Esquirol, who never attended a single performance but who, years after Coulmier died, repeated the outraged opinions of Hippolyte de Colins almost word for word). What Napoleonic bureaucrats and their successors found intolerable was the breach constituted, in the foreclosed world of the asylum, by that "other scene," one independent of all ideological control. Sade rehabilitated what revolutionary zeal and imperial propaganda jointly sought to crush in the abstract rigidity of their neoclassical poses: the materialization of bodies and the circulation of desire. Against an "educational and edifying spectacle of the world,"[66] against the moral value of a collective lesson, Sade proposed an exploration and theatricalization of the irreducible singularity of desire on a stage where the unique encountered the many. Therein lay the disgrace, in the view of an institution where an emerging medical field was struggling to achieve the exact opposite—to make insanity's wildness conform to normality and blend into the community.

The chimeras and sterile sensual delights promoted by Sade and Coulmier were countered by the advocates of mental therapy in a unanimous chorus on the useful, healing virtues of work. In February 1811 Royer-Collard drew up a "brief report on the asylum of Charenton" in which he listed the establishment's dysfunctions and enumerated needed reforms. In fifteen points he laid out the main lines of his future regulations, in which all power would reside with the chief physician. His two final recommendations were "the prompt establishment of workshops for convalescents of both sexes" and "the complete and permanent abolition of all kinds of balls and theatrical performances in the asylum."[67] Madmen should labor in the fields, madwomen in sewing workshops—such was the way to reestablish order at Charenton. Meticulous, monotonous tasks were supposed to tame insanity through the effort and hard work they entailed, draining the body to the point of exhaustion. Pinel provided a user's guide for these miraculous therapies, laying down the laws for the model asylums of the nineteenth century, whose ascendance was paralleled by the rise of factories. "The patients who are suitable for work are divided at daybreak into various separate groups, each headed by a guide who assigns tasks to them, and who directs and supervises them. The day is spent in continuous activity which is only interrupted by rest breaks, for tiredness at night brings sleep and calm."[68]

This model of servitude and controlled mental exhaustion was indeed the path down which the nineteenth century confidently headed. The name Marx gave it, of course, was none other than "alienation" (*Entfremdung*).

THREE * The Man Who Thought He Was Napoleon

In his sweeping survey of mid-nineteenth-century Paris, Alphonse Esquiros noted in an aside one unexpected consequence of the return of Napoleon's remains to France on December 15, 1840. "The year that Napoleon's coffin was brought back to Paris, Dr. Voisin at the Bicêtre asylum recorded the admission of thirteen or fourteen emperors. . . . This presence of Napoleon among us—all the images and external signs of the commemoration, which made his face spring up, so to speak, everywhere—indeed, everything about this event helped to create a particular cause of insanity."[1]

The picture of a monomaniac wearing a bicorne, with one hand tucked into his gray frock coat and eyes riveted on the horizon of glory, is perhaps even today associated with a commonplace that is never really questioned: All madmen think they're Napoleon. Yet is there any historical basis to this proverbial assertion? Did the French emperor crystallize a specific delusion actually recorded in the archives of asylums where monarchs competed hotly with prophets, and where Jesus Christ, Mohammed, and Louis XVI had already inspired so many contenders? If so, why and in what way did the image of Napoleon lend itself more willingly to megalomania than the figure of, say, Charlemagne or Louis XIV?

Underlying these questions is, in fact, a larger debate arising from issues of identity, subjectivity, usurpation, and projection within the context of madness and its relation to history, within the gap between *being* and *imagining, believing, claiming*, or *thinking oneself to be*. Hence the real question might not be the classic Who am I? but rather Am I who I think I am? It is a question that could well have been asked of Napoleon Bonaparte himself, or rather of Bonaparte *and* Napoleon. But before exploring these regions, we must understand how nineteenth-century psychiatry viewed and analyzed delusions of grandeur, which might well dethrone melancholia for the title of scourge of the century.

DELUSIONS OF GRANDEUR, OR THE SCOURGE OF THE CENTURY

The madness of believing you are a famous person—an avatar of the Greek concept of hubris (or *hybris*), the human propensity to overreach, to challenge the gods—was considered a specific disease in the nineteenth century, known in France as *monomanie orgueilleuse* (or *monomanie ambitieuse*), that is to say, "delusions of grandeur" (or "monomania with elated ideas"). According to a standard dictionary of the day (*Littré*), it was characterized by "an exaggerated desire for power and domination" and was just one of the many types of monomania defined by Esquirol in the 1810s as "partial delusion" or "delusion over a single object." Various attributes were added to *monomanie*—"homicidal," "incendiary," "reasoning" (or affective), "drunken," "erotic"—to describe what modern psychiatry labels *psychose délirante chronique* (chronic psychosis with delusional disorders). The term monomania would not long survive a certain theoretical confusion (notably between instinctive and affective monomania) and excessive conceptual vagueness.[2]

The reasons the medical community progressively abandoned the term monomania in the latter half of the nineteenth century are the same ones that ensured the widespread popularity of this catchall concept. In the 1830s, *la monomanie* became a part of everyday vocabulary; hardly a periodical or novel failed to mention it. The term is found in many places in the works of Honoré de Balzac and Eugène Sue; every courtroom was seen to convict its monomaniacal thief or other criminal. "Monomania! Everyone knows what that is," declared a character in an 1835 play by Charles Duveyrier titled *Le monomane*: "[It's an] urge that drives you to kill and steal. You cannot help yourself, though it does not make you any more evil. Monomania calls for showers, lots of showers!"[3] Perhaps this widely and variously used term was already drained of meaning. That, at least, is what Eugène Scribe seemed to be suggesting in a one-act comedy that made fun of an apparently rampant craze that excused everything. In it, a character scolded his nephew for trying to excuse the idea of faking his own suicide—in order to get people to talk about him—by saying it was "monomania." "You call that an excuse? But if we accept it this time, it will be used for every base act and every crime. . . . The man who has just demeaned himself by stealing will tell you, 'I'm a monomaniac.' . . . The murderer who strikes down an unarmed victim will tell the jury, 'I'm a monomaniac.' . . . And you yourself, misled by such sophistry, you have succumbed to your delusion by believing it to be legitimate. . . . Oh youth! Oh you who have displayed many kinds of courage, show now the rarest but most indispensable kind of all—reason."[4]

Scientific reality was significantly more complex. According to Esquirol, monomania was a chronic cerebral illness "characterized by a partial lesion of the intelligence, affections, or will."[5] People suffering from it might live, act, and reason normally apart from one delusion related to some particular thing. But even a harmless corruption of an intellectual, emotional, or moral faculty usually had unfortunate consequences. Many quiet and apparently reasonable patients, for example, had to be force-fed because they refused all food, convinced that someone was trying to poison them. Many an otherwise peaceful madwoman, convinced she was the duchess d'Angoulême or had the power to make it rain or shine, would go into a rage if her orders were ignored or thwarted. Subject to hallucinations and sensory illusions just like sufferers of maniacal insanity and melancholia, these patients sometimes had lucid periods when they suddenly realized the extent of their distraction and would fret with remorse and despair until they succumbed once again to their illusions.

People with a "sanguine temperament," a vivid imagination, or a "meditative or exclusive cast," according to Esquirol, were "individuals who, through self-love, vanity, pride, and ambition, abandon[ed] themselves to their reflections, to exaggerated projects and unwarranted pretensions, [and were] especially disposed to monomania."[6] He went on to stress an important point: "It is remarkable that these individuals almost invariably beguile themselves with the hope of a happy fortune when, stricken by some reverse, or disappointed in their lofty expectations, they fall sick. Thus a man who is actually happy and moderate in his desires and who, by some exciting cause, becomes insane, will not be a monomaniac, while an ambitious, proud, or amorous man who shall have become unfortunate, or have lost the object

FIGURE 19. Georges-François-Marie Gabriel, *a Soldier Who Claimed to Be the King of Sweden*. From *Heads of Lunatics Drawn at Charenton* (ca. 1823). Drawing. Bibliothèque Nationale de France, Paris. During the Restoration, Dr. Étienne Esquirol asked G.-F.-M. Gabriel to draw roughly a hundred heads of "lunatics" at Charenton. The most common symptoms of "monomania" were a passion for power or some overweening ambition, as in this soldier who claimed to be king of Sweden. (See also figures 20 and 25 below.) Photograph © BNF.

of his affections, will." Monomaniacs thus suffered for their own sins, victims of fundamentally tainted passions; monomania was merely "an exaggeration of the thoughts, desires, and illusions with respect to the future, with which these unfortunate beings amuse their fancy, previous to their illness." This moralizing vision of illness logically followed Esquirol's own famous thesis, published in 1805, whose very title underscores the link between source and effect, between normal passion and morbid excess: *Des passions, considérées comme causes, symp-*

tômes et moyens curatifs de l'aliénation mentale (The passions considered as the causes, symptoms, and means to cure insanity). If pride were indeed the "cause" and "symptom" of delusions of grandeur, it could also be used as a "means of cure" in mental treatment that sought to pique, wound, or repress the patient's vanity. "Here, more than in other forms of mental disease," stressed Esquirol, "and with better hopes of success, we apply to the understanding and passion of the patient, with a view to effect his cure. We have recourse to surprises, subterfuges,

FIGURE 20. Georges-François-Marie Gabriel, *Haughty Seamstress*. From *Heads of Lunatics Drawn at Charenton* (ca. 1823). Drawing. Bibliothèque Nationale de France, Paris. Photograph © BNF.

and oppositions, ingeniously managed, as circumstances suggest, the genius of the physician gives birth to, and as experience may hit upon, and appropriately pursue."[7] Specialists thus competed to come up with ways to bring down the most stubborn megalomaniacs; any expedient was valid, from flattery to repression, if it banished illness and defused conflicts. One of the most spectacular examples of such tactics concerns not a physician but Marguerite Jubline, the wife of Jean-Baptiste Pussin, the ward supervisor at Bicêtre. She worked alongside her husband, and Pinel praised her ingenuity here, as on several other occasions.

> Three deranged patients who thought they were the equal of sovereigns, and who each took the title of Louis XVI, fought one day over the rights to royalty and asserted them rather too vigorously. The lady superintendent approached one of them and drawing him aside asked in a serious voice, "Why are you getting into a dispute with those people, who are obviously mad? Is it not well known that you alone should be acknowledged as Louis XVI?" Flattered by this tribute the latter immediately withdrew, looking at the others in disdainful haughtiness. This same clever device succeeded with a second of the three, and in this way at once there was no longer any trace of the dispute.[8]

Of all monomanias, delusions of grandeur was the most common and most immediately recognizable. Dr. François Broussais held it to be "the principal monomania of intellectual origin,"[9] while Ulysse Trélat considered sufferers the most dangerous kind of "lucid madmen."[10] Hundreds of overlapping cases in the archives make it easy to assemble an Identikit portrait: haughty and disdainful countenance, pathological vanity, constant anger at not being obeyed, emphatic, self-assured pronouncements made right and left, although rarely consistent. If male, he was usually the ruler of the world; if female, she was empress of the universe. Their fortunes amounted to billions, their armies were invincible, they could annihilate the earth in a single breath. "Happy demeanor as usual, crown on head, making incoherent comments, calm as usual except when she is thwarted," summed up one observation on a patient convinced she was the queen of France.[11]

In the early nineteenth century, the specific and curable disease of delusions of grandeur was sometimes confused with a very serious illness that wreaked terrible damage over time: general paresis (paralysis) of the insane (or dementia paralytica). This disease, characterized by an inflammation of the meninges, was identified by Antoine-Laurent Bayle in 1822. It was a combination of neurological and psychological disorders that steadily brought dementia and death. Initially a victim of difficulty of speech and muscular weakness, the patient subsequently moved into a second phase typified by delusions of grandeur. "It is above all during this phase that [the patient] totally succumbs to illusions of silly vanity, whether he believes himself to be king, pope, emperor, grandee, millionaire, or owner of vast treasures. This one calls himself Napoleon and has won every battle of empire; another maintains that he has produced all the masterpieces now gracing our museums of painting and sculpture; yet another has only to nod his head to erect magnificent palaces, cities of crystal, houses of diamonds, and he makes bizarre movements; some paralytics think they are thirty feet, or forty or fifty cubits, tall."[12] The third and final phase led to mindlessness and total physical collapse.

Apart from a few specific symptoms, general paresis had the same etiology as monomania. "Intense passions, grief induced by jealous, thwarted romance, disappointed ambitions, impotent pride, and the fear of indigence after having known wealth are sometimes the only causes to which incomplete paresis of the insane can be attributed," asserted Louis Calmeil, a physician at Charenton who had become a specialist in the field.[13] Not until 1922, a century after Bayle identified it, was there definitive proof that general paresis of the insane was in fact the outcome of untreated syphilis. It was eradicated only once penicillin became widely available after World War II.

But in the nineteenth century, general paresis was a type of insanity that devolved solely upon psychiatry. In 1841 Calmeil estimated that it affected over 25 percent of the men at Charenton, and one woman out of fifteen (6.6 percent).[14] At exactly the same moment, the year 1841–42, delusions of grandeur (*monomanie ambitieuse*) was diagnosed in over 25 percent of the men at Bicêtre and 10 percent of the women in La Salpêtrière.[15] Whether of organic or psychological causes (which in no way affected their nature or recurring themes), delusions of grandeur, general paresis, and monomania together reached astronomical proportions in Parisian asylums in the period just after Napoleon's remains returned home.

Obviously, the return of Napoleon's remains was not the sole cause of such an increase. Delusions of grandeur was a fashionable illness of the day, just as hysteria would be in fin-de-siècle Vienna. It was at least in part a symptom of and a response to a society in which money and boredom reigned at the court of a bourgeois king whom the papers notoriously caricatured in the shape of a pear. Dreams of revolution had crumbled, and the legend of Napoleon belonged to a heroic past, leaving the romantic generation inconsolable. "The scourge of the present age stems from two causes," wrote Alfred de Musset in 1836. "People who lived through 1793 and 1814 bear two wounds in their hearts: everything that was is no longer; everything that will be is not yet. Look no further for the secret of our ills."[16] For a generation trapped in the gap between two pages of history—between the end of one era and a future with no clear perspective—the present was a source of anxiety and revulsion that translated into a dreadful disenchantment with the world.

That world—lacking in soul and panache, subject to bankers and speculators, dominated by priests and physicians—called out for new horizons. It was asking to be reenchanted, a task that the romantics carried out through marvelous stories, fantastic tales, historical novels, dreamlike accounts, travels, experiments with hashish, and so on, not forgetting the invention of outsized characters ranging from Balzac's Vautrin to Dumas's Count of Monte Cristo, who populated a new and strikingly lively gallery of contemporary literary figures. This heroic recasting of the world owed much to Napoleon's messianic image and found its social expression in the focus on personal fame and the unprecedented cult of great men; a veritable market in vanity spurred media visibility and self-promotion, thanks to the rise of the press and advertising. "The role of pride is so pervasive in society that one is almost surprised to see that exaggerations of this passion are included among mental aberrations. What excesses could be so large and manifest that they have not become, in a way, naturalized among ourselves? Does this passion spur men to misjudge themselves and believe they are superior in nature to other men? Yet that can be seen everywhere, every day," wrote Dr. François Leuret in his 1834 *Fragments psychologiques sur la folie* (Psychological fragments on madness), in which he listed delusions of grandeur as the leading form of monomania.[17] A few years later one of the contributors to the *Bibliothèque du médecin-practicien* (The physician's library) went further by stating that "we have no fear of being taxed with exaggeration in saying that the madness of the age is pride" and that never before in history "have we seen so many men make themselves out to be saviors, to have first-rank talents and abilities."[18]

The glorification of the self was on the agenda at a time when Victor Hugo—who chose *Ego Hugo* as his heraldic motto[19]—vowed that he would be "Chateaubriand or nothing," and when Balzac claimed he would accomplish with the pen what Napoleon had done by the sword. Whether real writers or imaginary characters, the nineteenth century was full of demigods and demiurges inhabiting self-contained fictional worlds and monumental novelistic cycles that offered extravagance and, above all, identification. On taking a closer look, in fact, if there is one trait typical of romantic characters, it is that they take themselves for the protagonist of a novel. Stendhal's Julien Sorel modeled his behavior on the Napoleon who exclaimed, "My life is a novel!" (as reported in the comte de Las Cases's memoirs of Saint Helena), while Balzac's characters identified with the likes of Manfred and Faust, and Théophile Gautier's Mademoiselle de Maupin played the role of Rosalind in *As You Like It*. In a lyrical century of commitment and intensity, when readers identified with heroes who themselves identified with heroes, delusions of grandeur was a typically romantic illness as characterized by the aggrandizement of self, the projection of identity, and obsessive allusion to a historical model.

This metaphorical link with the world of novelistic creativity went beyond mere analogy. Psychiatrists were worried by the actual effect of works of fiction. Literature acquired a negative image because it favored illusions and encouraged imitation—"novel reading" was listed by the faculty of medicine as one cause of madness. Nor it is unusual to come across comments in the archives such as the following passage on a woman suffering from delusions of grandeur and religious ravings: "It is thought that the derangement of her faculties must be attributed to the solitary life she led over the past eighteen months, along with her constant reading of novels. It is also thought that she was too eager to go deeper into the book of Revelations."[20] Beyond the potential damage of novels, it was "deeper" reading—even of sacred texts—that was generally considered inadvisable, especially for women (for whom, it was feared, mental reflection was a strain). According to Dr. Félix Voisin, "the impact of modern novels" was the cause of many mental illnesses, notably among the "misunderstood, independent, proud madwomen who are at war with their own sex." These forerunners to Madame Bovary bore "the perverted and distorted mark of books by Georges [*sic*] Sand, which they read without understanding them."[21]

So was delusions of grandeur a romantic *and* literary malady? Partly. Not to mention that the pathology also provided subject matter for literature of the day, as illustrated in a fine story by Gérard de Nerval in which the poetic themes of doppelgänger and reflection merge with an actual clinical description of delusions of grandeur. The story is titled "King of Bicêtre (Sixteenth Century): Raoul Spifame" and was published in *La Presse* in 1839. Raoul Spifame worked as a lawyer at the *parlement* of Paris in the sixteenth century. One day when the chamber sat in the presence of Henri II, everyone in attendance realized that Spifame looked just like the king, who himself was struck by the resemblance. From that point on, in the corridors of the palace Spifame was always laughingly addressed as "Sire" or "Your Majesty." This unfortunate mockery ultimately led Spifame to believe that he actually was the king. His royal posturings, harangues, and schemes for reform finally put him in the madhouse. Once in the asylum, Spifame became more convinced than ever that he was Henri II. He governed, decreed, and feasted, fully persuaded that "his dreams were real life and his prison was just a dream." Then one day the warder decided to hang a polished steel mirror in his cell. Spifame went up and believed he saw the king come toward him and speak, "at which point he hastened to make a deep bow."

> And when he rose, glancing at the alleged prince, he distinctly saw the figure rise also, a sure sign that the king had greeted him thus, giving him great joy and boundless honor. He then launched into intense recriminations against the traitors who had placed him in this situation, having most likely blackened his reputation in the eyes of His Majesty. The poor gentleman even wept, proclaiming his innocence and asking to be allowed to confound his enemies; at which point the king seemed singularly touched, for a tear glistened as it ran along the royal nose.

> At this sight a flash of joy lit up Spifame's face; the king was already smiling with a pleasant air; he held out a hand, Spifame put forward his own—the mirror, struck sharply, fell from the wall and crashed to the ground with a fearful noise that brought the warders running.[22]

The mirror perhaps reflects nothing so much as the perfect equation between fantasy (imagining yourself a monarch) and reality (so resembling a monarch that you *mistake* yourself for the sovereign): function and image merge, you can be yourself and another, a single individual yet two characters. In his face-to-face encounter, Nerval pushed the paradox of identity as far as possible: on glimpsing his own reflection, Spifame sees the king. Surely it is madness to take your own image in the mirror for someone else, to interpret symmetrical gestures as a form of empathy. And yet in his error Spifame proves, *simultaneously*, that he is not mad because *he acknowledges the difference* and proves that he dissociates himself from the king, someone who is distinct from the lawyer interned in Bicêtre. Don Quixote inevitably comes to mind, whom Esquirol cited as a perfect poetic incarnation of monomania, because his partial delusion left the rest of his understanding intact. Nerval conveyed this idea in the following terms: "Nothing could demonstrate better than Spifame's story how true is the depiction of that character, so famous in Spain, of a man insane in only one part of his brain, and highly reasonable in the rest of his logic; we truly see that he had an awareness of himself, unlike common lunatics who forget themselves and remain constantly convinced they are the characters they have invented. Spifame, before a mirror or in his sleep, recovered his sense of self and felt himself distinct; he could change role and individuality in turn, being identical and yet different, the way one often exists in dreams."[23]

What was the reality behind this syndrome during the disenchanted period when Nerval wrote his story? Who did people think they were during the July monarchy? They rarely took themselves, it must be said, for King Louis-Philippe himself. That, in fact, is one of the striking lessons to be drawn from the archives. People may have taken themselves for *a* king, but not necessarily the one sitting on the throne. A madwoman who was interned in La Salpêtrière in 1833, having sunk into dementia following delusions of grandeur, systematically answered her questioners with the reply, "Withdraw, knave, can't you see that I am the king of France?"[24] But was this king of France Louis-Philippe himself? In general, that bourgeois monarch—styled "king of the French" rather than "king of France"—was little conducive to identificatory urges. He did not stir the imagination or spark flights of fancy, demonstrating that the symbolism of the royal role must be physically incarnated if it is to become a *delusional* image. Which is not to say that there is no mention of Louis-Philippe in asylum archives; but the most striking—and, in fact, most amusing—thing is that patients usually mistook *another* inmate or even the director of the asylum for Louis-Philippe. In other words, the relationship was flipped: people didn't think *they* were the king, they thought the king was some ordinary or familiar person.

It is hard not to perceive this reversal of perspective—which humanized the king rather than aggrandizing oneself—as an effect of the extra lucidity ascribed to the insane, who thereby shed, by refraction, some original light on the reign of Louis-Philippe. "He lacked majesty," claimed Victor Hugo, "his great fault" was that "he was modest in the name of France." Hugo sketched a portrait of a monarch with very real good qualities yet lacking depth, who represented "the middle class" and incarnated the reign of "transition."[25] But people cannot identify with "a transition." Too human, too straightforward, too bourgeois, Louis-Philippe was an affable head of household who projected a conservative ideal, thereby defusing identificatory delusions. He was the opposite of grandeur. The staunch disdain for everything he represented was precisely what exemplified monomaniacs.

Reduced to the "middling" dimensions of the class he promoted, Louis-Philippe became an approachable human in the asylums, even if he retained his status of head of state. This accessibility extended to his family and entourage. "It was while advising us to keep the greatest silence that M. P. let us in on his secrets," reported the doctor at Charenton in 1831 concerning a forty-five-year-old landowner whom Bicêtre had sent to him with no information on his case.

> On traveling up from his home, he found himself in a stagecoach with the king and his son. He knew them well, had written in their defense, and was received at the Palais-Royal, etc. During his stay in Bicêtre he saw Louis-Philippe, in disguise, among the patients. He slept in the same room as the crown prince, who was also in disguise and who

FIGURE 21. Honoré Daumier, *Ministerial Madhouse*. From *La Caricature*, May 31, 1832. 33.7 cm × 563.5 cm. Honoré Daumier took Charenton as his model of a "ministerial madhouse" that compares King Louis-Philippe's ministers to madmen suffering from various kinds of political monomania: the comte d'Argout, astride giant scissors, "plays at censorship (his hobbyhorse)," while General Sébastiani juggles with Europe and François Guizot (arms raised, right) "preaches in the wilderness." To the right of the prime minister being subjected to a shower is the unnamed figure, seen from the back, of the "pear-shaped king," Louis-Philippe, who allegedly suffered from "the monomania of shaking hands" with people "who didn't want to." Bibliothèque Nationale de France, Paris. Photograph © BNF.

> confided government secrets to him. At mass, he found himself next to the queen, dressed as a peasant woman, and he recognized the prefect of police disguised as a cook. During this same period Lafayette and some twenty republicans were also hiding in Bicêtre. M. P. had no idea of the reason that led all these illustrious people to that place. Soon our questions aroused his suspicion; he believed we would betray him, hence he became angry and would say nothing more.[26]

Once his trust returned, M. P. admitted his fear of assassination if he revealed his secrets and said that by remaining at Charenton he was obeying orders from the king, of whom he was extremely fond. So, although defended by the patient who had written letters in his favor, Louis-Philippe retained the power to intern whomever he wished.

The same blend of deference and familiarity characterized the delusion of another patient who was convinced that Charenton was Louis-Philippe's royal residence. He also ascribed Louis-Philippe's name to one of the inmates of the asylum, where all the patients were descendents of the Bourbon family. Only too happy to be of service to the royal family, "he carried out all domestic chores, washing the dishes, sweeping the hall, and never speaking to anyone, including the nurses, without bowing low and addressing them as 'my prince.'" It is no coincidence that this patient confused the ruling Orléans branch with the historic Bourbon royalty. The monarchic principle remained firmly linked to the elder Bourbon branch, whose prestige and legitimacy were still intact as late as 1843 when this observation was recorded, even though Louis-Philippe d'Orléans had been on the throne for thirteen years. The physician, for that matter, was concerned about this historical inconsistency and tried to force the patient into a corner. "When I asked him how it happened that Louis-Philippe, who had driven out the Bourbons in 1830, was now living with them, he replied that Louis-Philippe had not driven out the Bourbons at all, that in 1830 some nasty people had indeed wanted to remove the family but that it got together and jointly agreed that Louis-Philippe should take up the reins of government since he was the most able to withstand the seditionists."[27] This unimpeachable logic cast Louis-Philippe as the opportunist he truly was.

The citizen-king's reputation hardly improved in asylums over the years. In May 1848 a female patient arrived at Charenton because she had been convinced since the revolution in February of that year, which had just driven out the Orléans family in turn, "that the person who lives above her, in her sister's place, is no other than Louis-Philippe himself. When she happened to encounter this person, she heaped insults upon him."[28] Abandoned, then forgotten, Louis-Philippe died in 1850 and was ultimately relegated to subordinate tasks in the memories of the insane. During the Second Empire (1852–70), a patient at Bicêtre who claimed to be related by marriage to Emperor Napoleon III asserted that "Louis-Philippe and his children are threshing the wheat in his barn."[29] Such a crime of (posthumous) lèse-majesté would have been unthinkable against a monarch who eclipsed all the others in the asylums of France: Emperor Napoleon I.

MASTER OF THE UNIVERSE

"Alive, he lost a world; dead, he owns it."[30] Chateaubriand's comment on Napoleon Bonaparte, prophesying a "despotism of his memory" can be best applied to the power that the emperor wielded over the collective imagination as his presence faded and his legend grew. As soon as he was exiled to Saint Helena, the henceforth invisible Napoleon sparked growing fascination. In 1818 the Charenton asylum recorded the admission of just one son of Louis XVI (who also thought he was Jesus and the prophets Elijah and Samuel) compared with five Napoleons. One of the latter group "appointed" and "dismissed" legislators, another "had purchased Italy and conquered Asia," yet another owned "forty thousand barrels filled with gold," and so on.[31] Five emperors out of ninety-two patients admitted that year represent 5.4 percent of the total madness at Charenton; this figure may seem low, but it lacks real validity, since many cases went undescribed or were not detailed enough to provide reliable statistics.

In contrast, the proportion of one to five for dauphin versus emperor is worthy of note. From the Directoire period up to the Second Empire, current events in France were regularly enlivened by "fake dauphin" incidents. The son of Louis XVI, who died in the Temple in 1795 at age ten—but who was said to have escaped or been kidnapped—inspired roughly one hundred impersonators all across Europe, including the son of a cobbler from Angers, Mathurin Bruneau, tried in February 1818 and imprisoned on Mont-Saint-Michel. Victor Hugo claimed that

Louis XVIII was haunted by two figures—Mathurin Bruneau and Napoleon—by which he meant two ghosts whose potential return the restored king feared more than anything else.[32]

Why did royalist imposters fill the courtrooms rather than asylums? They were all sent to prison—Jean Hervagault, Mathurin Bruneau, Claude Perrin, the baron de Richemont, and Karl-Wilhelm Naundorff. Why were they hounded by the justice system rather than the faculty of medicine? The answer seems self-evident. In people's minds, the survival of the dauphin—who would then have been Louis XVII—seemed a minute possibility but was nevertheless *credible*, abetted by the difficulty of recognizing a child in the features of a man in his thirties (or older, depending on the date of his appearance). Placing these claimants to the throne among the mentally ill would mean recognizing the absurdity of this historical possibility. That the French royal family wanted them tried rather than hospitalized perhaps suggests that the family itself, to whom these miraculous reappearances posed the most immediate threat, did not consider the possibility to be entirely *crazy*—or maybe it was the doctors who refused to consider false claimants true monomaniacs.

Bogus dauphins were adventurers who incarnated a character whose body had vanished and whose existence was therefore virtually conceivable. They took advantage of a fault line, a fantasy, and stirred doubts despite the feebleness of their arguments—most drew their information from a popular and highly fanciful novel, *Le cimetière de la Madeleine* (The cemetery of La Madeleine), which speculated about the substitution of Louis XVII. In contrast, phony Napoleons were all madmen who were *clearly* deluded because everyone knew that the original was languishing on Saint Helena. Indeed, rare were those who managed to convince their entourage of their imperial rank, apart from one monomaniac interned in 1826 (five years after the real emperor's death) who "thought he was Bonaparte, the father of Napoleon II" and whose "pretensions were strengthened by being believed by several dupes who gave credence to what he said and who viewed him as the victim of persecution."[33] The physician, however, did not specify whether those dupes were other patients in the asylum.

The difference between the phony dauphins and the phony Napoleons is simultaneously slim and vast, hard to define yet impossible to miss. In both cases there was impersonation. Yet whereas the first imposture represented a political danger and deliberate fraud, the latter was sheer farcelike madness of no consequence (except perhaps for friends and family). But were things really that clear-cut? For all we know, the dauphin impostors were *also* deluded and *really* thought they were heirs to the throne, like those compulsive liars caught up in their own lie, as witnessed by many examples down through history from the Anastasia mystery to the Wilkormiski affair.[34] For that matter, how can we explain the fact that Louis XVII appears so rarely in asylum registers—apart from one patient in Charenton in 1818, perhaps impressed by the recentness of the Bruneau affair—unlike his sister, the duchesse d'Angoulême, very much alive, whose name was enormously popular at La Salpêtrière?[35] Why was it only outside the asylum walls that people took themselves for the dauphin? The legend of Louis XVII rests on an absence: no one knew exactly what the child would look like as an adult. This disembodiedness, which paved a royal path for opportunist impostors, was perhaps what discouraged identificatory delusions in the asylums. Louis XVII lacked an *image*, unlike—to say the least—Napoleon I.

Never had a first name so conveyed strategic genius and a desire for power, nor had a physical image so incarnated the essence of hegemonic domination and authority: a cocked hat, a frock coat—and there you have the emperor. Napoleon was inextricably linked to his own caricature, down to his abrupt and tyrannical temperament.

The men who thought they were Napoleon always had the same profile: authoritarian, capricious, irascible—and imperial. Such a man did not merely rule France, he was the master of the universe. His power was limitless. Everyone had to bend to his will. His countenance was serious, he issued orders constantly, he demanded devotion from an entourage he largely despised. Foreign policy was the subject that most concerned him. Whereas many other monomaniacs dreamed of bringing about human happiness, seeking to end war and abolish taxes, the Napoleons were belligerent and violent, and they expected to be obeyed like a despot. One diagnostic report, dated 1831, serves as a good illustration:

> The first day we found him dressed elegantly, head held high with a proud, haughty air; his tone was that of command, and his least gestures indicated power and authority. He soon informed us that he was

> the emperor of France, with millions in riches, that Louis-Philippe was his chancellor, etc. Then, taking up a manuscript, he pompously recited verses of his own composition, in which he allocated kingdoms, settled the affairs of Belgium and Poland, etc. During the day he smashed everything because people would not obey his every order. He was calmed by a shower and then shut up in a cell. The next day we found him naked, having torn up everything, shouting, threatening, etc.[36]

At a loss when faced with such blind rage, many physicians turned to highly forcible methods of coercion and repression. Others preferred to employ ruse. One, a Dr. Leblond who ran a home for the mentally deranged with his father, dealt with a captain of the dragoons who lived in a perpetual rage, striking and insulting any servants who came near. He spent all his time in vituperation. "It is surely an indignity to treat Emperor Napoleon this way!" he declared to the doctor. "Those frightful valets bound me—I intend to have them shot." To which Leblond calmly replied, "Yes, you are indeed Emperor Napoleon, but Napoleon on Saint Helena." On hearing those words, the madman fell silent, then began repeating, "Saint Helena, Saint Helena." He then asked to be unbound and kept his promise to remain calm until he was freed.[37]

Should we believe these appealing tales of miraculous cures? There is a strong temptation to credit the efficacy of such theatrical ploys, which would reduce delusion to a play of language and lend madness a comic image. It would also turn psychiatrists into doctors able to share a patient's delusions even as they displayed a great talent for repartee. Denying the patient's title of emperor would only have increased his rage, whereas acknowledging that title while stressing his downfall was a way of setting him back on the path to reality. Like Napoleon on Saint Helena, the madman in the asylum was exiled, imprisoned, "alienated." The physician's shrewdness lay in exploiting the patient's delusion in order to establish a *logical* convergence with history, and to establish a metaphorical relationship between a truth and a fiction, thus making sense where none existed. The irony of the situation rests completely on the coherence of artificially layering a true image over a false discourse.

Many physicians promoted the marvelous effects of an approach to mental therapy that sought first of all to mollify uncontrollable patients and bring them back to reason, if by indirect methods. Dr. Guillaume Ferrus, an army doctor who had participated in all of Napoleon's campaigns up the retreat from Russia, and who had notably been present at the battles of Austerlitz, Eylau, and Wagram, was well placed to lend a sympathetic ear to the complaints of monomaniacs obsessed by the emperor. One day, for example, he saw a young man who claimed to be the son of Napoleon arrive at Bicêtre in "a state of intense agitation."

> "I was your father's physician," Dr. Ferrus said to him. "Come and talk with me, tell me your grievances, and I'll see to the problem." With those words Dr. Ferrus led him warmly, arm in arm, toward the trees gracing the courtyard. On asking him the reason for his agitation, he learned that the man had ridden twenty-five leagues on horseback. "But surely you know," he immediately interjected, "that whenever your august father, His Majesty the king and emperor, undertook similar rides, which happened often enough, he never failed to take a bath." The patient practically offered to do the same and indeed took himself to the baths. Encouraged by this initial success, Dr. Ferrus took his arm and said, "Did you know that Your Majesty has a strong, hard, erratic pulse and that it would do some good to draw a little blood? Not from your arm, which might prevent you from signing orders, but from a small vein in the neck." The patient allowed himself to be bled. In a fortnight Napoleon's son, having been bled, bathed, and consoled, was once again just his own father's son.[38]

It also took two weeks—although using different methods—for Esquirol's assistant, François Leuret, to fully succeed with Paul Dumont (not his real name), who was actually the son of a war department official but was convinced he was the son first of Joachim Murat (Napoleon's brother-in-law), then of Napoleon, then a schoolmate of the duc de Bordeaux (the Bourbon pretender), and finally a knight of the chamber to Queen Marie-Amélie. Obsessed by ancient nobility, he attributed a noble particle to everyone's name and identified himself, according to mood, as Paul *de* Murat, Paul *de* Napoleon, and so on. In the asylum he was called Monsieur Paul, "which in his mind did not contradict the status of being Napoleon's son." The physician then asked the nurses to address the patient only as Monsieur Dumont. The man became angry and complained bitterly to the physician, whom he insisted on calling Dr. *de* Leuret. In order to suppress this infatuation, Leuret prescribed a harsh cold shower every time the patient lapsed. "This patient was not in a state to profit from any exhortations we might have made; I acted upon his mind in a way that might be called mechanical, by linking, so to speak, a painful sensation to the action of his hallucinations."[39] For a psychiatrist who sought to describe mental therapy without hypocrisy and who openly acknowledged what was being quietly practiced in hospitals, there was only one way to cure the most recalcitrant patients: never get "taken in" by their ploys, but rather restore their *reason* through the *power of reasoning*, using carrot and stick, which meant using force when necessary. Leuret wrote, "A single string still vibrates within them, that of pain. Be brave enough to pluck it."[40]

Physicians were doing battle not only against madness but even more so against its terrific stubbornness. In this respect the man who thought he was Napoleon's son was at least as strong-willed as his father. "In his room almost all day long, he remains standing, hands in trousers pockets, and when he is asked a few questions he will answer, always concluding by saying that he is the emperor's son. He never addresses anyone," reads the 1836 register at Charenton.[41] Believing oneself to be Napoleon's son meant identifying not with his actual son, the duc de Reichstadt, but rather with a second Napoleon. Similarly, women who claimed to be the emperor's wife took themselves not for either Joséphine or Marie-Louise—who were powerless figures—but rather for a victorious rival. In an asylum, claiming to be married or related to Napoleon meant enjoying the same supernatural powers ascribed to the emperor. "She claims to have *the sun in her belly*," the head physician of Charenton noted in 1810 about an independently wealthy woman aged forty-six. "She thinks she is *Napoleon's wife*. She rules the universe thanks to electric fire in her body, which she can unleash at will."[42]

For the sake of thoroughness, it must be added—if with a twinge of disappointment—that those who thought they were Napoleon were rarely women. In the course of my research I came across only one case, a seventy-one-year-old monomaniac admitted in June 1852. She was firmly convinced of her identity—though it is not clear whether she thought she was Napoleon I or Napoleon III—and perfectly consistent. "She says she's Napoleon; she shouts, 'Long live Napoleon!'"[43]

The terrific surge of interest in Napoleon that occurred when his remains returned to France—a period when, recall, "delusions of grandeur" represented more than 25 percent of diagnoses—marked a turning point in the imperial legend. The grandiose ceremony, orchestrated by the July monarchy in an attempt at national reconciliation (despite the risk of reigniting a Bonapartist movement), occupied the government for many months in 1840. King Louis-Philippe dispatched his son, the prince de Joinville, to lead the expedition that brought back the body of Napoleon, who had died and been buried on Saint Helena in 1821. There the opening of the coffin in the presence of several witnesses, including a doctor, created surprise and a stir: his skin, hands, and face had been preserved. The body of Napoleon I was intact.

The convoy arrived in France in late November, and on December 15, 1840, a monumental carriage draped in purple crepe dotted with the imperial emblem of a bee, drawn by sixteen caparisoned horses. It passed through the Arc de Triomphe and headed down the Champs-Elysées toward Les Invalides. A huge, emotional crowd shouted "Long live the emperor!" and "Long live the great Napoleon!" The cortege included a white steed wearing the saddle Napoleon used at the Battle of Marengo. The crowd gasped, convinced—despite the laws of arithmetic and equine life expectancy—that the horse was the very one that had carried the emperor into battle.[44] Might Napoleon be immortal, like his steed? During the revolutionary events of 1830 a man who bore a striking resemblance to Napoleon had suddenly appeared in the midst of a riot at the Place de l'Odéon, wearing a frock coat and sitting astride a white horse. Amid all the clamor and confusion, the effect was instantaneous. "Long live the emperor!" shouted the crowd with one voice, as a woman crossed herself and fell to her knees, exclaiming, "Dear Jesus! I have lived to see him again!"[45]

The onlookers in 1840 were no crazier than the rioters of 1830. The myth of the man of the moment and the savior of the nation outlived the exile of the dictator and his corpse. His horse was "recognized" on the Champs-Elysées twenty-five years after Waterloo, just as he was "seen" to emerge in the tumult of 1830. Napoleon is always "with us," ever alive in people's imaginations.

Although the French conventionally refer to the return Napoleon's "ashes" (*cendres*) rather than his body, it was its physical intactness, interpreted symbolically, that imparted magic power to the corpse and to the image that neither death nor time apparently succeeded in diminishing. Proof can be found in a book published anonymously in 1836, titled *Napoléon apocryphe: Histoire de la conquête du monde et de la monarchie universelle, 1812–1832* (The apocryphal Napoleon: A history of the conquest of the world and the universal monarchy, 1812–1832). Having been withdrawn from circulation, it was republished after the return of the "ashes" under the signature of Louis Geoffroy, shorthand for Louis-Napoléon Geoffroy-Château. *Napoléon apocryphe* represented the first true work of political fiction, one that adopted a utopian view of history—history not as it was, but as it might have been. (Charles Renouvier would give the label "uchronia" to such works in 1857.) Geoffroy's alternative history was based on the following speculation: What would have happened if Napoleon had *not* been defeated outside Moscow? According to Geoffroy, the ruler of continental Europe would have pursued his conquests, becoming the master of the universe, from the Americas to Asia. The book thus helped to inflate and enlarge the ghost of Napoleon at a time when rumors concerning his death abounded. Did the emperor die of stomach cancer or was he poisoned? Did he really give up the ghost or did he escape from Saint Helena? Was it truly his corpse that was now interred in Les Invalides or had there been a switch?

This is the context in which we should interpret the impact on weaker minds of the return of Napoleon's remains, which worked as a trigger for delusional madness. In the months following the event, asylums witnessed the arrival of one emperor after another. Rarely has the phrase "The king is dead, long live the king!" seemed so apt. Strange and extreme behavior of all kinds was noted. "The day the emperor's ashes were interred, having drunk more than usual, he displayed great excitement at the sight of the hearse, gesticulating and making outrageous gestures and comments," it was reported of a forty-one-year-old farmer who subsequently came to believe that "*someone cast a spell on him*" and that "*he would use his influence to put an end to the dissension in the land and to bring harmony to all.*"[46] When it came to women, a thirty-five-year-old artist with a melancholy turn of mind attended the event, which triggered a series of mystical disorders. "The sight of the hearse bearing Napoleon's mortal remains (December 15) made an extraordinary impression on her. 'So that,' she cried, 'is what fame leads to!' The next day, on being congratulated at her success at sev-

FIGURE 22. François Rude, *Napoleon Awakening to Immortality* (1846). Bronze, 217 cm tall. Rude's statue of Napoleon was commissioned in 1846 by a former soldier in the imperial army, at a time when enthusiasm for the emperor was running high after the return of his remains to Paris in 1840. This period saw an increase in the number of mental patients who thought they were Napoleon. Musée Noisot, Fixin, France.

eral exhibitions: *'My fame,'* she said, *'is just like the emperor's, and will lead me to the same end!'* A few days later, she listened to a sermon on salvation. On leaving she was highly emotional, groaning and sobbing *that hell was opening before her eyes and she saw several people of her acquaintance there.*"[47]

An entire generation was marked by the return of the emperor's remains, which became a landmark date. Many years later the event still served as a reference point, as in the strange case of a thirty-three-year-old orange seller who was admitted to La Salpêtrière in 1851 in the early stages of general paresis.

> She said herself she was an army child, the daughter of Colonel de la Mauselière and a negress. She claimed that until age sixteen she passed as a boy and was part of a regiment of light infantry. She was abandoned by her mother, who always called her *my boy*, and who was called *Mother Black*. She added that this evil woman would destroy all girls; she also claimed to have been part of the expedition led by

> the prince de Joinville to bring back the emperor's ashes from Saint Helena. She described places on the island, the arrangement of the grave, the measures taken for the exhumation and for the return, and incidents of familiarity between the prince de Joinville and herself. What is surprising is that in the midst of her delusion this patient, who expresses herself fluently and has no lack of repartee, refers to her years of service and the pleasure she took in riding her little horse, apparently with total familiarity and knowledge of things. On being indiscreetly asked whether she ever had any lovers among the soldiers, she rose indignantly and walked out with these words: "I would have preferred a slap in the face to such contempt."[48]

This medical observation combines more than one problematic: delusions about race and aristocracy arising from mestizo roots; challenges to the role of women in society; change of sex and attribution of powers normally reserved to men. It left physicians both perplexed and mocking with regard to this Madame Chapiron (or "de la Maulière," as the register prudently added in the space for her name). Aged twenty-two in 1840, might this patient have joined the expedition disguised as a soldier, as certain wives had done in 1797 when their officer husbands sailed for Egypt? Or was she merely repeating tales recounted by one of her lovers among the soldiers, as the medical corps suspected? Or perhaps, quite simply, the patient was so struck by the event that she read papers and memoirs on the subject, becoming sufficiently well steeped in it to imagine that she had been there herself.

Like the guillotine, the figure of Napoleon was one of the most common, and above all most persistent, obsessions running through asylum registers. It survived down through various periods and changes of regime, oblivious to the results of the ballot box. "He thinks he's the son of Napoleon, and therefore a candidate for the presidency of the Republic," reads a note on a mason who was admitted to Charenton in 1848.[49] Whereas Louis XVI had vanished from the records by mid-century, the great Napoleon was still striding up and down the hallways of insane asylums long after the Paris Commune came and went in 1870.

The second great resurgence of acute "Napoleonic fever," after the return of emperor's remains, of course occurred with the advent of the Second Empire. But Napoleon III's accession to the throne sparked markedly different delusions. The same method (coup d'état), the same first name, and the same family did not produce the same effect. Karl Marx's famous opening lines of *The Eighteenth Brumaire of Louis Bonaparte* inevitably come to mind. "Hegel remarks somewhere that all great, world-historical facts and personages occur, as it were, twice. He has forgotten to add: the first time as tragedy, the second as farce."[50]

How would the farce play out in the asylum? Emperors of the second variety only rarely identified with Napoleon III himself. They claimed the throne as their own without being concerned to incarnate a specific character. "He is the emperor," reports the medical record, without specifying whether the Napoleon in question was the uncle or the nephew. In other words, the delusion involved title and role, but not the person of the reigning sovereign, who lacked distinguishing features. Viewed from this angle, Napoleon III begins to look like Louis-Philippe, as though a bourgeois emperor had succeeded the bourgeois king.

During the Second Empire, the vast majority of victims of monomania were picked up by the police in front of the imperial residences—the Tuileries and Saint-Cloud—where they had gone to claim their rightful place as emperor. There was the pharmacist's assistant who, "through reasoning, . . . convinced himself that he was the emperor"[51] and therefore intended "to have himself recognized," just as there was the wine broker who "wanted to speak to the emperor even while claiming to be the emperor himself."[52] Then there was the fruit seller who slipped into the courtyard of the château de Saint-Cloud "in order to discuss business with the empress and to offer to replace the emperor."[53] Whereas men who thought they were Napoleon I were perfect copies of that despot, steeped in the original model down to tiny character flaws, Second Empire monomaniacs simply wanted to claim their due without recourse to a coup d'état or other outburst of rage—they felt they merely had to come to terms with the current imposter or his wife. Others thought it possible to work with the emperor on useful social projects, as did a patient at Bicêtre who died a few weeks after arriving at the asylum in 1868. "He went into partnership with the emperor to purchase Europe and Asia. He will make war with flowers and gold coins. He will grow fodder on rocks, etc."[54]

Claims to the throne were often based on an imagined kinship, which always led back to the same figure. "He is the son of the great

Napoleon. His throne was stolen from him," read one report.[55] "He is the emperor's son; he instinctively knows it," stated another.[56] "He is the son of Napoleon and has come to Paris to claim his titles," read yet another.[57] And so on: "He is the prince [*sic*] de Reichstadt, related to the pope."[58] "He thinks and calls himself Napoleon II."[59] In this scheme of things, Napoleon III was rendered doubly illegitimate by two ghosts. He could claim neither the direct descent of Napoleon's son, the duc de Reichstadt, who died in 1832 yet who still enjoyed the role of heir to the throne in the popular imagination, nor the prestige of the great man himself, who in every instance provided the ultimate, overwhelming frame of reference.

THE USURPER

This quick overview of the delusions inspired by Napoleon and by his legend has left one question hanging: Why? *Why* did people identify with Napoleon I more than any other monarch? The answer initially seems obvious. If any role is going to be adopted, it may as well be that of the most powerful, most feared figure—who also happened to be the most recent one. Napoleon was the image par excellence of a superman, the very symbol of modern omnipotence and domination. Fair enough.

Yet the singularity of this case also rests on another feature that sets Napoleon apart from every monarch who preceded or followed him. Compared with kings who incarnated the dynastic past of an age-old monarchy based on divine right, Napoleon was the Usurper, the little corporal from Corsica who came to rule Europe all on his own. His legitimacy was not *inherited* but *won* through political genius and armed might. Whereas a king was crowned by the grace of God and the luck of birth, Napoleon assumed his crown on his own authority even as he placed another on the head of Joséphine, turning his back on the pope who had been summoned to Notre-Dame in Paris, as seen in the famous painting of the *Coronation* by Jacques-Louis David. It matters little whether he was a savior or a dictator, adored or hated: in the eyes of his contemporaries, Napoleon represented the unique case of an adventurer who climbed to the head of a country all on his own. In the end, he was a perfect example of the American ideal of a self-made man.

FIGURE 23. Jacques-Louis David, *Emperor Napoleon Crowning Himself* (early nineteenth century). Pencil and ink sketch on paper, 29.2 cm × 25.2 cm. David's sketch is a striking composition that captures not only the strong will of the sword-wielding Napoleon Bonaparte, who climbed to the top all on his own, but also the infatuation with Napoleon as an incarnation of temporal power turning its back on the spiritual power represented by Pope Pius VII. Musée du Louvre, Paris. Photograph: Thierry Le Mage, © RMN-Grand Palais/Art Resource, New York.

As an *enfant de ses œuvres* (the nineteenth-century French equivalent of self-made man), Bonaparte first had himself named consul through a coup d'état and went on to be proclaimed emperor by a Senate decree ratified by an overwhelming plebiscite. Having arrived at the summit free of any genealogical trappings, in 1804 he nevertheless turned the French Empire into a hereditary system of government by reestablishing the principle of dynastic legitimacy and by concocting in just a few years a "costume nobility" with no roots or past. His countless enemies, like the European courts who detested this product of the French Revolution, felt that Napoleon had seized power illegally. Tacitly denied his rights, the Usurper was nonetheless acknowledged by most of the major powers, subject as they were to the forced march of his victorious campaigns. Along with military domination there came a cult of personality and a legend—whether glowing or sinister—that extravagantly singularized Napoleon's temperament and character. Never had the power of government been so personified, so literally embodied.

"A monarch" wrote Benjamin Constant, "remains, in a way, abstract. He is seen not as an individual, but as an entire race of kings, a tradition spanning several centuries. . . . The monarchy is not a preference accorded to one man over others, it is a supremacy established in advance; it discourages ambition but does not offend vanity. Usurpation demands immediate abdication by all in favor of one person alone; it nurses every pretension and places every personal conceit in ferment."[60] It is safe to bet that such "ferment" stimulated all those projections in the minds of men and women whose lives had often been rendered fragile and who one day decided to identify with Napoleon, the man Balzac described as "a prodigious phenomenon of will . . . who could do everything because he wanted everything."[61] Through Napoleon's self-confident, all-conquering image—"'impossible' is not a French word," he reportedly said—power became accessible to anyone who wanted to set up a new dynasty and change the world. Such a person was Pierre Carra, a mental patient in Charenton who declared himself "Emperor Pierre Carra, who has reigned since the fall of Bonaparte,"[62] not to mention all those villagers who left their provincial homes for Paris in order to claim their rights and be proclaimed emperor, only to be locked up in Bicêtre, as a rule, for vagrancy.

A man who thought he was Napoleon was therefore usurping the identity of a usurper, not to mention that, as a monomaniac, he imitated a monarch who was himself said to suffer from delusions of grandeur. In other words, anyone who took himself for Napoleon was a usurper who thought he was a usurper, and a megalomaniac who thought he was a megalomaniac. Should we then conclude from this phenomenon raised to the second—indeed, third—power that a madman who thought he was Napoleon was a madman who quite logically thought he was mad? There are very few eyewitness accounts or specialist studies that fail to imply that Napoleon was "mad" and that the Napoleonic wars were lethal "folly." Obviously such terms were used in their common, everyday sense, designed to express the extravagance or excesses of Napoleonic schemes.

In the face of such intellectual and psychological assertions, what was actual medical opinion on the emperor's brain, on the puzzle of its ostensibly miraculous workings? Pinel, who had been a consulting physician to Napoleon since 1805, had an opportunity to see the emperor upon his return from his initial exile on Elba, at a reception in the Institut de France. Napoleon asked the doctor if there were greater numbers of madmen. "I said 'no,' but I thought to myself (. . . with a mischievous smile) that great geniuses, and famous and ambitious conquerors, were perhaps not free from a touch of madness."[63] Napoleon himself is said to have subscribed to this theory. According to another source, one day he told Pinel that "you couldn't slip a farthing [into the gap] between a genius and a madman," then added, "I must take care not to fall into your hands."[64]

By the time these apocryphal anecdotes were making the rounds, the link between madness and genius was becoming commonplace in medical literature. Psychiatry, eager to stake out its own area of expertise, appropriated a topic previously discussed by philosophers ranging from Aristotle to Schopenhauer and from Montaigne to Diderot. It did so by turning to the famous men of the past: memoirs, anecdotes, and recollections, everything became fodder for psychiatrists seeking to reconstruct, interpret, and theorize about the psychology of artists and statesmen, from Rousseau's persecution complex to Louis XI's melancholy. The extravagant personality and fate of Napoleon could hardly escape this fad for retrospective diagnosis.

It was not only temperaments and dispositions that came under scrutiny. In the early nineteenth century Franz Joseph Gall founded a new science, dubbed phrenology, by asserting that there were correlations between the shape of the head and an individual's intellectual and moral dispositions. People immediately began mapping skulls. Gall's theory stated that cerebral functions or faculties, as they grew larger, would affect the shape of the skull (an idea still reflected in the popular French expression "having the bump [i.e., a gift] for math"). By manually feeling bumps or depressions on the skull (including casts and sculpted busts), phrenologists claimed to be able to decipher a patient's psychological aptitudes and deficiencies. The favorite guinea pigs for this new doctrine were the heads of extraordinary people such as geniuses, criminals, the insane, microcephalics, and so on.

Napoleon felt only contempt and loathing for phrenology. So when Gall and Johann Spurzheim submitted a paper on the anatomy and physiology of the brain to the Académie des Sciences in 1808, their path was blocked—probably at the emperor's order—by the committee responsible for evaluating their work, which was chaired by Georges Cuvier and included Pinel. Napoleon was also keen to promote French scientists, since an Englishman had just won the award in chemistry, and a victory by these Germans would have put French science in the shade. Even from his exile on Saint Helena the fallen emperor confirmed his thorough annoyance with the charlatans' theory.

> A little hunchback can be a great genius; a tall, handsome man can be an idiot. A large head with a big brain is sometimes devoid of ideas, whereas a little brain can harbor vast intelligence. Just consider Gall's own stupidity: he ascribes certain bumps with inclinations and crimes that do not exist in nature but come from society and human conventions—what would happen to the bump for theft if property didn't exist? Would the bump for drunkenness exist if fermented beverages did not? Or the one for ambition, if society did not exist?[65]

In an 1835 study titled *La phrénologie et Napoléon*, Dr. David Richard, a psychiatrist, magnetizer, and phrenologist who was a friend of George Sand, suggested that Napoleon's hostility to the materialism of Gall's theory stemmed from a combination of philosophical conviction, superstition, and political opportunism. "The metaphysical opinion that the soul and its actions cannot be manifested by external forms flattered Napoleon's penchant for the miraculous, and it tended to reinforce popular preconceptions of the emperor as driven by an elusive, supernatural, divine spirit, found only in him and to which everyone must silently bow."[66] It is tempting to follow Richard down this path. Napoleon obviously thought phrenology was useless and intellectually worthless; but it was in this great propagandist's own interest to maintain the mystery of his genius, which he would never dare subject to a common cranial measurement. His wariness was such that he even forbade Joséphine to "have her bumps read," although the empress went behind his back and secretly presented her head to Gall in the studio of painter François Gérard. No report of this meeting ever surfaced, even though Gérard was an early member of the Société de Phrénologie. Obviously Gall was unable to get anywhere near Napoleon's skull, but for lack of putting his hands on the original the German doctor based his study on existing busts of the emperor, which unsurprisingly revealed the same carnivorous, murderous instinct—located just above the ears—found on the skulls of Caligula, Nero, Sylla, Septimus Severus, Charles IX, Richard the Lionheart, and François Ravaillac (Henri IV's assassin).[67]

War was declared between world's greatest soldier and the science of skulls. It was one that took unexpected turns, even beyond the grave. In 1821 Dr. François Antommarchi attended Napoleon in his dying moments on Saint Helena. Upon the emperor's death, Antommarchi made a death mask, the only "true" record of Napoleon's face, which included the front part of his skull. As a amateur phrenologist, Antommarchi drew fanciful conclusions that appeared in a volume of memoirs published in 1825. Napoleon was allegedly endowed with an "organ" for conquest and another for imagination, which did not even exist in the nomenclature employed by Gall (who brusquely dismissed Antommarchi's report).[68] The incident might have ended there, but in 1833 a government commission was charged with producing and disseminating a bust of Napoleon cast from the original mold, the missing back of the skull to be inferred from the front part. The following year the *Gazette Médicale de Paris* exploited the event to publish a serialized—but unsigned—article titled "Phrenological Commentary on Napoleon's Head."

The sober title was in fact a cover for an attack designed to ridicule Gall's theories. The author began the article by noting that Napoleon's death mask—the only authentic element on which any serious study could be based—did not resemble the emperor's portraits as idealized by artists. Paintings and sculptures obviously smoothed features and added height, but above all "they made the skull larger. Gall's doctrine perhaps had something to do with this latter modification. At the time, people were highly disposed to believe that great genius could not reside in a small head, and it was felt that it was better not to skimp on space when it came to Napoleon."[69] On examining the "real head," however, the author found the "smallness of the skull" to be striking. However well proportioned and regular it was, it was judged to be "small, narrow, petty" and of ordinary circumference (alleged to be the same size as 50 percent of men).[70] Other disillusionments followed. Contrary to Antommarchi's assertions, the organ of dissimulation showed no protuberance. The famous "bump for math" was nowhere to be seen, replaced by a hollow—yet everyone knew that Napoleon excelled in mathematics and had produced a famous theorem. The same thing was true of the organ for destructiveness, which was nonexistent. In short, it was vain to seek what was sought at all costs. "Neither Napoleon's genius, nor his passions, nor his well-known aptitudes appear on his skull. Never has there been a more striking rebuttal to the phrenological hypothesis."[71]

It was a bitter pill for the phrenologists to swallow: apparently the very skull of their legendary adversary had just proved the inanity of Gall's system, as he thumbed his nose from beyond the grave. Indignant responses from specialists proliferated. They unanimously stigmatized the anonymous study as sloppy, but their rebuttals were contradictory. Some writers argued that it was impossible to conduct a phrenological examination on an incomplete cast; others stated that the existing section sufficed but had been poorly interpreted. Opinions also diverged on the legitimacy of recourse to paintings and sculptures of Napoleon, sometimes considered too imprecise and therefore of little interest, sometimes thought to be rich in information. The study by Richard was the most complete and thorough. The keen phrenologist methodically addressed the arguments of the anonymous commentator—whom he identified in a postscript as Dr. Louis Peisse[72]—pointing out errors of computation on the size of the head (Napoleon's was allegedly larger than average in volume) and correcting many imprecise statements, all the while pointing out that the "bump for math" (or aptitude in calculations), located at the outer corner of the eye, displayed a size proportional to Napoleon's predispositions. Despite its drawbacks, then, Richard concluded that the death mask confirmed the validity of Gall's doctrine, for Napoleon's skull notably revealed combativeness, destructiveness, secrecy (wiliness), firmness, and self-esteem. And even if everything was not apparent in this relic, that was because it did not reflect the emperor in his prime but showed him as a worn-out man whose morphology was atrophied by the distress of illness and exile.

If phrenologists — and their opponents — were able to make Napoleon's skull express anything and everything, were mental specialists capable of uncovering the secrets of his soul and revealing potential disorders of his mind? The vogue for medicohistorical studies was in full swing during the July monarchy. Louis-Francisque Lélut became the first leader of the field of pathobiography thanks to his polemical books on Socrates and Blaise Pascal, both of whom suffered from hallucinations and therefore, as far as Lélut was concerned, from mental illness.[73] Now, Napoleon also apparently suffered from hallucinations, as reported by Alexandre Brierre de Boismont, followed by Jacques-Joseph Moreau de Tours in the latter's substantial volume on "morbid psychology and history" (*La psychologie morbide dans ses rapports à la philosophie de l'histoire* [1859]). Napoleon actually "saw" his lucky star. One day in 1806 he reportedly took General Jean Rapp by the arm and said, "Do you see it up there?" Rapp remained silent, but when asked a second time admitted that he saw nothing. "What!" exclaimed the emperor, "You can't make it out? It's right in front you, shining." Becoming more and more heated, he shouted, "It has never abandoned me, I see it on every great occasion. It tells me to push ahead, and it's my constant sign of good fortune." Yet does an anecdote, repeated by a third party who himself heard it from yet another person, make Napoleon mad? Moreau de Tours preferred to argue that "certain hallucinations, far from creating the least disorder in overall faculties, *could be a strong stimulant for the execution of preconceived plans*."[74] Although genius may well be neurotic, that did not necessarily make it insane. Genius and mental illness were not the same thing, though they might share a common basis in an irritable nervous system and a hereditary predisposition to morbidity.[75]

This was the line taken by Italian physician and anthropologist Cesare Lombroso in his 1864 *Genio e follia* (Genius and madness) and later in *L'uomo di geio in rapporto alla psichiatria, alla storia ed all'estetica* (The man of genius in relation to psychiatry, history, and aesthetics) (1888). Lombroso's books were a hit with the general public but more controversial in medical circles. When analyzing the case of Napoleon, Lombroso relied exclusively on a portrait written by Hippolyte

Taine, published in the *Revue des Deux Mondes* in 1887 (which, for that matter, won praise from Nietzsche).[76] The full text of Taine's article took up five pages of Lombroso's book and in fact constituted the only pages on Napoleon. It described the emperor as a medieval tyrant, a "condottiere of the worst sort" as well as a "superior artist" whose "colossal self," instead of serving the nation, subordinated the nation to his own person. With his brutal, intense temperament, Napoleon was irritable and subject to convulsions and weeping. "There had never been," claimed Taine, "even among the Malatestas and Borgias, a mind more sensitive and impulsive, capable of such electric charges and discharges, in whom the inner storm was more continual and more thundery, more sudden in its lightning bolts and more stunning in its shocks." This latter comment certainly fueled Lombroso's conclusion—which was also the only sentence on the subject from his own pen: "To anyone acquainted with the psychological constitution of the epileptic, it becomes clear that Taine has here given us the subtlest and precisest pathological diagnosis of a case of psychic epilepsy with its gigantic megalomaniacal illusions, its impulses, and complete absence of moral sense."[77]

This inconsistent conclusion was perhaps inevitable given the offhand nature of Lombroso's approach, which involved simply copying a text without substantiating its argument at any point. Nevertheless, a fuse had been lit. There followed a burst of publications on Napoleon's convulsions, especially since epilepsy was associated with mental illness and—in Lombroso's opinion—genius. Caesar, Saint Paul, the Holy Roman emperor Charles V, Martin Luther, Dostoyevsky, and Gustave Flaubert were afflicted. In 1902 a publication such as *Les Archives d'Anthropologie Criminelle* was still asking, Was Napoleon epileptic? It was a thorny issue on which no one agreed. The article set Louis Antoine Fauvelet de Bourrienne's memoirs and Constant's account (denying epilepsy) against Talleyrand's recollections (supporting it).[78] It noted that in 1893 Drs. Corre and Laurent had rejected the possibility in the *Revue Scientifique* with the argument that epilepsy impaired the intelligence, so that "even though they believed that rabble-rousers were neuropaths, they concluded that Napoleon I had a hysterical temperament."[79] Meanwhile, Dr. Augustin Cabanès pursued the question in a successful series of publications titled *Les indiscretions de l'histoire* (1903–6), ultimately concluding in the negative, since Napoleon had not had a single epileptic fit on Saint Helena. Cabanès, a prolific writer who founded the *Chronique Médicale* and ran the Société Médico-historique, wrote dozens of highly commercial pathobiographies and returned to the charge in 1924 with *Au chevet de l'empereur* (At the emperor's bedside). Readers of that book were spared none of the great man's hereditary defects and private diseases: Bonaparte descended from a line of arthritics, caught the mange in Toulon, had the yellow complexion typical of a bilious temperament, purportedly suffered from dysuria (inflammation of the bladder), irritation of the stomach, and various wounds, ultimately dying of stomach cancer complicated by tuberculosis. And yet Cabanès referred not once to psychological disorders, melancholia, or delusions of grandeur. Even Napoleon's attempted suicide at Fontainebleau in 1814 inspired no comment from the doctor, who devoted his energy to discovering the composition of the poison employed, and this at a time when *folie-suicide* ("suicidal derangement") was still considered a mental illness. And for Napoleon's mental blanks at Waterloo, which incited talk of "dullness, cerebral torpor, and a 'fog of lethargy,'" Cabanès had a markedly more prosaic explanation. Although the emperor was perfectly lucid when it came to strategic and tactical genius, he suffered from an "in no way serious but very painful indisposition," namely "an attack of hemorrhoids, which made riding a horse a painful exercise."[80]

It is surprising to discover that this medical literature—which is rather sparse, by the way—contains so few serious monographic studies on Napoleon by reputable psychiatrists. The school around Professor Alexandre Lacassagne, who founded *Les Archives d'Anthropologie Criminelle* and was a great promoter of medical archaeology, preferred to study the likes of Olympe de Gouges, Rousseau, and Marat rather than Napoleon. The medical corps was far more interested in elucidating the causes of Napoleon's death (cancer of the stomach versus poison) than in studying his legendary megalomania. A more thorough clinical analysis of the emperor's ambitiousness might have been expected. But apparently not. At most he was given brief mention in articles on the subject. Even Maurice Beaujeu, who published a dissertation on "caesaritis," a concept developed by Lacassagne to indicate "a special form of delusions of grandeur" specific to rulers, went no further than a single sentence: "This was the illness Napoleon felt he had contracted when he would say, 'I have slept in the bed of kings, where I caught a fearsome disease.'"[81] Napoleon certainly deserved more than this brief comment. Wasn't he the perfect embodiment of the modern Caesar, the soldier who became *imperator*, afflicted by delusions of grandeur that grew with the attainment of power, who owed nothing to heredity and everything to political circumstances?

Historians, whether sympathetic or hostile to Napoleon, were much more prolix and categorical on this issue. "Who could have predicted that the sensible man of 1800 would be the madman of 1813 and 1815?" asked Adolphe Thiers in his *Histoire du Consulat et de l'Empire*. "Indeed, it could have been predicted," he went on, "by remembering that absolute power brings with it an incurable madness, the temptation to do all when one *can* do all, including evil after [having done] good."[82] The great historian Jules Michelet, author of *Histoire de France*, agreed, although it might be pointed out that Michelet entertained complex relationships with Napoleon, madness, and the two combined. His father was a printer who went bankrupt after the imposition of Napoleonic censorship laws and who found a job in Dr. Duchemin's nursing home on rue de Buffon, where he rose to become superintendent. From 1815 to 1818 Michelet therefore spent part of his youth, ages seventeen to twenty, among mental patients. Every night he dined with the unrestrained boarders and observed the influence of political upheavals on the life of the mind. "Never was there so much mental illness as after the storms of the Revolution and the forays of the Empire," he asserted. "The very roots of nervous existence seemed to be affected."[83] Michelet's assessment of Napoleon was perhaps not totally uncolored by these youthful memories when, in his history of the nineteenth century, he invoked specialists to explain the emperor's "state of pride and insane rage" during the Russian campaign. "It is up to psychiatrists to describe it. What they call 'lucid monomania' sometimes transcends insanity."[84]

Many historians, in fact, tip Napoleon into a state of madness after 1812. His military debacle was allegedly accompanied by a mental debacle, a loss of his senses owing to a blind, raving thirst for power that had crossed the line. In an entry in his *Grand dictionnaire universel*, Pierre Larousse took this idea even further. He wrote that Napoleon may have been "what could be called the most insane politician if Alexander had never lived," because "he displayed to the world the sad spectacle of a genius who fell to the state of a poor madman." Worse,

Napoleon's "powers of calculation when it came to details merely served to justify his madness to himself, while his insane dreams and speech, even after Waterloo, confirm that in this respect his illness was incurable."[85]

Larousse's loathing for Napoleon is well known. He never forgave the man for abandoning revolutionary ideals, as demonstrated by the opening lines of his famous dictionary entry on Bonaparte. "General of the French Republic, born in Ajaccio, Corsica, on August 15, 1759, died in the chateau de Saint-Cloud outside Paris on 18 Brumaire Year VIII of the French Republic, One and Indivisible (November 9, 1799)." Over a period of several generations the distinction between the all-conquering emperor and the megalomaniac stuck outside Moscow was preceded by a far harsher criticism that was ideological in nature—Napoleon had betrayed Bonaparte. Indeed, hadn't Beethoven altered, in anger, the dedication of his symphony "to Bonaparte" upon the latter's proclamation of an empire, changing it to "*Symphonia Eroica* [Heroic symphony], composed to celebrate the memory of a great man"? When Napoleon died on Saint Helena, Beethoven is alleged to have commented drily, "I've already written the music for that sad event."

Those symbolic deaths demonstrate how easy it is to separate the terms Bonaparte and Napoleon. Just as the revolutionary ideals of 1789 are contrasted with the Terror of 1793, the romantic figure of the military victor at Arcole seems incompatible with the pudgy tyrant of the Empire. "Yes," insisted Larousse,

> there were two men within that character, in that singularly gifted being, whose double name and double face with its highly particular nature were wonderfully appropriate to the double role he played in the world. Augustus may have called himself Octavian, Octavian may have called himself Augustus, but he was always the same man, wily, shy, artificially polite, and shrewd, disowning his friends when his self-interest spurred him to sacrifice them. Whereas here, it should be repeated, we have two distinct men, as well as two separate names.[86]

Now, this duality—or rather this successive appearance of two characters in one—is theoretically rich in implications for any analysis of splitting of the mind, yet psychiatrists seem to have overlooked it. It did not, however, escape Jacques Lacan, who commented on the general infatuation with the subject. "If a man who thinks he is king is mad, a king who thinks he is king is no less so."[87] What was Lacan insinuating? That anyone who thinks he's a king when he works in an office is obviously deluded and has lost touch with reality, but that the king who thinks he is king has also fallen into a trap, since he mistakes himself for the image of the character that the world reflects back to him. The illusion is not the same, yet is analogous. One man takes himself for a monarch, the other takes himself for the fiction of monarch. Napoleon, whom we might consider a caricature of the insanity of power reflected back on itself, may in fact have avoided this error thanks to the existence of Bonaparte. "Don't think that I am being witty," added Lacan in paralipsis, "certainly not with the quality of wit that shows in the saying Napoleon was someone who thought he was Napoleon. Because Napoleon did not think he was Napoleon at all, since he knew full well by what means Bonaparte had produced Napoleon and how Napoleon, like Malebranche's God, sustained his existence at every moment." According to Lacan it was on Saint Helena that Napoleon finally thought he was Napoleon, when dictating his exploits to Emmanuel Las Cases and forging his legend, and thus may have slipped into a kind of madness. By staging his own life, the fallen emperor arguably relinquished his salutary mental split in order to cleave to the myth of Napoleon, whose tale he composed in that masterpiece of propaganda, Las Cases's *Mémorial.*

Lacan's hypothesis is appealing insofar as it helps to draw a dividing line between Napoleon and all his epigones in the asylums. Ultimately, what is the difference, in *theory*—in practice, the answer is simple—between the Napoleon on Saint Helena and a man who thinks he is Napoleon? One of Leuret's patients, who thought he was Mohammed, perfectly demonstrated the blurring of the line in a letter to his doctors. "You reproach me with nothing more than speaking with energy and passion, with having what is called a vivid imagination. But many young people have vivid imaginations. In periods of revolution and battle the imagination grows vivid, and it did not occur to any doctor to impose showers on Mirabeau, Alexander, or Napoleon."[88] This objection seems valid except that the patient identified himself with the prophet *in an unmediated way*, whereas a dialectical process was presumably at work within Mirabeau, Alexander, and Napoleon.

At what point, and to what extent, do people cleave to their pipe dreams? At what moment does identification become delusion? These questions become all the more acute during periods of revolution, when the process of identifying and cleaving no longer applies to important people (or not solely), but applies to political ideals. The fine line that separates the mentally ill from the mentally healthy never gets thinner than during these episodes of passion for democracy, which psychiatry attempted to turn into a disease of the mind. That, however, is another story—to be continued.

FOUR * *Morbus Democraticus*

The identification of revolution with madness has long been accepted as a truism. The spontaneity and intensity of popular uprisings have been associated with wild impulses and irrationality, while movements to reform and overhaul society have allegedly led to abuses and disorder—yet no one ever questions the established order's own dormant madness and muted violence. That, during the ancien régime, a fifteen-year-old girl was hanged for stealing a silver-gilt spoon and a boy was drawn and quartered for lampooning the king will never spark debate over the insanity of the legal system under a monarchy by divine right. Instead, what gets discussed is the spectacular fury and collective hysteria of the revolutionary massacres of September 1792, designed to illustrate the theme of political madness dear to conservatives such as Edmund Burke and François-René de Chateaubriand. The latter, addressing readers potentially nostalgic for the revolutionary spirit, wrote, "The Terror was not the invention of a few giants; it was quite simply a mental illness, a plague."[1]

Is revolution therefore a pathological symptom? Throughout the nineteenth century most psychiatrists thought so and said so, stigmatizing the nefarious effects on people of any exaltation of democratic aspirations, including anxiety, stupefaction, persecution complexes, and so on. France, sure enough, offered a good vantage point on a century rich in revolutions and civil wars: 1789, 1830, 1848, and 1871. This rate of at least one great upheaval per generation led Freud to comment that the French were a "people of psychical epidemics, of historical mass convulsions."[2] Confronted with a growing asylum population, doctors tried to rationalize and describe this urge for emancipation, freedom, and progress in medical terms. They spoke first of "political monomania," followed by *morbus democraticus* (democratic disease), and finally "revolutionary neurosis," or *paranoia reformatoria*.[3] The escalation in terminology testified to an increasingly psychiatric perspective on politics. Thus, as silly as such inventions may appear in hindsight, they should not mask the serious attention psychiatrists paid to the correlation between madness and ideology. What do asylum archives reveal about their assertions? Do repeated traces of revolutionary trauma as documented in medical records suffice to demonstrate the impact of political upheaval on madness? What roles did factual reality and physicians' subjective decisions play in explaining mental illness? And even if nineteenth-century insurrections indeed triggered certain delusions, what was the effect of psychiatrists' political and epistemological construction of insanity?

Such questions are not meant to cast systematic, pointless discredit or suspicion on physicians' prose. Rather, they aim at exploring the meaning of a diagnosis, reestablishing the context in which it was elaborated, and analyzing its presuppositions and motivations. In short, this approach means unfolding—opening out—an interpretation that becomes more complex as time goes on, as revolutionary anxiety became layered in French history. Indeed, the events of 1793 cast their shadow throughout the nineteenth century, hovering over the revolutions of 1830 and 1848 and triumphantly resurfacing in the midst of the Commune of 1871. The great primal scene, whether admired or dreaded, spoke to each generation in a ventriloquist's voice. This eternal return to roots imbues the word "trauma" with its underlying connotation of "reminiscence."

And it is precisely on—and from—memory that psychiatry works. It digs into a patient's background, unearthing heredity, retracing genealogy, going over family history. It tries to understand a patient's character, acts, and drives through an interrogation designed to reveal a physiology, a psychology, and even—during that strict century—a morality behind illness. The parade of heretics marching toward nineteenth-century asylums not only featured masturbating males, licentious women, antisocial individuals, vagabonds, and alcoholics but logically included rebels, protesters, and feminists. The point here is not to challenge in hindsight the medical validity of a diagnosis or to make anachronistic claims of arbitrary confinement—after all, an onanist or a revolutionary might *also* suffer from delusions—but rather to question the hierarchy of criteria used by psychiatrists who, just like everyone else, had their own personal histories, memories, religious convictions, and political opinions. So the encounter between patient and psychiatrist is the nexus where we must seek to unravel the ins and outs of medical interpretations and the ideological construction they entailed.

THÉROIGNE DE MÉRICOURT, OR REVOLUTIONARY MELANCHOLIA

During the Empire and Restoration periods, physicians treated numerous patients traumatized by the Revolution who still lived in dread of the guillotine in particular. Some of those patients were former revolutionaries, such as Jacob Dupont, mentioned in chapter 2, who was sent to Charenton in 1810 for advocating atheism. The most famous case, however, was that of Théroigne de Méricourt, whose story is worth briefly recalling.

Born at Marcourt in the Ardennes in 1762 to an affluent farming family, Anne-Josèphe Therwagne (later Théroigne) lost her mother at age five. Her father remarried a few years later. Subjected to a kind of slavery by her stepmother, the girl fled from home and began a wandering life, working as a milkmaid and then as a lady's companion until she was dismissed, and finally becoming a courtesan in Paris, where she contracted venereal disease. When the Revolution broke out, the young woman—whose life had been a series of misfortunes—adhered to the new ideas with unmitigated fervor, convinced that this wave of freedom would help to overcome the alienation women experienced.

Thus arose the myth of a revolutionary Fury, a bloodthirsty militant feminist at the head an army of Amazons. Élisabeth Roudinesco's biography of Théroigne, however, has reestablished the facts and recast the career of "the fair Ardennaise" by stripping away the myths. It turns out that, contrary to legend, Théroigne did not take part in the revolutionary events in Versailles in early October 1789 (although she may have been a spectator). She was indeed summoned to the trial and massacre of royalists on August 10, 1792, but she did not slay anyone by her own hand, any more than she killed with a thrust of her sword a sworn enemy, the journalist François-Louis Suleau; nor did she participate, as was often alleged, in the massacres of September. Théroigne was an advocate for women's rights, notably the right to fight, and thus proposed forming phalanxes of armed women to defend the nation. Her militarist feminism—distorted and ridiculed by monarchist calumny—greatly helped to blacken the portrait of an intelligent, skilled, and brave woman whose revolutionary zeal primarily involved fueling the debate of ideas through a club known as Les Amis de la Loi (Friends of the Law), haranguing the crowds, and working toward the emancipation of women. Targeted by the royalists, who detested her, she was cast as a harlot (whereas she was cool and cerebral) and as a spy who hatched far-fetched plots (which in fact never existed). Théroigne was ultimately kidnapped and imprisoned in the Austrian Tyrol on trumped-up charges. After vigorously defending herself during months of interrogations, she was finally released by the Holy Roman emperor Leopold II for lack of evidence.

On returning to revolutionary France, she sided with Jacques Pierre Brissot and the Girondin group. Thus on May 15, 1793, she was surrounded at the entrance to the Convention by shrews who accused her of selling out to the moderates; the women pulled up her skirt and whipped her bare buttocks in public. Jean-Paul Marat intervened and released her from the clutches of her persecutors, taking her under his protection, but Théroigne never recovered from her humiliation. After this public spanking she withdrew from the scene, never to reappear. She remained at home alone, unable to write. In 1794, at her brother's request, she was officially declared insane—probably to spare her the guillotine, a fate that had overtaken two other revolutionary women, Madame Manon Roland de Platière and Olympe de Gouges, beheaded in November 1793. Théroigne then spent the next twenty-three years being shuttled between various specialized institutions, from a madhouse in faubourg Saint-Marceau (1795–97) to l'Hôtel-Dieu (1797–99), to La Salpêtrière for one month (December 1799 to January 1800), to Les Petites Maisons (1800–1807) and then back to La Salpêtrière, from 1807 until her death in 1817.

For her final ten years Théroigne was treated by Esquirol, whose career paralleled Philippe Pinel's in certain respects. Like Pinel, Étienne Esquirol was born in southern France and became a cleric destined for a career in the church until he decided to study medicine, first in Toulouse and then in Montpellier and finally in Paris, where he arrived in 1798. The ninth of ten children in an affluent Catholic and monarchist family, Esquirol, unlike his mentor, never experienced the humiliations of the ancien régime. But the Revolution shattered his family: it bankrupted his father (a prosperous Toulouse merchant and administrator) and killed his elder brother, François-Antoine, who was tried as one of the leaders of a royalist uprising in Haute-Garonne in Year VII and executed on 22 Vendémiaire Year VIII (October 14, 1799).[4] Did Esquirol perhaps meet Théroigne during her brief stay at La Salpêtrière in December 1799, just after he had lost his own brother? It is not impossible. By that time he was already frequenting the mental ward run by Pinel, becoming his favorite student. Whatever the case, he would encounter Théroigne eight years later. These biographical details are difficult to ignore when analyzing the famous medical file Esquirol compiled on Théroigne, which does not necessarily mean they distorted the physician's diagnosis or induced intellectual dishonesty on his part.

Esquirol published the case of "Téroenne, or Théroigne de Méricour" in 1820 as part of the entry for "lypemania" (melancholia) in the *Dictionnaire des sciences médicales*, later republished in his major treatise on mental illness.[5] At forty-four, Esquirol's authority and reputation had earned him the post of chief physician at La Salpêtrière, where the ailing Pinel had retired that same year. Esquirol's article in the dictionary summed up years of research into what the ancients called melancholia but Esquirol proposed labeling by the more scientific term lypemania. Although the name did not stick, his study helped develop the concept of depression. This was the context in which Théroigne's case, supposedly illustrating the Revolution's effect on mental illness, was presented as being of interest to "those who are fond of political phenomena and who seek . . . extraordinary facts in medicine." Esquirol's observations can be divided, roughly, into three parts.

The first part is biographical, covering the years before Théroigne's hospitalization. Esquirol here faithfully followed an error-riddled entry in the *Biographie moderne*, a dictionary of people who had left their mark on French history since the Revolution. The main interest of Esquirol's plagiarism obviously lies in the little adjustments he made to the original. The examples speak for themselves, hardly requiring comment.

Biographie moderne: She played a remarkable role in the early years of the Revolution.

Esquirol: [She] played a most deplorable role in the early years of the Revolution.

Biographie moderne: [She] became friendly with various leaders of the common people.

Esquirol: She became intimate with various leaders of the common people.

Biographie moderne: On October 5, [she] above all helped to undermine the Flanders regiment by leading other wenches under her command into the ranks.

Esquirol: On October 5 and 6, [she] above all helped to undermine the Flanders regiment by leading whores into the ranks.[6]

The biography entry makes no mention of Théroigne's putative participation in the massacres of September 1792 but asserts that it was she who called for the killing of her sworn enemy, the royalist journalist Suleau, on August 10. Esquirol ignored (or perhaps altered) that information by stating that Théroigne "took an active part" in the events of September (which we know to be false) and reportedly used "her sword [to] cut off the head of an unfortunate man they were conducting to the tribunal of [that] prison. We are assured that it was a former lover."[7]

This series of "corrections," which speaks volumes about Esquirol's opinion of his patient's previous life, is striking for the implicit or explicit sexual dimension introduced into the quoted examples. Théroigne *became intimate* with party leaders, led *whores*, and beheaded her *lover*. Of course, by misrepresenting reality (or at least his source) in this way, the physician was merely repeating an old refrain: for a woman to become involved in politics meant abandoning her "natural condition" and inevitably falling into freakish, hybrid sexual anomalies, which in this case led to a portrait of a shameless, castrating female. Most of the women active in the Revolution—Olympe de Gouges, Claire Lacombe, Madame Roland—were castigated for embodying a distasteful blend of unnatural power and lewd insanity, which even included Queen Marie Antoinette, accused of incest during her trial. As Augustin Cabanès would put it a century later in his *Névrose révolutionnaire*, "Whether revolutionary termagants or royalist harpies, all women are the same once they become involved in politics."[8]

Esquirol not only succumbed to the usual fantasies and preconceptions of his day, he proffered disturbing misinformation concerning Théroigne's political opinions. He rightly copied from the *Biographie moderne* that she harangued the people "in order to bring them back to *moderation* and the Constitution." But he hastened to add a little phrase of his own, that "this course [could] not suit her long." Soon she would be seen alongside the Jacobins, "a red bonnet upon her head, a sword by her side, and a pike in her hand, commanding an army of women." So her feigned moderation was belied by her raving behavior and deeds. Esquirol's denial was pretty extreme, because he made no mention of Théroigne's arrest during the Terror or the public spanking that played such a crucial role in the history of her illness.[9] The physician also pointed out that, once in La Salpêtrière, the patient continued to blame moderates as well as royalists. Yet perhaps she was blaming them because they had abandoned her?

The second part of Esquirol's study concerns the medical observations themselves. It is characterized by a highly significant grammatical shift. Indeed, Esquirol recounted Théroigne's early years in La Salpêtrière in the past tense, reporting that she constantly insulted and threatened everyone, speaking incessantly of liberty, of revolutionary committees, and so on. "In 1808," he continued, "a distinguished personage, who had been the leader of a party, visited La Salpêtrière. Téroenne [*sic*] recognized him, raised herself from the bed of straw where she was lying, and heaped abusive language upon the visitor, accusing him of abandoning the people's party and being a moderate, to whom a decree of the committee of public safety would soon do justice." But as soon as his patient sinks into dementia and feebleness, the doctor slips suddenly into the present tense, thereby reinforcing the dramatic tension and impact of his tale. In fact, this second part of his study would be frequently reprinted, cited, or summarized by historians rightly struck by its powerful imagery.

> In 1810 she becomes more composed and falls into a state of dementia, which enabled us to observe traces of her early prevailing ideas. Téroenne is unwilling to wear any clothing, even a chemise. Every day, both morning and evening, and many times a day, she waters her bed, or rather the straw of it, with several buckets of water, lies down, and covers herself with her sheet only, in summer, and with both sheet and

> coverlid in winter. She amuses herself in walking with naked feet, in her cell flagged with stone, and inundated with water. . . .
>
> Although in a small and gloomy cell, very damp and without furniture, she enjoys good health, and pretends to be occupied with very important matters. She smiles at persons who accost her and sometimes replies hastily, *I know you not*, and conceals herself under her covering. It is rare that she replies correctly. She often says: *I do not know; I have forgotten.* If they insist, she becomes impatient and talks to herself in a low voice. She articulates phrases, interspersed with the words *fortune*, *liberty*, *committee*, *revolution*, *rascal*, *warrant*, *decree*, etc. She greatly resents the moderates. She is angry and transported with passion when opposed, especially when they desire to prevent her from taking water. She once bit a companion with so much fury as to take out a piece of flesh. The disposition of this woman had therefore outlived her understanding. She rarely leaves her cell, generally remaining there in bed. If she goes out, it is in a state of nudity, or covered only with her chemise. She takes but few steps, most frequently proceeding on all fours, and stretches herself on the ground. With a fixed eye, she collects all the scraps she finds on the pavement and eats them. I have seen her devour straw, feathers, dried leaves, and morsels of meat lying in the dirt. She drinks cistern water while they wash the courts, although it may be dirty and charged with filthy matter, preferring this drink to every other.[10]

Théroigne de Méricourt, or A clinical history of decline: in this moving portrait of a female activist who foundered, Esquirol skillfully weaves revolutionary violence, dementia, and animality into a fabric whose threads can no longer be distinguished. Indeed, as Esquirol announced at the start, at the core of her illness lay the "dominating ideas" of revolution, ideas that we are led to understand are incoherent, unintelligible, and reduced to the same tirelessly repeated words. The new ideas thus became obsolete—worse, senile—via a patient stuck in an irrevocable past. All that survived was the savage violence. When Théroigne bit a piece of flesh from a companion, it was not madness that drove her or dementia that ruined her mind. On the contrary, it was her "disposition," which had "outlived" her intelligence. Could Théroigne still be called civilized? "I endeavored to induce her to write," noted Esquirol. "She traced a few words, but was

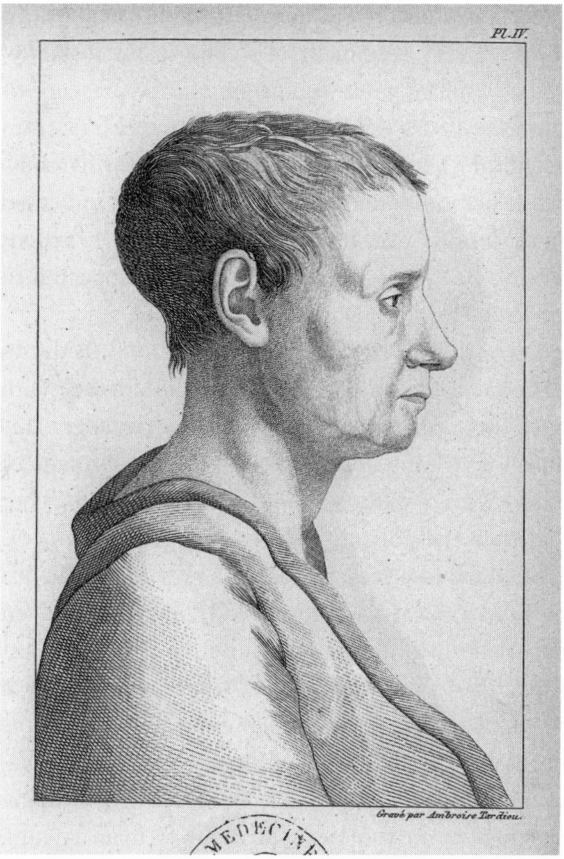

FIGURE 24. Ambroise Tardieu, engraving of Théroigne de Méricourt (pl. IV), for Esquirol's *Maladies mentales considérées sous les rapports médical, hygiénique et médico-légal* (1838). Théroigne de Méricourt took up arms for the French Revolution but went mad during the Terror. She was treated at La Salpêtrière by Esquirol, who ascribed her illness to her revolutionary commitment. The second volume of the French edition of Esquirol's monumental treatise on insanity, *Des maladies mentales*, included engravings by Tardieu that allegedly illustrated various kinds of madness, such as dementia (figure 26 below) and maniacal insanity (figure 27 below), even as they presented a picture of the asylum as a place where violence can be controlled. Photograph © BIU Santé, Paris.

never able to complete a sentence." He then returned, for the third time, to her nakedness. "Every sentiment of shame seems to be extinct, and she is habitually naked without blushing, in the presence of men." If writing and modesty are the factors that distinguish us from animals, what remained for Théroigne? She incarnated a world of outmoded, dead ideas while her indifference to her surroundings indicated her withdrawal from the world of the living. When Esquirol "wish[ed] to obtain her portrait in 1816, she willingly sat for it, but appeared to attach no importance to the [artist's] work."[11]

An engraved version of this portrait has come down to us. It shows a woman of indeterminate age, somewhat round-shouldered, with very short hair brushed forward, staring glumly into the distance. This zombielike figure makes a striking contrast to the romantic image of a blazing-eyed Amazon with a feather in her hat and a sword in her hand. The artist who drew the portrait was Georges-Marie-François Gabriel, known above all for two sets of drawings now in the Bibliothèque Nationale de France. One set featured individuals sentenced to death, most of them about to die by the guillotine. The other set comprised pencil portraits of mental patients in Charenton, drawn at Esquirol's request. The result is a striking encounter between people about to lose their heads and people who have already lost their minds; above all, Gabriel's strange specialty comes to the fore, his sketching of portraits in a courtroom, at the foot of the scaffold, or in an asylum. That said, during this particular period the likes of Théodore Géricault painted not only decapitated heads but also portraits of monomaniacs commissioned by a disciple of Esquirol, Dr. Étienne Georget.[12]

The third section of Esquirol's study was devoted to his autopsy of Théroigne. Autopsies were increasingly performed in asylums, where physicians who believed in a material physiology sought to locate the seat of mental illness in the body's organs. Esquirol was a great advocate of this school, even though he was obliged to admit that "pathological anatomy has taught us nothing positive with respect to the seat of melancholy."[13] Indeed, opening Théroigne's body and examining her brain explained nothing. At best Esquirol noted that her transverse colon had shifted position, which he had noticed among many other mental patients, and which he considered making a rather unlikely anatomical criterion of madness.

So is Théroigne de Méricourt a textbook case? Yes indeed—but a

FIGURE 25 (above left). Georges-François-Marie Gabriel, *An Officer Driven Mad by His Political Opinions*. From *Heads of Lunatics Drawn at Charenton* (ca. 1823). Drawing. Bibliothèque Nationale de France, Paris. (See also figures 19 and 20 above.) Photograph © BNF.

FIGURE 26 (above right). Ambroise Tardieu, engraving (pl. XIII), "Dementia." For Esquirol's *Maladies mentales considérées sous les rapports médical, hygiénique et médico-légal* (1838). Photograph © Adoc-photos/Art Resource, New York.

FIGURE 27 (left). Ambroise Tardieu, engraving (pl. VII), "Maniacal Insanity." For Esquirol's *Maladies mentales considérées sous les rapports médical, hygiénique et médico-légal* (1838). Photograph © Adoc-photos/Art Resource, New York.

case of manipulation and biased construction in the way Esquirol recounted, exploited, phrased, and above all interpreted the facts the better to provide a "clinical" demonstration of the ravages supposedly caused by revolutionary ideals. According to Roudinesco's biography, Théroigne apparently showed signs of mental disorder as early as 1782; her writings suggested a "split" personality with alternating highs and lows. The events that began in 1789 apparently channeled and transformed this disorder until the Terror brought them permanently to the surface.

> If her involvement with original feminism had enabled her to live her life under the banner of liberty, and thereby to express her latent madness in acts of positive revolt, the collapse of the revolutionary ideal plunged her into a state of definitive alienation that brought out her latent psychosis. In moving from a "free" and "traveling" madness to a chronic psychosis, she then lapsed into the repetitive lethargy of asylum dementia. When, under the Restoration, Esquirol wrote his famous observation of Théroigne, he reversed her destiny. Instead of realizing that the Revolution had "carried" Théroigne's madness to such a degree that it had effectively masked it, he set out prove that, on the contrary, her involvement in revolutionary politics lay at the root of that madness, and of a madness at large in the world as a whole.[14]

The French Revolution thus perhaps provided not only a screen for the projection of delusion but also a space for its translation. In a broader context, this hypothesis offers new perspectives on subsequent revolutions and their relation to madness, their ability to simultaneously mask and reveal individual and collective psychological disorders or illness. What drives might revolution unleash? What madness might it conceal? And how did psychiatry interpret the rebellion of minds?

DOWN WITH THE BOURBON MONARCHY: CIVILIZATION AND ITS DISEASES

For most psychiatrists, it all seemed clear: "Political agitation produces mental illness, even as it increases the rate of suicide and crime," wrote Félix Voisin in 1826, echoing many of his colleagues who made similar figurative use of words such as "agitation" (*commotion*) and "convulsions" to naturalize a body politic compared to an unwell body.[15] In this respect most doctors followed the line laid down by Esquirol, who addressed this issue on several occasions during his career. In 1838, two years before his death, he devoted a long passage to it in his entry "insanity" for the *Encyclopédie du dix-neuvième siècle* (Encyclopedia of the nineteenth century). In fact, that passage was a faithful rehashing of earlier texts embedded inside one another, demonstrating that in twenty years Esquirol's opinions had hardly changed.

His position on the relationship between politics and pathology was nevertheless not as clear-cut as it may seem. Riddled with contradictions, it needs to be dissected and placed in perspective. Esquirol felt that the link between political events and mental illness was indeed one of cause and effect, but the causes had merely a triggering rather than a predisposing effect, and the impact was temporary. His examples of colonial conquest, the American war of independence, and the French Revolution all stirred passions and displaced people and thus were disorders that he argued revealed and favored monomania rather than suddenly creating it. Yet these events not only triggered but also shaped insanity—the arrival of the pope in France was accompanied by a rise in religious monomania, Napoleon's domination of Europe and allocation of kingdoms increased cases of delusions of grandeur. Nevertheless, these events or periods of history had an impact on predisposed temperaments, acting simply as catalysts for aberrations that would have taken form in other circumstances. "The individual who now becomes insane by the loss of his fortune and rank would have become so fifty years before in consequence of the loss of his fortune at sea, or after a disgrace at court; that, whom the terrors of the revolution rendered insane, would have become so two centuries ago though fear of sorcerers and the devil."[16] In other words, history does not cause the symptoms of madness, but latent madness emerges as a function of the vagaries of history.

The other issue, of course, was whether political upheavals increased the rate of mental illness. In 1805, Esquirol was categorical. "By bringing all the passions into play, by giving greater flight to feigned passions and exaggerating hateful passions . . . political agitation increases the number of madmen; this was observed during the revolution in England and has been observed in France ever since our revolutionary turmoil."[17] But by 1824 the physician had changed course, going so far as to suggest that mental illness decreased during periods of political excitement, such as 1786 to 1792, a period when "all of society seemed struck with dizziness. . . . Political fanaticism and its accompanying ills brought out a few cases of madness, but all physicians noted that when it weighed upon our country with greater fury, there were fewer nervous diseases and less madness."[18] In contrast, the Restoration—a period when "the mass of people had never been so calm or less prone to excitement"—saw the number of mental illnesses increase at all levels of society.[19]

Despite appearances, Esquirol is not contradicting himself in these two passages, written some twenty years apart. The Revolution, and particularly the Terror (note that Esquirol ended his period of "excitement" in 1792, just before the Terror began), might have been largely responsible for increased madness in France, but only over the long term and with delayed effect. Turmoil puts a temporary hold on madness, which gets caught up in the heat of the action, erupting all the more once calm has returned. The case of Théroigne de Méricourt was thus a perfect illustration of Esquirol's theory. He summarized his argument in three points: (1) Théroigne was predisposed to madness, as demonstrated by her excitable temperament and eccentric behavior; (2) revolutionary events interrupted the evolution of her madness; and (3) "when the Directoire was established and political clubs were closed, Téorenne lost her reason," concluded Esquirol logically[20]—a logic that dispensed with historical accuracy, since in fact Théroigne was officially declared insane during the Terror.

If Esquirol minimized events that were by definition temporary, considering them a smokescreen behind which an outburst was brewing, it was also to better underscore his profound belief that madness was a moral affair and that the real reason for the increase in insanity in France lay in the debasement of social behavior since the Revolution. During the Restoration, those profound changes in society and mentalities resulted in an abandonment of religion, in moral laxity, and in the "cold egotism" of a society in which generational ties withered and "each [person] live[d] for himself." On one hand, the absence of proper upbringing among the lowest classes spawned almost all of society's ills, while on the other hand the "vice" of indulgent upper-class parents who gave their children a lax upbringing aggravated the situation. "Accustomed to follow all his inclinations, and not being habituated by discipline to contradiction, the child, having arrived at maturity, cannot resist the vicissitudes and reverses by which life is agitated. On the least adversity, insanity bursts forth."[21]

Esquirol felt that madness was above all "a disease of civilization," contingent less on political events than on moral ideology.[22] The more civilization advanced, the more insanity spread. Few cases of insanity were found in lands groaning under the yoke of a despot, or among savage tribes, whereas "a republican or representative government, in giving more play to all the passions, ought, other things being equal, to be more favorable to the production of insanity."[23] The entire nineteenth century was marked by this idea of madness linked to progress and the form of government. All studies agreed that madness spreads first in large cities, where industrial activity, social and political tensions, and the effervescence of ideas and passion trigger a mental excitement conducive to mental illness. In 1881 Dr. Paul Jacoby conducted an overview of the scientific literature on the question and again identified the spread of civilization as the leading cause of the spectacular increase in madness in Europe and particularly in France, where cases of mental illness went from 5.24 per 10,000 inhabitants in 1836 to 24.28 in 1869, an increase of 363.35 percent, some thirty-two times faster than the 11.23 percent growth in population during that same period.[24]

What role did the revolution of 1830, which brought down the Bourbon monarchy, play in this inexorable rise? We might start by looking at a chart Esquirol drew up of the causes of madness in patients admitted to Charenton between 1826 and 1833. In the first years, the physician reported not a single admission caused by "political events." However, in 1830 thirteen patients were admitted to the asylum with illnesses caused by political events, rising to fifteen in 1831, then dropping to two in 1832 and one in 1833. In all, then, these thirty-two cases over three years represented 2.3 percent of the overall total of 1,375 admissions, figures that seem paltry compared with the 337 admissions (24.5 percent) ascribed to hereditary causes during that same period; in an earlier period, the years 1811 and 1812, the madness of thirty-one of the patients in Esquirol's own private establishment was ascribed to political events, representing 18.5 percent of the total.[25] Why then did Esquirol write that "homes and asylums for the mentally ill in Paris were for a time overwhelmed by the great number of madmen produced by the events of 1830"?[26] The answer is that he assimilated political events with other ills, listed under different causes. "The social disturbances of that period [1830 and 1831]," he wrote, "exercised their influence on the production of insanity not only through alarm and political exaltation, but even more so through the reversal of the social fortunes of many individuals."[27] Indeed, between 1829 and 1830 "domestic troubles" rose from twenty-six to forty-seven cases, and "fright" from eight to fourteen, while from 1830 to 1831 "reverses of fortune" leaped from three to fifteen. Although it is impossible to be more specific about these figures, they may well be related to the upheavals that overthrew the Bourbons and offered the French throne to the Orléans family, known as the July monarchy. There must have been collateral damage (bankruptcies, losses of jobs and positions), although it is hard to measure. Dr. Alexandre Brierre de Boismont, who ran his own private nursing home, followed his mentor Esquirol in cultivating a certain vagueness by asserting that "the three days [of uprising] in July must have triggered a loss of reason among many people; our establishments thus witnessed the arrival of a goodly part of the victims of internal strife. . . . Later we admitted other patients whose intellectual faculties became disordered owing to disappointed ambitions, reversals of fortune, and shattered affections."[28] That's all he had to say?

Turning to the records at Charenton, the peak in cases caused by political events unsurprisingly occurred in August 1830, representing six admissions out of ten, four of them women. Three of those patients had already spent time in an asylum, suggesting that the revolutionary events revived a latent manic or melancholic state. The registers include comments such as: "This patient has been admitted to the establishment five times, remaining one month each time. The current fit is ascribed to the events of July 27th, 28th, and 29th. The delusions are absolutely identical to previous years."[29] So one wonders what real impact the revolution had, apart from being a trigger like any other event devoid of political import.

Men and women were taken to Charenton after the revolutionary events in July 1830 as a result of intense fear or other emotional shock. There was a landowner from Versailles whose reason left him as troops approached nearby Rambouillet: convinced that his life was in danger and that people wanted to shoot him, he "cringed at the approach of nurses, whom he looked upon with a kind of horror."[30] Then there was a woman who "was in the street when the king's troops clashed with the citizenry" and became so frightened that she lost her mind: in the asylum she constantly repeated that she did not deserve to live because she was "the cause of the massacres that have just occurred in Paris."[31] In general, the trauma afflicted individuals whose upbringing or education was "narrow" or "almost nonexistent," and whose character was "uncompromising," "difficult," "restive," "irascible," or "unsympathizing," suggesting that other circumstances might also have driven them to the asylum, as with the inveterate onanist who had already been treated at Bicêtre and who became delusional after nearly falling victim to working-class rioters: "This event was the immediate cause of the illness to which he was predisposed by his private habits, just like the last time."[32]

Patients' political opinions can be read between the lines and occasionally are explicitly stated, as with Madame T., who was "devoted to the former king, Charles X, and his family," and with Madame J., the wife of a pastry cook at Versailles and the mother of four children, who did not share her husband's views as he enthusiastically joined the Paris uprising. More important, however, Madame T. was "sharp yet somber in character" and had a "feeble temperament"; moreover, "people say that she has faulty judgment." Married and the mother of one child, "it is suspected that, being pregnant before marriage, she took some violent physic to induce an abortion."[33] As to the "excessively coquettish" Madame J., she "had very little upbringing because she would never accept any kind of subjugation"; furthermore, since her marriage her behavior had apparently been "far from blameless."[34] Despite the official attribution of their madness to the July revolution, it was indeed their allegedly reprehensible habits that led such patients to the asylum, in accordance with Esquirol's theory of insanity as a disease of civilization.

In this context, where were the manic, feverish defenders of the barricades—republicans suffering from "political monomania"? There weren't any, at least not at Charenton. At best we come across the admission on February 21, 1831, of a grocer's assistant who "ever since he has lived in Paris . . . , reads a good deal, mainly newspapers" and reportedly played "a very active role [in the uprising], which appears to have considerably excited his mind."[35] The connection between his political convictions and his delusions of grandeur was not clearly established, however. Esquirol employed the same rhetorical caution in his diagnosis of a woman who admitted to "opinions that were more than liberal" and who, on hearing about the events of July, "went into such joy that she seemed considerably excited for several days."[36] Yet this incident was not the cause of her melancholia, which was attributed to her fear of witnessing massacres like the ones she had seen in Marseille in 1815.

This quick overview of the medical records seems to show at least two things. On one hand, the impact of the July revolution on mental illness was statistically negligible. On the other, the delusions were basically triggered by fear, with no categorical correlation being established between political upheaval and loss of mind by Esquirol, who was a liberal and therefore favored the new Orléans monarchy.

So do the statistics and comments at Bicêtre and La Salpêtrière for the same period produce conclusions similar to those at Charenton? In a report on the mental health wards of both hospitals, published in 1835, it was indeed specified that during 1831–33 the number of cases rose one-eighth over the years 1827–30, then subsequently dropped. "These results were probably caused by the July revolution, whose impact must have continued beyond the closing months of 1830, plus the cholera epidemic and the poverty that still weighed on the working classes in 1832."[37] Yet does this hasty, very general conjecture, covering very different causes over a three-year period, have any true value? The study did not even include "political events" in the charts listing the causes of mental illness, indicating that they were quantitatively negligible. In fact, it seems that the relation between revolution and madness during this period was an issue addressed above all by eccentrics and firebrands such as the Grenoble physician Sylvain Eymard, who in 1832 published an ultraconservative diatribe titled *La Politicomanie, ou De la folie actuellement régnante en France* (Politicomania, or the madness currently reigning in France). In bombastic language the doctor castigated, pell-mell, the scourge of revolution, the mania for popular sovereignty, and the obsession with democracy and republicanism. It is doubtful that many people read Eymard's pamphlet. But in a revamped edition it enjoyed several print runs at the start of the Second Empire, under a more ambitious title that indicated how far revolution was henceforth viewed as a structural phenomenon: *La Politicomania, ou Coup d'oeil critique sur la folie révolutionnaire qui a régné en*

Europe depuis 1789 jusqu'au 2 décembre 1851 (Politicomania, or A critical glance at the revolutionary madness that reigned in Europe from 1789 until December 2, 1851).

UP WITH THE SECOND REPUBLIC: THE PLAGUE OF DEMOCRACY

Talking the Talk

The revolution of 1848 was longer, more convulsive, and far deadlier than the three-day affair in July 1830, thus reawakening the interest of psychiatrists. Right from the month of May in that year, Dr. Jacques-Étienne Belhomme, son of the same Belhomme who ran the nursing home during the Terror, presented a paper at the Académie de Médecine titled *Influence des événements et des commotions politiques sur le développement de la folie* (The influence of political agitation and events on the spread of insanity). Belhomme's study followed the path of earlier ones drawn up after the revolution of 1830, and it came to similar conclusions: the number of mental patients increased during revolutionary periods because such events affected "feeble minds" and fragile temperaments predisposed to mental illness. "The revolution last February was sudden," it read, "and occurred with incredible swiftness; the population of Paris was profoundly disturbed by the military maneuvers, the firing of rifles and cannons, and the presence of evil-looking men seen only during riots, so it is not surprising to see madness arise."[38] Belhomme's demonstration, based on ten clinical observations, nevertheless failed to convince his colleagues. Guillaume Ferrus, the inspector general of asylums, sought a middle ground by asserting that an increase had indeed been noted in certain establishments but that it was far from universal. Jules Baillarger agreed, providing figures for the number of patients admitted to La Salpêtrière and Bicêtre: 1,220 in 1847 compared with 1,354 in 1848, representing an increase of 134 cases; but in 1843 there had been 1,335 and in 1846 the number was 1,331, which mitigated, not to say invalidated, the significance of the 1848 figures. In fact, a later study would show that, throughout all of France, the number of admissions actually dropped in 1848 (7,686 admissions in 1847 as against 7,341 in 1848) yet subsequently rose to 7,536 in 1849 and 8,814 in 1850.[39]

Baillarger also added, perhaps unexpectedly, that "while political disturbances bring with them real and powerful causes of madness, it should also be acknowledged that they defer other influences that often produce this disease in times of great prosperity and calm. There are many passions within the family itself that can unsteady the mind, little by little, and for which political events can provide a fortunate diversion!"[40] Countering the usual preconceptions, Baillarger apparently supports Esquirol's observation that madness declines, proportionally, during periods of disturbance and increases during periods of calm. He even seems to be going further, suggesting that civic excitement is healthier for the mind than withdrawing into the family, insinuating a dichotomy between public and private, external and internal, political and familial that favors the first term in each pair. The same idea is found in Benedict-Augustin Morel's *Traité des maladies mentales* (Treatise on mental illness). Morel was chief physician at an asylum in Maréville that housed a thousand patients, and he claimed that between 1848 and 1856 he "had not recorded the exaggeration of political ideas as a cause of insanity in more than three individuals."[41] This theorist of mental degeneracy went on to write:

> As to political agitation literally speaking, perhaps we should acknowledge that it has passed sentence on more nervous diseases than it has caused. At first sight this may seem paradoxical; but once we look at the facts resulting from the salutary effect of crises, we perhaps have the right to say that many neuropathies have been healed by major social agitation. From this perspective, what was observed in 1789 was also seen in 1848, and similar consequences have stemmed from all major events that, by changing the face of societies, impart a more vigorous direction, a more useful goal of activity, to the unhealthy, sickly, indifferent constitution of throngs of individuals by reforging them, so to speak, in the crucible of great misfortune.[42]

Meanwhile Belhomme, in the conclusion of his address to the Académie de Médecine, complained that his work had been overlooked, bitterly noting that his peers never cited it. Two months later, however, Brierre de Boismont defended Belhomme's theory in an issue of *L'Union Médicale*, fearlessly extending the ravages of revolution to the entire range of political activists: conservatives were afflicted by "sorrowful monomania," whereas progressives suffered from "joyful monomania." The latter particularly inspired Brierre de Boismont's eloquence: "A considerable number of individuals who threw themselves wholeheartedly into the utopias of the day were not considered mad, but simply passed for bold innovators. Yet it is impossible for me, a physician, to forget the faces, gestures, and speech of many of those people I observed in the clubs, there being no difference to distinguish them from the residents of our homes; and even if any advantage were seen, it would go to our patients, whose fits of fury are infinitely rarer."[43] Here Brierre de Boismont introduced an already venerable figure who would enjoy an ever brighter future in psychiatric circles: the mad individual who hides behind a mask that only a psychiatrist, endowed with second sight, is able to pierce. Pinel, referring to the September massacres, had already mentioned a recluse in Bicêtre who presented himself to the revolutionaries as a healthy man unjustly incarcerated, and who was therefore released despite Jean-Baptiste Pussin's repeated warnings, only to shed blood all around him by snatching up the first sword he came upon.[44] This type of madman, undetected by lay observers but recognized by specialists, was "the lucid madman" who suffered from "mania without delusions" or "reasoning insanity," as amply described some years later by Ulysse Trélat. There was something of the traitor and the devil in this protean figure, able to deceive the naive but unable to fool science.

How reliable, then, were statistics on madness that overlooked "those maniacs" who "died in street battles"[45] or disappeared into prisons or exile? These same statistics failed to include, in Brierre de Boismont's words, "those unwell people who, almost all incurable, slowly pass away within families" that prefer to keep them at home rather than suffer the shame of public hospitals.[46] In other words, although the statistics had spoken, they proved nothing, since they did not take into account all those who were dead or out of sight—who were also, as we know, out of mind. But facts were facts, and Brierre de Boismont was determined to face up to them, even as he threatened future generations with a worrying prophecy that women who became pregnant during the Revolution would give birth to children doomed to go insane. The newborn, like the missing, were thus taken hostage by Brierre de Boismont's argument. "A comment we feel we must repeat is that this madness, *although perhaps not increasing the number of the insane in special establishments*, has nevertheless left a trace of its passage, for which proof will be supplied, several years hence, by those who were conceived under the imprint of those wretched days."[47]

That Brierre de Boismont, along with Jacques-Étienne Belhomme, was one of the few men to contest the relative stability in the number of insanity cases during revolutionary periods probably came about because both men ran private nursing homes that catered to a wealthy clientele—the one most threatened by revolution. It would hardly be surprising if they admitted more patients to their establishments during those periods. But from their particular experiences they drew ideologically driven generalizations. As dramatic as the two men's opinions were, they remained in the minority, as the German psychiatrist Wilhelm Griesinger pointed out.

> It is a remarkable fact that great political agitations appear to have less influence on the frequency of mental diseases than might at first be supposed. Esquirol remarked this at the time of the first French revolution. According to many French and German physicians (excepting Brierre), the revolutionary movements of 1830, and especially of 1848, gave rise to little or no increase in the number of cases of insanity. To the laity the influence of the revolutions appeared very considerable, because in these times politics formed the subject of the delirium in many patients; this, as we have seen, is a purely accidental and superficial relation.[48]

Griesinger here makes a crucial distinction and simultaneously unravels a stubborn confusion: the increase in political delusions during revolutionary periods creates the *impression* of an epidemic of madness triggered by the disturbances, whereas admissions to the asylums do not markedly increase. There is apparently a kind of optical illusion between talking the talk (the very real increase in political discourse) and walking the walk (the illusory number of cases of insanity).

Study of the archives substantiates this viewpoint. Never before did politics so prey on people's minds, never had the ideological content of delusions been so fully reported and described by psychiatrists. As early as 1847, when France was struck by a subsistence crisis and corruption scandals were sullying the final days of the July monarchy, an example of the role political passions played is offered by the case of Jules S., a twenty-three-year-old law clerk admitted to Charenton. The young man—the perfect portrait of a young socialist republican straight out of a novel by Eugène Sue—was repelled by his father's butchery business and had gone to Paris to study law.

> His fiery spirit and noble sentiments soon found favorite nourishment in the philanthropic and humanitarian meetings to which he was introduced by a few of his friends. Totally neglecting his law studies, he turned to books that flattered his thinking the most. Thus Lamennais, Fourier, and Pierre Leroux became his regular reading. He felt that the working classes were the ones that deserved the most attention from philanthropic individuals. Thus he enthusiastically defended all social reforms designed to provide relief to the people. His father, however, perceiving that his son was not fulfilling his expectations, summoned him home.[49]

On his returning home, everything went wrong. Jules S. fell in love with a young woman "far above his station" and was rejected. He sank into sorrow and misanthropy, threw himself into religion, and saw apparitions when he entered churches. His behavior become more unpredictable every day. "The duc d'Aumale having visited his region recently, [Jules S.] introduced himself to the duke and gave him a tin box containing a *pea*, a *bean*, and a piece of paper on which were written the following three words: honor, liberty, charity. According to the young man, this gift had an enigmatic meaning that only he could interpret." Did political commitment mark the start of an overexcited state that would soon turn unhealthy? Or, on the contrary, was it because he left the excitement of Paris, because he became oppressed by paternal authority and dropped politics for religion, that Jules S. wound up in Charenton? Although the diagnosis does not mention it, what springs to mind is Baillarger's suggestion that political events provide a felicitous distraction from those pernicious passions that families have such a knack for.

Melancholy Republicans and Stubborn Communists

The repercussions of 1848 were distinctly different from those of 1830. In a matter of months, politics went from just one element in the origin of illness to the main theme of delusions recorded at Charenton. Starting in February, almost all cases of madness were rooted—either explicitly or by direct or indirect inference—in the revolution and its aftershocks. "His illness is ascribed to the events of June and to politics in which he became much too involved," read the notes, for example, on a thirty-seven-year-old road mender, although we never learn what "much too" actually meant.[50]

Broadly speaking, cases fall into two categories, depending on whether madness is considered the *consequence* of revolution or its *cause*. On the one hand are the victims, the men floored by the spectacle of insurrection and crushed by the loss of their wealth, the women whose houses were invaded by rebels, who went into shock or fell into a stupor on seeing barricades go up in the streets. These were the trauma cases, which always constitute the majority of mental disorders during revolutions, from the imaginary guillotine victims of 1793 to the appalled populace of 1830. On the other hand there were the culprits—the rioters, the haranguers, and the activists who participated in the uprising either in theory or in practice. The hallowed figure of 1848, without being a totally new invention, was the unkempt, verbose madman galvanized by political passion, an heir to the Jacobins, the September rioters, and the insurgents of July 1830. In a major twist, however, this figure now acquired a sister, with a henceforth clear profile: she was a virago, heiress to the *tricoteuses* of the Terror and an avatar of George Sand, who abandoned her role of wife and mother to spend her time reading newspapers she couldn't understand and prating in peculiar political clubs. These caricatures, whose twisted grins were constantly reproduced in the press, represented a modern mode of madness that profoundly modified the debate over the relation of psychopathology and politics.

In a sign of the times, Charenton henceforth established separate registers for male and female patients. The growing visibility of women in society was accompanied by a new awareness: women's role as "players in history" was confirmed by the rise of a feminist movement allied to the utopian movements of Claude-Henri de Rouvroy, comte de Saint-Simon, and François Marie Charles Fourier that called for civic and political equality, by the participation of women in political debate and in battles at the barricades, and by the publication of women's periodicals that discussed work, salaries, and education (*La Voix des Femmes*, edited by Eugénie Niboyet, and *La Politique des Femmes*—later *L'Opinion des Femmes*—edited by Jeanne Deroin and Désirée Gay).[51] Such women were perfect targets, sparking either hatred or a "conspiracy of silence" rather than admiration. They prompted irritation and sarcasm even within their own political camp, where women on the barricades were held to be out of place and militant feminists were accused of making untimely demands when all efforts, without exception, were supposed to focus on the fate of the proletariat. "We seek the most virulent terms of disgust and contempt, in order to throw them in the faces of those shrews who have fled hearth and home, or rather their cells in Bicêtre!" Thus Alexandre Dumas exclaimed in 1849[52] when, as an unsuccessful election candidate and disappointed republican, he was drifting toward the conservative Parti de l'Ordre.

As though echoing the newspapers of the day, the Charenton archives are blithely ironic about the "women of '48" and sympathizers with the revolutionary movements. Physicians even displayed a self-indulgent tendency to stigmatize allegedly arrogant pretensions and picturesque situations and attitudes. They even openly employed irony, strangely undermining the status of their own "record of medical observations." Take the following "diagnosis" whose tone seems more suited to the opening passages of a satirical story:

> Hardworking and very active, Madame Rosty was at first totally committed to her trade. In the early years of her marriage her sole entertainment was a subscription to the *Constitutionnel*. Little by little she acquired a taste for politics, becoming thoroughly knowledgeable about the ministers to [King] Louis-Philippe, whose policies she detested. Indeed, Madame Rosty passed, in her shop, for a *republican*.
>
> When the events of February occurred, she greeted the advent of the Republic with enthusiasm. Madame Rosty suddenly found herself fashionable.
>
> Although, on one hand, our patient's political dreams were coming true, unfortunately the same was not true of her plans for wealth.
>
> The Republic chugged along, but the sale of items of bedding came to a halt, a halt so thorough that she began to fear the very ruin she had wished upon Louis-Philippe.
>
> Constantly fretting about the grim situation in which the stagnation of business placed her, she fell into melancholia.[53]

The comic tone of this opening description bears little relation to the shock that triggered Madame Rosty's illness, namely a saltwater bath prescribed by her doctor the week before her internment. The bath was supposed to be a substitute for the ocean bathing she had desired as a way of taking her mind off things, but it had such an impact that she instantly lost her memory and became infantile. Subject to bouts of hysteria and hallucinations, she was nevertheless cured and left Charenton less than two months after her arrival, proving that her republican melancholia was not all that serious.

These cardboard revolutionaries, with their hearts to the left but their money to the right, were not to be outdone by stubborn communists such as Mademoiselle Cirnéa de Villot, the daughter of the last military governor of Corsica, who lost his social rank following political reverses. To make matters worse, the woman's mother was already a mental patient at Charenton, and she herself was unmarried at age thirty.

> She threw herself headlong into politics and favored the ideas of Louis Blanc. The revolution in February overexcited her imagination. She greeted the name of Lamartine with enthusiasm, considering him a messenger from God who would regenerate France. She spoke constantly of Lamartine and Blanc. Some confusion in her thinking could be detected in the midst of all this overexcitement.
>
> Mademoiselle de V. is now afflicted by acute maniacal insanity. She is prey to extreme agitation, she talks constantly, and her speech reveals great disorder in her intellectual faculties. "I deny madness," she says. "I maintain that madness doesn't exist. I know full well that my mother is here! I have pains in my head, I'm very thirsty. I used to be a chatterbox, that's why I need to drink. I have a disease of the larynx, that's why I have to go to Italy. I'm a communist! I haven't slept for three weeks. I'm much too busy to govern France, everything is awry.[54]

Everything about this finely etched diagnosis rests on a rhetoric of discrepancy, in which everything is expressed by omission. There is a total absence of transition from one paragraph to another, a void between the description of political opinions and the description of illness. It is as though the shift from "some confusion in her thinking" to "acute maniacal insanity" (accompanied by "great disorder in her mental faculties") tacitly expressed the logical connection between political excitement and verbal delusion, accompanied—as the physician went on to note—by "highly expressive gestures." The description of her ravings plays on a similar grammatical construction in that the patient spouts a chain of statements that are themselves acceptable but whose linkage, or rather uncoordinated assembly, reveals their absurdity. Denying madness even as she acknowledges her mother's internment is a contradiction, just as establishing a causal relationship between larynx and Italy is irrational. The height of absurdity in these non sequiturs is also a logical conclusion: being a communist, an insomniac, and too busy to govern France, Mademoiselle de Villot could only conclude that the country is in disarray, an allegory for the state of her own mind.

So politics brewed the poison, revolution caused the illness to erupt. This view was accepted by all doctors, some of whom did not hesitate to explicitly blame "social heresies" for injecting minds with disorder and madness. One was Louis Bergeret, the chief physician at a hospital in Arbois in the Jura region, who wrote an article on the ravages of 1848 in the area, where he estimated that the number of the mentally ill increased tenfold. It is safe to wager that this unverifiable figure owes much to the personal beliefs of the doctor, who, it should be noted, was not a psychiatrist but a specialist in forensic medicine. He claimed there were millions of "half-mad" and "quarter-mad" people stricken with a revolutionary fever more dangerous than typhus or cholera. Of the ten cases he discussed in the *Annales d'Hygiène Publique et de Médecine Légale* (Annals of public health and forensic medicine), seven were women whose delusions largely consisted of rebelling against injustice and calling for the elimination of poverty. As of February 1848, these women—farmworker, factory worker, winegrower's wife, craftsman's widow—had been corrupted by a "wave of bizarre and subversive ideas" and a mass of "demagogic" publications. They heard voices, thought they were imbued with a sacred mission on behalf of the people, and went into raving fits. "No more poverty, no more exploitation of men by other men, nor more rich, no more police. The people must govern themselves. . . . I want to save the country," shouted one of them.[55] "When will the people break down the doors of prisons and labor camps?" asked another, who took Louis Blanc for the messiah. "No more executioners, no more victims! As Victor Hugo said, all this must go. There will be no more wretches, all men must be the same. Socialism will make them all equally happy."[56] Bergeret concluded that "a sense of exacerbated pride had gone to everyone's head, everyone was so impatient to leave their stations that one young woman who had thoroughly studied the phalanstery became so full of Fourier's ideas that she lost her mind." Not only was "she seen going out in a man's clothing," but she refused to allowed herself to be auscultated, "declaring that she would never allow a doctor to treat her until women were allowed to study for a doctor's diploma."[57] She ended her days in a mental home.

Bergeret waited fifteen years before publishing these edifying observations—out of a concern for impartiality, he claimed at the end of his article, in order to let time restore calm. What would have happened had he published them right after the uprising? Perhaps we're better off not knowing.

Compared with the outrageous remarks by Bergeret, who made no distinction between political agenda and raving madness, hospital diagnoses were generally more subtle. Ambiguity, rather than sensational demonstration, is the usual effect of this archive material.[58] This is partly due to gaps and lacunae in the registers, as demonstrated by the records of male patients in Charenton. Among the patients who had taken part in the riots, there were a few political prisoners transferred from jail to asylum. Did they actually go mad, or were they simply feigning insanity to escape worse punishment? A wine merchant, for example, who was arrested and charged with plotting to overthrow the government, "spoke passionately and wrote constantly," believing that "God had bestowed on him the title of head of government and the right to give orders to ministers, the people, and the representatives of the nation."[59]

When dealing with physicians' written comments, it is not always easy to distinguish political passion from illness. What conclusion, for example, should we draw from the following diagnosis by Dr. Jacques-Joseph Moreau de Tours of a patient called P., a traveling sponge salesman locked up in Bicêtre at the orders of the prefect of police, who refused to wear any clothes and had to be straitjacketed: "In the course of his mental disorder, political ideas can be seen to dominate; he speaks most often of Barbès and other rebel leaders and says he took part in all the uprisings, which is possible; in any case, [his] current state is one of true maniacal excitement." Thus it hardly matters here whether P.'s claims were delusions or reality—his highly excited state would have condemned him to insanity *whatever the case*, just as his behavior, although nonviolent, condemned him to internment *in any case*, based on a questionable determinism: "P., however, is rarely violent, being merely turbulent and extremely irksome, and it is possible that this condition will disappear, even heal, yet it is also certain that sooner or later it will recur and will require his confinement within the hospital for a fourth time."[60]

The line between political prisoner and madman sometimes seems very thin. In addition to legalistic issues that are impossible to judge after the fact, there are many cases of ideological "ravings" accompanied by hallucinations, such as a patient afflicted with acute maniacal insanity "characterized by ideas of social reform." He "claimed he wanted to sacrifice himself for the Republic" and considered himself "a political prisoner" but also claimed he was locked up because he obeyed a voice that instructed him to "kneel before the statue of Henri IV, go the Chamber of Peers, break three panes, and be arrested there."[61] At that time he would have come across another patient, a tailor, who "first proposed highly advanced philanthropic ideas, wanting to pay the debts of every Frenchman, etc., which was his way of healing the large wound called Pauperism." This well-intentioned patient said he could employ ten thousand workers as the "tailor to the Chamber of the new Emperor Napoleon," an assertion made in November 1848, four years before the Second Empire was proclaimed. "Now," added the doctor, "[he says] his nephew, a young tailor, has just been appointed president of the French Republic."[62]

Utopia and Loss of Reason

The blend of discourse on the improvement of humankind with truly delusional behavior as found in mental health archives for the year 1848 raises a philosophical and historical question. In the nineteenth century, what did political utopia have in common with a certain conception of madness? To what extent was the dream of a better society synonymous with a loss of reason? These thorny questions are partly dependent on the ideological stance of the person who raises—and potentially answers—them.

A famous session of the National Assembly on May 15, 1848, represented one of those moments in history when the link between political passion and madness was raised directly. Briefly, these are the facts leading up to it: elections on April 23 had resulted in a National Assembly with a majority of "latter-day republicans" (moderate republicans, monarchists, and conservatives) at the expense of the radical republicans who had spearheaded the February uprising. Various reasons have been advanced to explain this outcome (some candidates camouflaged their true leanings behind a progressive label, inexperienced voters were influenced by local priests and notables in the provinces, and so on), which left a bitter taste in the mouths of the February rebels. For leaders of the extreme left who remembered the events of 1830, the revolution was being stolen from them a second time. On May 15 they organized a demonstration in Paris to support insurgents in Poland (whom the French government had decided not to aid); the demonstrators ultimately invaded the Bourbon Palace where the legislature met. "Just picture market hawkers mingling with senators," wrote Victor Hugo, recalling the waves of men and women shouting and gesticulating on all sides, carrying flags crowned with the revolutionary red cap. "Everywhere were heads, shoulders, shouting faces, raised arms, clenched fists. No one spoke—everyone shouted. The legislators sat motionless; it lasted three hours."[63] Gesticulating petty merchants, impassive senators: the stage was set for a confrontation between "lower" France and "upper" France.

As Hugo watched the scene unfold, Alexis de Tocqueville was approached in the crowd by Dr. Ulysse Trélat, the elected representative from Puy-de-Dôme. Trélat was a psychiatric physician who was then in charge of the fourth ward of La Salpêtrière and whose sympathies were republican. He had previously belonged to various secret societies linked to the Charbonnerie and had participated in many plots. Arrested on several occasions, Trélat notably found himself in court in 1832 alongside the likes of François-Vincent Raspail and Louis Auguste Blanqui at the "trial of the Fifteen." Frail health, exacerbated by a stay in Clairvaux prison in 1835, limited his political activity for a while. But by 1848 he was back on the scene, playing several roles—mayor of the thirteenth arrondissement, chair of the colonization committee, lieutenant colonel of the twelfth legion commanded by Armand Barbès, vice president of the Constituent Assembly, and, as of May 12, minister of public works. The anarchist Pierre-Joseph Proudhon held Trélat in "fond admiration," whereas the socialist activist Louis Blanc thought

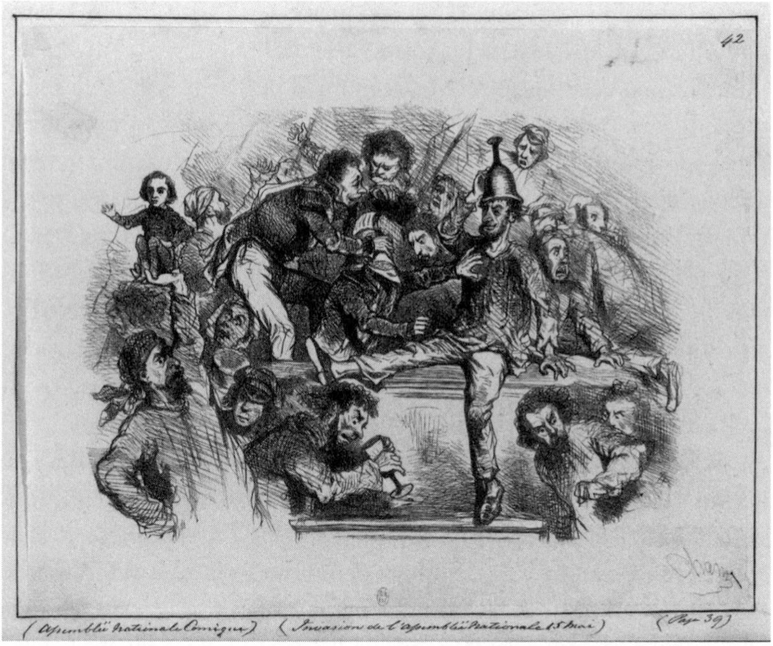

FIGURE 28. Cham (Charles Amédée de Noé), *May 15th*. Illustration for Auguste Lireux's *Assemblée nationale comique* (Paris: Michel Lévy Frères, 1850). On May 15, 1848, demonstrators invaded the National Assembly. The cartoonist Cham offered his version of the event, presenting it as a fit of madness. In the middle is Auguste Blanqui, with the speaker's bell on his head; on the left Louis Blanc is being held aloft in the palm of a demonstrator's hand. Bibliothèque Nationale de France, Paris. Photograph © BNF.

he was a "nonentity."[64] Tocqueville, meanwhile, described him as a "a revolutionary of the sentimental kind, a dreamer . . . [and] moreover a physician of distinction, who was at that time at the head of one of the principal madhouses in Paris, although he was a little cracked himself." On May 15, then, Trélat went up to Tocqueville, who recorded the incident. "He took my hands effusively, and with tears in his eye: 'Ah, monsieur, what a misfortune and how strange it is to think that it is madmen, real madmen, who have brought this about! I have treated or prescribed for each one of them. Blanqui is a madman, Barbès is a madman, Sobrier is a madman, Huber is the greatest madman of them all: they are all madmen, monsieur, who ought to be locked up at my Salpêtrière instead of being here.'" Tocqueville commented that Trélat "would certainly have added his own name to the list, had he known himself as well as he knew his former friends."[65]

Supposing that this anecdote, recounted by Tocqueville himself, is accurate, did Trélat really think his comrades-in-arms were truly mad? The assertion might seem worthy of interest, especially coming from a recognized specialist in mental illness who was, furthermore, to the far left. Yet at the same time, what credit should we lend his judgment if the physician was "cracked" himself, as Tocqueville claimed? Whatever the case, the assertion that men should be sent to La Salpêtrière, an asylum reserved for women, will have to be attributed to the use of metaphor or to an absent-minded lapse (whether on the part of Trélat or Tocqueville we cannot tell).

Trélat alternated between political activity and medical activity all his life. He also mingled the two, for better and for worse. A highly devoted physician who spent most of his career at La Salpêtrière, he was considered a saint by his staff and patients and showed concern for the fate of the poorest by setting up support committees to aid patients who left the asylum penniless. While he tried to align his work with his political and philanthropic principles, in a somewhat more disturbing way he also conceived of his political role in terms of psychiatry. On May 27, 1848, Trélat the government minister ordered the arrest of Émile Thomas, director of the highly contested Bureau Central des Ateliers Nationaux, who had come to the minister's office to submit his resignation; Trélat justified his unfortunate act to the National Assembly with the astonishing explanation that it was a "medical decision."[66]

Perhaps Trélat had the awkward tendency, due to either political opportunism or professional bent, to consider all his peers ready for the asylum. His key publication, *La folie lucide* (Lucid madness), at any rate showed that he was broad-minded on the matter, for in it he jumbled together monomaniacs, adventurers, kleptomaniacs, sex fiends, and dipsomaniacs along with the feeble-minded, the suicidal, the merely nasty, and the arrogant.

The conclusion Tocqueville drew from this incident raises another issue. "I have always thought," he wrote, "that in revolutions, especially democratic revolutions, madmen, not those so called by courtesy, but genuine madmen, have played a very considerable political part. One thing at least is certain, and that is that a condition of semimadness is not unbecoming at such times, and often even leads to success." On studying the ugly, unhealthy portraits that Tocqueville penned of the leaders of 1848, it becomes obvious how much his commentary is indebted to the antirevolutionary tradition and to a class consciousness that blithely associated insurrection with insanity. Just take Auguste Blanqui, dubbed "l'Enfermé" ("Old Putaway") for having spent more than thirty years in government prisons: "He had wan, emaciated cheeks, white lips, a sickly, wicked, and repulsive expression, a dirty pallor, [and] the appearance of a moldy corpse," having apparently spent "his life in a sewer, and hav[ing] just left it."[67] Armand Barbès, meanwhile, was "one of those men in whom the demagogue, the madman and the knight-errant are . . . closely intermingled," but Tocqueville immediately added that "it was the madman that predominated in him, and his madness became raging when he heard the voice of the people."[68] These sinister comments and harsh diagnoses might easily be contrasted with the opinion of Dr. Cyrille Lacambe, who praised Blanqui's exceptional intellectual machinery in a letter designed to reassure the latter of his lucidity at a time when Blanqui feared he might be neurotic. "I am convinced that you have no organic lesion, and that all this is [due to] the impact of imprisonment and labor. Your mind is an immensely powerful spring, and I am surprised that it has not yet shattered into countless pieces the slender cogwheels that drive it."[69] Then there is the letter from George Sand to Barbès: "You do not *protect* yourself from anything when all the others are running for shelter. That is why they call you mad, those who cannot imitate you. I feel, however, that you are the only one with wisdom and logic, just as you are the finest and most upright of all. . . . I am telling you all this, and yet I do not approve of [the events of] May 15."[70]

However obvious the limitations of Tocqueville's comments, by postulating the existence of a link between revolution and madness he was nevertheless the only writer to clearly articulate an idea many of his contemporaries shared. This postulate rested on a series of shared physical features based above all on a cliché that perpetuated the image of a man who is "beside himself," notably popularized by Gustave Courbet's 1843 self-portrait, known as *The Desperate Man*. Mad gestures, cries, gazes, faces, poses—it can hardly be overstressed that these first and foremost characterized the insurgent bodies of "the people in tatters." Such bodies were marked by social difference, creating a separate barbaric, hostile class that sparked rejection, fear,

FIGURE 29. Cham (Charles Amédée de Noé), *Pierre Leroux Borrowing His Little Poplars from an Inmate at Charenton*. Lithograph. Socialist Pierre Leroux's 1848 plan for constitutional reform included planting poplar trees in every town and village in France as a symbol of the people and equality. Cham exploited the idea to ridicule Leroux, seen here taking his poplars from an inmate at Charenton. Bibliothèque Nationale de France, Paris. Photograph © BNF.

distaste, and disgust—emotions similar to the ones visitors to insane asylums experienced when confronted with unusual behavior and strange faces. To middle-class eyes, insurgency and insanity visually resembled one another. In the press, similar terms described the two: fanatical, frenzied, rabid, hotheaded, raving. Once liberated from their social fear, such people no longer had anything to lose, alarming the bourgeoisie. Insurgents undermined the established order just as the insane undermined the order of reason. As Dr. Bergeret pointed out with dread, the madman "displays his mental state in all its nudity before the beholder's eyes"[71]—as did the men and women in the riots and on the barricades.

There is nothing terribly original or new in the fact that a revolution depends on the boldness and fervor of a few leaders whose energy and excesses may seem similar to mad gesticulation. Revolutionaries counter official violence, which provides the immanent framework for order and reason, through a kind of "madness," an agitation that translates into a transcendence of self and a boundless energy, both of which were required in 1848 to transform French society and establish a democratic, socially conscious republic. Now, it is very striking to see that a *positive* value was also ascribed, subliminally, to this energy and to periods when the people allegedly went astray. Alphonse de Lamartine described the faces of the February insurgents as "pale and excited to [the point of] madness . . . their eyes fixed as in insanity." He added that "it was the madness of liberty!"[72] Marie d'Agoult, meanwhile, referring to the events of May 15, spoke of "men led astray by passion, but *well intentioned* in their madness"[73]—rather than the opposite. Even Tocqueville acknowledged—practically over his own dead body—the moral integrity of the "madness" of revolutionary ideals; he felt Barbès was his most formidable adversary precisely "because he was the most insane, the most *disinterested*, and the most resolute of them all."[74]

Whether pilloried or tacitly praised, why is the violence of insurrection always associated with madness, whereas the violence of repression never is? Blanqui was a madman who should be "put away," whereas Louis Eugène Cavaignac, who turned the events of June 1848 into a bloodbath, was hailed as the savior of the nation. It is singularly crazy to castigate popular uprisings but reward massacres; this weird rule systematically relegates revolution to insanity but attributes to reaction all the virtues of common sense. Indeed, the demands of "governmentality" are perhaps imbued with the *reason* underpinning the French term for "national security," so appositely called *raison* d'état.

These issues would arise again with redoubled intensity during the Paris Commune, where the horrors committed by the reactionary Versailles forces were never subjected to any diagnosis of collective insanity. The government cannot be mad, especially a purportedly "democratic" one. And yet it is tempting to agree with Eugène Ionesco that, in many respects, "Reason is the madness of the strongest. The reason of the weakest is madness."[75]

François Pardigon was a young student arrested during the disturbances of June 22–26, 1848. Among the one thousand prisoners crowded with him in the cellars of the Tuileries Palace, he saw nearly two hundred "lose their minds" when national guardsmen pointed rifles through ventilation grates, ready to fire on the first person to approach in search of fresh air. One prisoner called for his wife, another claimed he had to go open his shop, and a third demanded to leave and go have a beer, as though this sudden mindlessness would save them from the horror of their situation. "Nothing was more droll," reported Pardigon, "if anything could be droll at such a time, than the air of sovereign contempt with which they looked at us when we told them, 'It's not possible, you're going to get yourselves killed!' Their astonished eyes looked for the danger, but found none."[76]

Alongside madness as a cause of revolution, largely inspired by ideological preconceptions establishing a *visual* connection between desperate rebels and the insane, the various forms taken by madness as a product of repression—from haven to redeeming obliviousness—appear to be much more relevant on the clinical level. Most studies that followed the revolutionary events analyzed the experience of terror much more than the inflicting of it, whichever side was favored. One example is the case of a house painter who participated in the June uprising and nearly went before the firing squad, only to be sent to the hulks (decommissioned naval ships anchored near the coast to serve as prisons for the revolutionaries of 1848): he was described by Dr. Paul Briquet in 1850 as one of the earliest cases of male hysteria (convulsive fits, dizziness, lump in the throat, fainting, sobbing on awakening) caused by "intense emotions."[77]

Delusional Democrats

The question of a link between revolution and madness appeared in a special light in 1848 once the introduction of universal male suffrage implied the sovereignty of the people. For the first time in history, what Marie d'Agoult called "the real revolution" made the unimaginable concrete: all adult males, including servants, the poor, and soldiers, could participate in the political process.[78] The number of eligible voters ballooned from 250,000 to 9,500,000. In psychiatric terms, this new passion for equality was given a name: the democratic disease.

Even before science adopted it, this expression was employed by the poet Alfred de Vigny, who wrote as early as 1832 that "elections are the democratic disease."[79] Above all, it appeared in a visionary essay by Tocqueville, "De la classe moyenne et du peuple" (On the middle and lower classes), in which he discussed "the great battle" that was looming over the right to property. "Who can fail to recognize," he asked in October 1847, "this final symptom of the old democratic disease of our times, whose critical phase is perhaps approaching?"[80]

In 1850 a doctoral thesis defended the year before under the title "De morbo democratico, nova insaniae forma," was published in Germany as *Die demokratische Krankheit, eine neue Wahnsinns Form*. That very same year it was translated into French as *De la maladie démocratique, nouvelle espèce de folie* (On the democratic disease, a new form of madness). A quick glance at the table of contents reveals that the author intended to discuss the etiology, diagnosis, and treatment of this disease. That author, Carl Theodor Groddeck (father of Georg Groddeck, whom Freud called a "splendid analyst"), was not a specialist in mental illness. On the other hand, he was extremely conservative and nationalistic, as his book reveals when he describes the conflict between individual and society, between self and nonself, within a universe where the state must maintain order. According to Groddeck, the foundations of society were marriage, upbringing, discipline, morals, obedience, national identity, and love of country. To flout them by giving in to "egotistical passions" or advocating a "system of negation" and love of freedom "with no aims or limits" would mean sinking into depravity and madness. "The revolution of February [1848] tore down all the barriers of containment. From the blood and wreckage of the barricades there emerged the alarming specter of the sovereignty of the people."[81] The epidemic then spread throughout Europe, owing to "the instinct for imitation." Germany underwent a revolution in March. Anarchy proliferated, as did insanity. Groddeck, who devoted fifty pages to the causes of the disease but a mere twelve to its description, diagnosis, prognosis, and treatment, made no attempt "to recount all the ridiculous aberrations that the mania for progress has produced,"[82] but he sought to reassure readers by predicting a steady extinguishing of the epidemic, given that "the entire history of Germany is basically monarchic."[83] The treatment he proposed was to work toward "national unity" by imparting a new meaning to that concept, which had so favored the revolution.

The interest this partisan essay in psychopathology sparked among specialists was without doubt largely due to its attention-grabbing title, as Alain Chevrier pointed out in an essay on the book's reception in France.[84] Scholarly circles in Berlin had also taken note of it—Groddeck considered it a point of pride that he was booed during his dissertation defense, where he had been hard pressed by young German democrats in the packed room of witnesses to his *disputatio* in Latin.[85] Whatever the case, within a year the leading publisher on mental illness in Paris had brought out a French translation, which was noted in the *Annales Médico-psychologiques*. Unsurprisingly, the review was written by Brierre de Boismont. He adopted a satirical tone and employed the time-honored trick of inventing a dialogue with a friend, an imaginary physician counterpart whose ideas he corrected. The friend had not yet read the book (a boon to avoiding discussion of it) but claimed to be able to guess its contents, or at least its spirit, from the title, providing Brierre to Boismont with an excuse for delivering his own political opinions on the subject.

The very first paragraph of Brierre de Boismont's article set the tone: "'Now that's a poor title,' he said to me. '*Morbus democraticus* is not new, it dates back to the beginning of the world. Satan was afflicted with it when he declared war on the Lord.'" The speaker felt that that title should have been *De morbo demagogico, antiqua insaniae forma, hodie epidemica* (On the demagogic disease, an ancient form of madness, now an epidemic). Reduced to a "fever of revolt against any principle of authority" and the "seed of every revolution,"[86] the democratic disease was allegedly as ancient as the passion it sprang from: pride. Pride, greater and greater pride, repeated the speaker (quoting Spanish counterrevolutionary Donoso Cortès, who defended dictatorship in a famous speech given in response to the events of 1848), was an age-old impulse that spurred the demagogues known as "democrats" to seek to take the places of the rich, the noble, and the powerful. The novelty was that it had assumed epidemic proportions.

Brierre de Boismont clearly had nothing to say about Groddeck's work, yet he gleefully jumped on the subject, adapting the canonical classification of mental illness to democrats, categorized into "maniacs, monomaniacs, the demented, and idiots." He deployed the entire antirevolutionary repertoire, from the description of symptoms to diagnosis, beginning with an Identikit portrait of a rebel foaming at the mouth:

> Maniacs are generally seen in fraternal gatherings called clubs. They have bristly, often unkempt hair, their eyes are wild, their mouths are twisted; their speech usually comes out as raucous noises, vociferations, threats, and cries of rage in which one can catch the words "infamous capital, wretched bourgeoisie, do away with the old society. . . ." One of the main varieties of this maniacal insanity is *delirium tremens*. . . . The disease can be easily recognized from the following signs: the individual who wishes to speak trembles all over, his tongue is thick and does not articulate clearly, his eyes bulge, his face is red, and his breath has a peculiar odor; his imagination is prey to frightful hallucinations.[87]

It was when discussing the category of monomaniacs, however, that Brierre de Boismont refined his ideas and addressed the ideological dimension.

> Communist monomaniacs tear down all artificial separations and arbitrary distinctions. With them, brotherhood will rule the world; the only title they recognize is that of virtue; their only concern is the general good; they forget themselves the better to think of others. Armies will disappear for want of need, battle will be done only with nature; passions will fade, the wildest animals will meekly obey the orders of mankind. The sons of Adam will finally enjoy their laboriously acquired heritage, becoming the sovereigns of the land. Achieving this magnificent outcome calls for a trifling effort: renouncing one's individuality, depositing everything one owns in the common chest, and refraining from writing letters from America to spiteful minds in Europe.[88]

The concluding allusion indicates that Brierre de Boismont was attacking not so much Marxism as a brand of utopian communism spearheaded by Étienne Cabet, the theorist for an ideal community, Icaria, that roughly one hundred followers had attempted to set up first in Texas and then in the rest of the United States. The title page of Cabet's *Voyage en Icarie* (Travels in Icaria), published in 1840 and reprinted several times, advertised the founding principle of this perfect republic: "First right: To live. To each according to his needs." "First duty: To work. From each according to his strengths."[89] Cabet's great passion was equality—to the point of totalitarianism. In the imaginary capital of Icaria there were neither masters nor servants; everyone was a worker, all professions were equal, and all houses (including furniture) were alike, as was all clothing. The same schedule governed the lives of Icarians in strict discipline from 5 a.m. until lights out at 10 p.m. This classless, stateless society had neither prisons nor money, and the people were sovereign, sharing all their property.

Cabetism, which Engels described as a pioneering initiative despite its crudeness,[90] was of course just a stand-in for the entire communist movement targeted by Brierre de Boismont, whose aversion to workers' movements would culminate in 1871 when he urged the establishment of special asylums for Communards. Yet what he refused to see—so blinded was he by class hatred—were those things the communist ideal in fact shared with the utopian asylum. The connection was obvious to someone like Dr. Jacques Bouchet, a disciple of Esquirol who headed an asylum in Nantes. Communism provided a direct source of inspiration, even if it was hard for Bouchet to admit as much in the agitated context of 1848.

> It is with regret that I am obliged to employ language that has become political at the present moment, but it is true that the very principles of communism are applied to treatment of the insane. The reason is simple: most of the time the illness is merely the result of the principle of individualism taken to an extreme in the context of family, property, work, and freedom. The remedy is therefore to be found in an opposite system, that is to say the renunciation of self and the regularization of activity guided by an external mind. Struggle ceases under the authority of these principles, the brain and its faculties steadily enter a state of rest. A communist feeling steadily seeps into thoughts and acts, putting a halt to individualist impulses and the deviations they cause. But they are merely suspended; if the bonds restraining them are suddenly removed, they will all reappear.[91]

It is no coincidence that Bouchet made this comment in an article devoted to putting mental patients to work. It is worth recalling Pinel's recommendations on the discipline of work, the measures advocated by Pierre-Paul Royer-Collard at Charenton, and the subsequent initiative in 1834 by Guillaume Ferrus to set up a farm, called Sainte-Anne, where patients from Bicêtre could work the land. In 1848 asylums were being transformed into a huge machine to right wrongs, to discipline bodies, and to guide minds in a determined effort to combat the "individualism" of patients often reproached for their "egotism." Psychiatric "communism," an image Bouchet employed not only "with regret" but in a sense that went beyond the political context of his day, in fact represented a very precocious complicity between psychiatry and totalitarian impulses.

Meanwhile Brierre de Boismont, as the director of a private nursing home, preferred to attack the utopians in a sniggering tone by padding his politicomedical nomenclature with concepts such as "monomaniacs with passionate attractions" for whom "work becomes an endless party" and who go home in the evening "to fairy-tale palaces" (a clear allusion to Fourier's phalansteries). This was the setting for a new, loving world that advocated the liberation of women and sexual freedom. "Earthly paradise exists; women, endowed with a spouse, a genitor, lovers and successives [*sic*], sing of bliss time and time again. There is no point in the envious crying 'Orgy,' for the good times have finally arrived."[92] Brierre de Boismont's pitiful procession of pathological democrats, composed of the demented (politically fickle and stricken by amnesia), the imbeciles, and the idiots, ends with the "worshippers of all the spurious ideas abounding in this world."[93]

Although the significance of his article should not be exaggerated (it was, after all, just a book review), Brierre de Boismont here carried out what Groddeck failed to provide: a "psychiatric" interpretation of left-wing sympathizers about 1848. Obviously his ironic approach and diagnostic parodies seem to preclude an overly literal reading of a text that is closer to a humorous sketch than a scholarly article. Yet is that really so? In 1871, surveying the ruins of the Commune, Brierre de Boismont directly expressed his deepest convictions, demanding that, in retrospect, they be taken seriously:

> Twenty-one years ago, I reviewed a German booklet titled *Morbus democraticus* for the *Annales Médico-psychologiques* (1850). I myself had been struck by the seriousness of the events of 1848, for at the time I was living in faubourg Saint-Antoine, and in my analysis I pointed to the democratic, egalitarian, and social insanity, with its maniacs, its monomaniacs, its lunatics and its idiots, whom I had been able to study in depth among the workers of that neighborhood. . . . Study of that world led me to view it as a collection of the worst sort

> of madmen, far more dangerous than criminal lunatics. The distinctive quality of the latter involves killing and robbing a few individuals and burning a few buildings, whereas that of the former is to murder an entire society and burn down all the buildings on which a nation prides itself.[94]

The democratic disease was therefore a serious, chronic illness. And it was a disease rife among one class, the proletariat, whose pathological, anatomical, and symptomatic profile was being closely monitored by the bourgeois science of psychiatry with an alarm that expressed, in Louis Chevalier's words, "the truly racial nature of social antagonisms."[95]

ASYLUMS FOR THE WRETCHED

In 1848 the working class represented 40 percent of the people living in Paris, whose population of one million had doubled in the preceding half century owing to industrialization and the rural exodus. The workday was limited to twelve hours—in often harsh, unhealthy conditions—reduced to eight hours for children, who could legally begin work at age eight. In 1851, however, a new law allowed for many exceptions. The workday often stretched to fifteen hours, for an average salary that rose from 3.82 francs per day in 1847 to 4.99 francs in 1871 in Paris, where wide disparities were prevalent depending on the trade, age, and sex of the worker. This 30 percent hike in pay over twenty-five years made Paris wages the highest in Europe, apart from England. Income was nevertheless totally insufficient given the explosion in rents caused by Baron Haussmann's urban redevelopment (which pushed workers toward the outskirts and forced them to move constantly) and skyrocketing food prices (up 50 percent for wine and oil, 80 percent for butter, cheese, and eggs, and 100 percent for meat in the years 1847–57 alone). Periodic structural unemployment hit household incomes and made a decent living impossible. In 1860 half of workers were in debt and were threatened with debtors' prison. Between 1860 and 1868, the number of poor who registered at the Montmartre charity office tripled.[96]

Whether labeled poverty, destitution, or pauperism, the condition was a major scourge of the nineteenth century. Hospitals and poorhouses witnessed it every day when confronted with bodies shattered by fatigue and indigence. So did mental asylums, as illustrated by the case study that opens *Les ouvriers des deux mondes* (Laborers of both worlds), a major survey headed by Frédéric Le Play based on information gathered in 1856. The study focused on a traditional journeyman carpenter in Paris, who suffered from congestion of the lungs from frequent outdoor work, as well as five injuries to his upper limbs. His wife—who had given birth to six children in eight years, four of whom died young from intestinal ailments—suffered from nervous fits associated with hysteria. She first worked at the trying job of metal polisher, which triggered paralysis of her right arm, then sold vegetables in the market. The carpenter's brother suffered from softening of the brain and had lost his reason; his deceased sister had been an epileptic, and his father's life was cut short by alcohol. The couple were living with their two children in a two-room apartment totaling 210 square feet in the heart of today's Marais district.[97]

On average, 60 percent of the inmates at Bicêtre and La Salpêtrière came from the working class, including craftsmen, day laborers, and salvagers such as water carriers and rag-and-bone men. The other residents were junior office workers, small tradesmen, servants, and vagabonds, almost all of them scarred by the vicissitudes of work and life. Women, above all the single and widowed ones, were the first to suffer the consequences of insecurity and destitution, which often brought them, as a last resort, to La Salpêtrière. In 1851 the hospital's head physician, Trélat, decided to compile a set of observations dating back to as early as 1820. This register, now in poor condition, contains 330 cases and provides a unique overview of thirty years of madness and poverty among Parisian women, for some of whom the asylum was their sole outlook.

Jeanne C. was admitted on October 19, 1796, to La Salpêtrière, where she died in September 1852. "Admitted at age twelve, she spent her entire life in the hospital, unable to do anything other than shred linen or unravel wool."[98] Marie Marguerite V., a seamstress admitted at age fifty-seven on October 25, 1821, and transferred elsewhere on December 15, 1852, had a "weak intellect; she knows how to read a little, and replies fairly well, can talk, but has always been unable to take charge of herself. She ran after men; has no support, no one comes to see her. . . . If she is harassed in any way, she begins to rave: 'One day she was offered three francs a day for washing chemises of victims of the guillotine, but she didn't want to earn her bread in that way.'"[99] The entry for Désirée M., admitted on October 2, 1822, reads: "Congenital intellectual weakness. She sews fairly well and sticks to her work; but cannot count above twenty, does not know what month or year it is; cannot take charge of herself and is one of the unfortunately overly numerous beings for whom confinement is required by the lack of a prosperous family."[100]

Although profession was not always indicated, the most commonly represented trades included thirty-five seamstresses, sixteen domestic servants, fourteen laundresses, thirteen day workers, ten linen maids, seven prostitutes, six embroiderers, five cleaning women, four passementerie makers, three teachers, three gardeners, three fruit and vegetable sellers, three lace sellers, three vest makers, and three boot stitchers. Others worked with needle and thread in various ways (spinner, feather worker, mattress maker), in the wood or metal trades (gilder, polisher, burnisher), in the garment industry (makers of caps, suspenders, gloves, corsets), or were small merchants or peddlers (from flowers to oranges).

This socioprofessional breakdown altered little during the nineteenth century. By the end of the Second Empire, seamstresses (estimated to number 100,000 in Paris at the time) were still the most numerous profession in La Salpêtrière, where the proletariat constituted an overwhelming majority. For these women, who arrived there bereft of any other refuge, the physician personified the dominant class on two levels—bourgeois and male. He was the judge, the protector, the embodiment of law, knowledge, and charity. Intimidation, which was an integral part of mental therapy, rested directly upon this unstated social difference, immediately perceived through the dress, bearing, gaze, gestures, and knowledge of the "doctor" in relation to his patient. As Esquirol, who treated some of the patients included in this register, commented almost ingenuously in 1818:

> Circumstances have allowed me to be the physician in an asylum where only poor patients are received and at the same time to head a private home that takes only rich patients. In the private home, I enjoy greater influence in the women's wing than in the men's; and this influence is even more marked among the female patients at La Salpêtri-

ère. The inmates there see me in a station much superior to their own; thus on several occasions I have managed to return a patient to reason, almost like magic, by granting her an interview in my office; some of them showed signs of a cure right at that very instant.[101]

Fifty years later, Dr. Voisin reported the case of a patient at La Salpêtrière who would weep when she came near him, saying that she did not dare come toward him because she was not "dressed well enough to go into society."[102]

Throughout the century poverty wreaked its havoc, a sinister trace of which can be glimpsed, in anamorphosis, in the registers of the asylums. "This overexcitement seems to be produced by excessive poverty and destitution. She ate the remains of her child," indicates an 1853 report on a woman abandoned by her lover, whom the physician apparently hesitated to diagnose as maniacally insane.[103] In 1857 Dr. Jean-Étienne Mitivié noted with annoyance that one patient was "not truly insane. The asylum should not be burdened with these old people who require nothing more than a good infirmary."[104] The seventy-six-year-old woman in question died two months later of senile dementia. The same doctor wrote in 1860: "Does not seem to be insane; this woman has been very weakened by poverty, hardship, and a stubborn cough."[105] Jacques-Henri Girard de Cailleux, meanwhile, diagnosed a woman who attempted suicide in 1868 as having a "melancholic attitude: feelings of fear at not being able to provide for her family, at total destitution; despair."[106] In 1869 Voisin was even more explicit regarding another patient: "Is in a pronounced state of cachexia; cannot use her limbs; but *is not insane*, and her admission here is as contrary to the law as many other admissions that I have already reported."[107] Dr. Prosper Lucas summed up another case in 1871: "Fear of not having work; worried about poverty; suicidal ideas; genuflections."[108]

Even more chilling than these desperate salvage operations was the detectable rise in *deliberate* internments that imbued "asylum" with its meaning of final refuge. The pit of despair is easy to sense here. "Arrested after smashing a shop window in order to get herself arrested; vague persecutions, she is being prevented from taking a job; she wants certificates from former employers that she can't find; delusions dating several months back," wrote Dr. Charles Lasègue in 1863.[109] The following year a young woman was "arrested at her request. Refuses to

FIGURE 30. Antoine Wiertz, *Hunger, Madness, Crime* (1853–54). Oil on canvas. Musée Antoine Wiertz, Brussels, Belgium. Belgian artist Antoine Wiertz was an advocate of democracy who depicted the horror of nineteenth-century living conditions. Here a woman driven insane by destitution is reduced to eating her own child, whose leg is being cooked in the pot. Photograph: Hermann Buresch. Photograph © bpk, Berlin/Art Resource, New York.

work or to return to her parents. Insistent requests to be rehired. Declares that she will misbehave until she is taken back."[110] In 1870 Trélat commented on a forty-six-year-old linen maid: "Today the patient is a hypochondriac. She nevertheless answers accurately and does not want to leave the establishment."[111] That same year the doctor noted the case of a fifty-five-year-old woman with no profession: "This patient, on whom we have no information, is sad and weepy, saying she has been told several times that she can leave but that she does not feel in a position to go."[112]

In the light of this litany of unhappiness, madness seems to be nothing more than the ultimate expression of helplessness. It is impossible not to feel moved by certain cases, such as a thirty-year-old woman afflicted by "hysterical mania dominated by the idea of being poisoned." She was convinced that people wanted to harm her and that "there must be a victim"—indeed, according to her husband, she "married before the age of sixteen and has had ten children and fourteen miscarriages."[113] Although the asylum was indeed a tool of social control designed to put prostitutes and "rebellious" (or "insubordinate") women who "refused to follow any rules" back on the straight path, it was also a place where women who had had lost everything, from means of subsistence to the most basic physical integrity, came to await death.

Given this context, the situation at La Salpêtrière was particularly dramatic because surrounding hospitals shamelessly unloaded their most awkward cases on it. "The woman named X was sent to us from Hôtel-Dieu in the most critical state—cold, almost no pulse, heavy diarrhea, cyanotic hands, displaying the most alarming signs. She will die. / As I am writing this report, I have learned that the patient has died. How could they order and conduct her transfer in such a condition?" wondered a powerless Trélat in real time in 1866.[114] The situation worsened when Sainte-Anne Hospital opened in 1867. Inaugurated with great pomp by Empress Eugénie, this mental clinic, designed to serve as a central admissions office for dispatching cases within Paris, found itself on the front lines of poverty: "insufficient nourishment" and "total indifference to his situation past, present, and future" are phrases that recur again and again right from the first register.[115] Overwhelmed but wishing to publish model accounts, Saint-Anne apparently exploited its prerogatives to shift the burden to other asylums. Three times in 1868 alone Voisin, the physician on La Salpêtrière's ward number one, complained about the arrival of patients with contusions to the head, or gangrene, or pleurisy, but not displaying the least signs of insanity. This behavior was "contrary to the most basic sense of charity" and was solely designed "to lower the mortality statistics at Sainte-Anne."[116] Many of these women, hardly in a condition to bear transfer, died on arrival or in a matter of days.

Beyond a shadow of a doubt, poverty functioned like an enthusiastic procuress for public asylums during the Second Empire. The victims it dispatched to La Salpêtrière usually suffered from a persecution

FIGURE 31. Jules Gaildreau, *Hydrotherapy*, Sainte-Anne Hospital, Paris (1869). Engraving. The Sainte-Anne mental hospital, which opened in 1867, actively practiced hydrotherapy, based on water's three main effects: sedative, tonic, and revulsive. Only doctors were allowed to prescribe showers and baths in closed tubs (see also figure 32), in which patients might remain up to ten hours a day. Photograph © Roger-Viollet/The Image Works.

FIGURE 32. French school, *Bath Therapy Room*, Sainte-Anne Hospital, Paris (1869). Engraving. Photograph © Roger-Viollet/The Image Works.

complex combined with a "compensatory" delusion designed to counteract the threat to their existence. Delusions were thus converted into a consoling refuge. The most wretched of women suddenly found themselves to be employers, duchesses, millionaires. Madness represented the final rampart against the horror of a hopeless situation. "People owe her billions, but a lawsuit is challenging her right to the money. She is the wife of Louis-Napoleon, Rothschild serves as her intendant, etc., etc."[117] A baker's wife could forget her sorrows because she owned "all of Paris, all of France, all of Europe."[118] A corset maker spent her time writing offensive letters to government bureaucrats, the Senate, and the emperor in order to lay claim to an inheritance of 900,000 francs that she had allegedly been deprived of.[119] Women not yet entirely over the edge might travel from the provinces to Paris, where they simply headed to the Tuileries Palace to petition the emperor to remedy their fate, requesting "an authorization to beg"[120] or a "change of employment."[121] They would be arrested and sent to the asylum, where they remained at best for a few months before recovering their freedom—and their unchanged, impoverished lives.

Appeals to the emperor were even more common among the inmates at Bicêtre. Each month the police arrested more or less manic individuals who presented themselves at the gates of the imperial palace to ask for a job, to establish their right to the crown, to demand an important position in the government, or to denounce a plot, thanks to a mission God had imparted to them. In delusions that nominally involved the emperor (ranging between 2 and 5 percent of all cases from year to year), Napoleon III represented the ultimate recourse; he was simultaneously the answer to, the witness of, and, occasionally, the cause of the people's destitution. Delusional discourse—persecution and megalomania, recriminations and praise—was marked by great confusion when it dwelled on the economic situation. "He is a count, he is rich, he has no position";[122] "Everyone will turn to dust, he will create a new world, he will dress in gemstones like the emperor";[123] "God and the Blessed Virgin . . . have told him that the emperor will pay his debts."[124] One man came to borrow four hundred francs from the emperor, another wanted eight million in cash, while a third claimed that people were preventing him from getting a job and that the emperor was part of the conspiracy.

On occasion, financial worries could take a political turn. Insults, seditious comments, and shouts of "Long live the Republic!" or "Down with the emperor!" sporadically served as markers of a "rant" often triggered by alcohol with its tongue-loosening effect. "Ideas of reform," like "political plans" and "social concerns," were symptoms of dominant anxieties whose details were rarely indicated. We never learn exactly what was said by a twenty-nine-year-old clockmaker arrested in 1860 on top of the column in Place Vendôme, "making a speech and haranguing the crowd," but whose ideas, according to Dr. Lasègue, "were not very coherent."[125] Nor do we know how an old man "took revenge on General Cavaignac in June 1848."[126] Some patients heard voices, like the pork butcher who was told that "we all live in a republic, everyone is free and everyone can have and carry off whatever they can take."[127] One day laborer, meanwhile, was convinced he was being "summoned to rule the world, to obtain bread at low cost,"[128] while a landowner who had recently arrived in Paris asserted that "the republicans are asking him to become dictator."[129] Insanity was talking politics, whether insisting on justice for workers, on lower prices for wheat, or on an end to shortages. And above all it was talking about living conditions and the angst of the lower classes in Paris during the Second Empire.

In this respect, reasons for arrest provide more information than many disquisitions on the torments of extreme poverty. Theft (usually for something pathetic like a blanket, an apple, a sausage, or a pair of boots), insolvency, and bankruptcy were rivaled by the increasing incidence of alcoholism, while certain motives for arrest ring out like heartrending cries of alarm: "Arrested in Nantes for tearing down a sign forbidding begging";[130] "farmer, arrested lying on a bench, said he'd lost everything he owned and had come to Paris to ask the emperor for a job";[131] a sculptor "arrested at his own request, declaring himself without a home and without resources";[132] a joiner "who fired a pistol at a policeman and said he wanted to go to prison in order to have work";[133] "chimney sweep, arrested wearing a sign on which he had written that he demanded work and his rights as a citizen . . . his wife said he was worn out from overwork."[134]

We should not misconstrue things, however, or let the magnifying effect of the archives at Bicêtre and La Salpêtrière, asylums reserved for the underprivileged, blur the true socioeconomic picture of mental illness. Madness afflicted every level of society, making no exceptions and showing no preferences—an observation that remains valid today, as demonstrated by the variety of categories of population affected by schizophrenia. On the other hand, what the nineteenth-century records at Bicêtre and La Salpêtrière clearly reveal—despite the Second Empire's wish to halt and to hide poverty, unemployment, and vagrancy by increasing the number of workhouses (which had nearly disappeared under the July monarchy) from twenty-one in 1853 to forty in 1870[135]—is the confusion between psychiatric hospital and penal institution, between charity and punishment. The physicians who received countless patients sent by the police reluctantly confessed as much. In a moment of discouragement in 1866, Dr. Pierre Berthier ended his diagnosis of a penniless seventy-year-old man "in an infantile state" with the comment that "it is deplorable that the Bicêtre asylum is tending to become a poorhouse."[136] The tendency was all the more deplorable in that poverty, in return, was being linked to deviance in an inevitable process that saw fringe existences sprout via parthenogenesis.

This was the political, economic, and socially stigmatizing context in which the "democratic disease" should be understood. A final bout of fever would erupt with the Paris Commune of 1871, bringing a century of French revolutions to a close.

FIVE * Reason in Revolt

On July 19, 1870, subsequent to the famous "Ems telegram" rewritten by Otto von Bismarck himself in order to provoke a clash, France declared war on Prussia. In a matter of weeks German troops were pouring into France. A crushing defeat at Sedan on September 2 signaled the collapse of the Second Empire; on September 4 a provisional government proclaimed a new republic, but the enemy army continued to advance through fields and towns, so that by September 19 Paris was encircled. The Prussians set up a blockade. Paris fought back, holding out despite cold weather and famine, but on January 28, 1871, the government of national defense headquartered in Versailles capitulated in the name of France. Feeling betrayed by their leaders in Versailles, the people of the capital rose up and on March 18 founded the Paris Commune, simultaneously an insurrectionist movement and a revolutionary government. The Commune survived until it was crushed by forces loyal to Versailles during the "bloody week" of May 21–28, 1871, when much of Paris was deliberately burned down.

The period 1870–71 constitutes an uninterrupted whole even though the Franco-Prussian War was not the same as the internecine fighting, nor is a blockade the same as an insurrection. Yet as different in nature as they may be, the events that occurred in Paris between September 19, 1870, and May 28, 1871, must be viewed here in a historical continuity that alone makes sense of the phenomenon of an accumulation of psychological traumas. This can be read not only between the lines of asylum archives, where dreadful fears of enemy bombardment and incendiary riots inextricably overlap, but also in the intense debates in the *Annales Médico-psychologiques* that continued to question, several years after the conflict, the relation between war, insurrection, and madness, even as they once again discussed the controversial scourge of the day, alcoholism.

The ravages of war and civil strife hit the asylums directly. As Prussian troops approached Paris, La Salpêtrière closed its outpatient clinics and freed up 240 beds; Bicêtre was handed over to the military authorities and totally evacuated, its patients dispersed to a dozen provincial establishments. Saint-Anne, a hospital founded in 1867 to receive mental patients of both sexes, transferred over two-thirds of its patients to various asylums in the region in order to make room, thus becoming the only hospital in Paris to deal with cases of madness; its records are consequently the main archival source documenting mental illness in the capital during this period.[1] And it did not treat all madness, only the most urgent cases, since some types of admission were denied, notably epileptics and idiots, condemned to wander the streets of Paris. Indeed, the asylum was soon overwhelmed. There were shortages of food, medication, and even pharmaceuticals (employees of the city's pharmacy department having been drafted in large numbers). From November 1870 onward, the spread of smallpox and extremely cold weather (8.6°F on Christmas Day) increased the mortality rate in a city that lacked everything including food and fuel. The rising death rate affected mental patients in considerable numbers, mortality in the asylum being primarily due to shortages provoked by the blockade. Many patients arrived "in an advanced state of cachexia" according to a statistical study of Sainte-Anne's admission records, which yielded the following figures:

Deaths in 1870:
226 men, of whom 170 were admitted within the month
108 women, of whom 80 were admitted within the month

Deaths in 1871:
246 men, of whom 153 were admitted within the month
194 women, of whom 124 were admitted within the month[2]

In January 1871 the Sainte-Anne neighborhood was the target of intensified bombardment. Enemy fire caused just one death at the asylum, which used its cellars to shelter a particularly vulnerable population whose insanity and fits of convulsions were sometimes triggered before internment by the shock of having a shell land nearby. Might that mean there was a type of madness specific to the events of war?

JOAN OF ARC AND GROANING PANOPHOBICS

Long before Freud identified "war neuroses" after World War I, disorders related to violent shocks and war had been variously described in medical literature. Surgeons appointed to Napoleon's Grande Armée identified a "narrow escape syndrome" in which the whistle of a cannonball could paralyze an infantryman; following early train crashes, a concomitant notion of "traumatic neurosis" was elaborated in both England and France; the siege of Sebastopol in the Crimean War (1854), the battle of Solferino during the French campaign in Italy (1859), and the American Civil War (1861–65) all sparked accounts and studies of syndromes such as "soldier's heart" (or "irritable heart"), describing "neurovegetative manifestations of war trauma."[3]

In the fall of 1870 Paris indeed found itself in a war situation, or more precisely a state of siege. The civilian population was trapped and famished. The mass psychosis of a besieged people was dubbed "obsidional fever" [*la fièvre obsidionale*], a term apparently used mainly by military authorities and literati.[4] Physicians referred instead to what Benedict-Augustin Morel attempted to identify by the name "groaning panophobic insanity" (from *pan*, "all" and *phobia*, "fear, dread," meaning dread of everything). Characterized by intense anxiety expressed through continual groaning and sometimes spasmodic reactions triggered by constant fright, this kind of insanity might even manifest itself as imitating death, to escape imagined torments. It primarily afflicted women who, thrust into an unbearable angst, were convinced they had been ruined, had been sentenced to death, or were about to be tortured or burned at the stake. The illness was not new, but war supposedly "increased the number of victims of terrifying impressions to unprecedented proportions."[5]

At Sainte-Anne, lypemania (or melancholia), including groaning panophobics, was the leading illness diagnosed in women, afflicting 33.23 percent of female patients in 1870 and 42.52 percent in 1871. These were astronomical proportions, especially when compared with men suffering from melancholia, representing only 14.45 percent of patients in 1870 and 15.78 percent in 1871.[6] A peak was reached between June and September 1871, when ideas of persecution, anxieties over inability to earn a living, and uncontrollable fears were at their most intense. Similar statistics could be noted at La Salpêtrière in the months following its reopening. The terrors of the Commune overlapped with the torments of war, siege, and hardships in a tangle impossible to unravel. Prussian shells were replaced by incendiary flames, the horrors of siege were joined by those of civil war, and famine was aggravated by alcoholism. "She sees men armed with rifles who want to kill her," wrote Dr. Valentin Magnan about a thirty-one-year-old passementerie maker. She saw "policemen coming to arrest her, she saw a lion, fireworks, red cannon balls. . . . This patient was already treated in June 1870 for alcoholic delirium with suicidal tendencies."[7]

Doctors unanimously observed that war plunged women into despair and thrust men into maniacal agitation. The latter teemed with battle plans and martial schemes, especially sufferers of general paresis (representing 22.12 percent of the male population in Saint-Anne in 1870), who outdid one another in imagining all kinds of paths to victory. "They will blanket France with fortresses, cast cannons with extraordinary range, surround Paris with unbreachable ramparts. One of them believes he has come up with a system of dirigible balloons that can carry explosive machines destined to destroy all the German armies in a single blow . . . ; they devise sure means of getting abundant provisions into the city, or else to make succulent food from the most indigestible substances."[8] At Charenton, despite the laconic quality of the records during that period, we come across three patients admitted in November 1870 in a similar state of rapture. One "want[ed] to leave the asylum to become president of the republic," another "won battles and killed 40,000 Prussians, etc.," while a third "claim[ed] to be capable of driving off the enemy army all on his own."[9]

This perhaps looks like male braggadocio versus female faintheartedness, but such conclusions need to be qualified. The first patients admitted to Sainte-Anne in the months following the outbreak of war displayed a nearly inverse trend. "He is afraid of being taken for a Prussian and shot," reads a report on one man,[10] while another "believes he sees Prussians everywhere, and constantly runs off to flee them."[11]

The register for female patients, meanwhile, reveals delusions full of patriotic pride and an unexpectedly poetic audacity. "She is France's heroine," reads the comment on a fifty-one-year-old seamstress. "She has revived all of history, has reconciled kings; she is Saint Anne in person, daughter of the wandering Jew, in search of her father, etc., etc."[12] Meanwhile, Dr. Lucas reported that a forty-seven-year-old peddler of trinkets was "the second Joan of Arc, whose mission was to stop the bloodshed; she has to drive back the Prussians by throwing banknotes and pepper in their eyes. It was their capture of Wissembourg, her hometown, that disturbed her mind."[13]

The reference to Saint Anne, even within an asylum of the same name, was less common than reference to Joan of Arc. It was in 1869 that the question of canonizing the maid of Orléans arose (a process that finally culminated in 1920), once historian Jules Michelet had turned Joan into a "lay saint," an incarnation of patriotic feeling within the republican pantheon. Many women who, like Joan, came from modest backgrounds identified with the heroic soldier and martyr on whom the fate of France depended. These women, noted Magnan, "belong to the working class, have little education, and are of very ordinary intelligence" but believe they have been summoned to repeat her role. "'God assigned them the task of saving the country,' and they calmly accepted everything that happened to them as trials designed to reveal the providential nature of their mission, reinforced by hallucinations. In their speech, in their words, there was sometimes a kind of sincerity so confident that at other periods it would have drawn the attention of crowds."[14] Joan was adopted as an emblem even by men, such as one patient who inscribed the name of France's new patron saint on his flag. In a letter dated September 23, 1870, he wrote to General Louis Jules Trochu, the head of the government of national defense, that "If the government of national defense adopts my ideas, I hope to lead the French army and citizens to a striking victory in a vigorous attack at night, composed of wonderful shouts uttered simultaneously by us all: *In the name of God and Joan of Arc, death to the Prussians!*"[15]

This crusading spirit did not carry all before it, however. According to Henri Legrand du Saulle, the doctor at the holding cells at Paris police headquarters, the hardships that Parisians suffered triggered depressive forms of madness among patients who displayed all the features of "physiological wretchedness."[16] Yet most of these "delusions from hunger" arose *after* the armistice with Prussia, even though food began reappearing in the markets by February 1871. "They have neither energy, nor appetite, nor desires. Their organism has profoundly deteriorated, their loss of weight is striking, their intelligence inert."[17] This sudden anorexia after the harshest of shortages is an eloquent expression of the psychological collapse of some Parisians following military defeat, just as a rejection of that capitulation was the starting point for the Commune.

JACKALS, MAGPIES, MONKEYS, AND ARSONISTS

On March 10, 1871, the National Assembly, which had taken refuge in Versailles, voted to end the moratorium on payment of rents, debts, and other financial transactions, at the same time halting pay for the national guard. This series of measures asphyxiated laborers, craftsmen, and petty merchants among a population already obliged to bear the draconian conditions of the armistice and to endure the shame of a capitulation felt to be treasonous. The local watch committees that had been organized during the siege began to talk of insurrection. The call for the establishment of a Commune in Paris, drafted as early as January 7 and disseminated via red posters plastered on the walls of the city, was evolving into a reality. Fearing the reaction of the people of Paris, Versailles leader Adolphe Thiers ordered the arrest of Auguste Blanqui on March 17 and dispatched the army to recover the artillery stationed in the neighborhoods of Belleville and Montmartre. But the residents felt that these cannons, financed through a national subscription, were their property, and they opposed the measure. Given the crowd of women and children blocking access, the troops who arrived in Montmartre on March 18 refused to obey orders: downing rifles, they began to fraternize with the people. It was the start of an uprising and proletarian revolution that gave birth to the Paris Commune, which would be bloodily crushed on May 28.

March 18 to May 28, 1871: between those two dates, the registers at the Sainte-Anne asylum recorded diagnoses day by day, constituting a strange seismograph of insanity during the Commune. In that two and a half months the asylum admitted 353 male and female patients, significantly below the average of 250 admissions per month when Sainte-Anne first opened, but almost perfectly balanced in terms of gender—176 women and 177 men.

What do the documents have to say about them?[18] Any analysis requires preliminary technical comment, notably concerning the difficulty of establishing pertinent and reliable statistics. How can the socioprofessional breakdown of patients be accurately determined? The vast disparities in professions and the vagueness of their descriptions makes classification awkward. Without knowing whether "jeweler" referred to an apprentice or the owner of a shop, it is impossible to decide whether someone was an employee, a craftsman, or a businessman. And was a fruit and vegetable seller a small businessman like a wine broker? Did a "railway employee" work in an office or on the roadbed? The line between laborers and craftsmen was extremely vague in the nineteenth century, and the registers never specify whether an upholsterer, for example, was a simple workshop hand or was self-employed, which would make him a craftsman or even a businessman—whereas craftswomen were automatically considered workshop hands, since female workshop owners were practically nonexistent. Despite these difficulties, it appears that the main socioprofessional categories of the men interned at Sainte-Anne during the Commune break down roughly as follows:

Craftsmen (30%) and manual workers (30%)	60%
Office workers, basic employees	20%
Small businessmen:	10%
Sundry (farmers, soldiers, 1 student, 1 concierge, 1 servant)	5%
Person of private means	0.5%

The first thing that leaps to the eye is the overwhelming majority of craftsmen and manual workers—the least privileged part of the population, which was also one that largely supported the Commune. Tailors, shoemakers, and upholsterers arrive at the head of this group, constituting 9 percent of all patients. In the ledgers for the male patients—unlike those for women—the doctors specified whether the patient was able to "read and write" and indicated his religion. "No education" was the case for 9 percent of them; 99 percent said they were "Catholic," while 1 percent were "Jewish."

In comparison, the picture of women internees is as follows:

Manual workers	45.5%
No profession	17%
Servants	13.6%
Profession not specified	9.7%
Small businesswomen	6.2%
Persons of private means	2.8%
Concierges	2.8%
Sundry (1 actress, 1 photographer, 1 teacher)	1.7%
Prostitute	0.6%

Here again the working class largely predominates. Seamstresses (14.2 percent), day laborers (7.9 percent), and laundresses (7.4 percent) alone accounted for 29.5 percent of the female population admitted during this period. The most notable feature, however, is the "no profession" category, which, when added to the "profession not specified" group, equals 26.7 percent, a contingent almost equal to the section above (and one that does not exist among the men). One-third of the "no profession" group was too old to work—an impoverished old age was primarily a woman's lot. Whereas among the men there was just one valet, the female servants number twenty-four, that is to say 13.6 percent of the total, another considerable difference, probably exacerbated by the fact that when the bourgeoisie fled Paris en masse, they often left female servants behind to look after the property.

A similar, perhaps even thornier, problem concerns the establishment of statistics on the etiology of the illnesses. At Sainte-Anne, patients first passed through the admissions office, where Dr. Magnan either drew up a "momentary certificate" and sent them to a ward appropriate to their sex or else decided to transfer them outside Paris. Prosper Lucas was the physician in charge of women, Henri Dagonnet handled the men. They would then establish a diagnosis that would not necessarily agree with Magnan's (for instance, an "alcoholic delirium" suddenly became a "maniacal condition"). Just to complicate matters, Lucas and Dagonnet would not always employ the same terms or follow the same priorities, sometimes mentioning the category of illness (mania, melancholy, dementia, etc.) or the symptom (persecution complex, hallucinations, etc.). In many instances "lypemania" might be complicated by a "maniacal condition," or "dementia" by "subacute alcoholism," with no indication of which outweighed the other. Any attempt to draw up a coherent picture is thus doomed to failure.

Here we will therefore rely on the overall figures, in percentages, given by Bouchereau and Magnan for the year 1871.[19]

	Men (%)	Women (%)
Maniacal insanity	4.96	8.50
Melancholia	15.78	42.52
General paresis	18.79	8.31
Dementia	19.41	23.27
Epilepsy	14.09	9.06
Alcoholism	25.88	5.70

The remaining cases involved hysteria, chorea, and idiocy in individual patients not included by the two physicians in their percentages. Among the figures above, two stand out: the melancholia among women (as mentioned above) and the alcoholism among men (which topped the nosological charts, a rank it would retain into the twentieth century).[20] The percentage of alcoholics admitted to Bicêtre, for example, continued to rise throughout the period of the Second Empire, going from 12.78 percent in 1855 to 25.24 percent in 1862. At Sainte-Anne, Dr. Louis Gustave Bouchereau and Magnan published comparative statistics for the periods of March–June 1870 and March–June 1871 showing that, despite official propaganda, the Commune did not provoke a morbid inflation in alcoholic delirium (21.2 percent of patients diagnosed as alcoholic in 1870 as against 22.6 percent in 1871). The month of March 1871 even recorded a drop compared with the previous year.[21]

In contrast, during the Commune there was a dramatic rise in cases of delusion related to current events, whether they involved the trauma of war or of insurrection. This observation seemed to pertain primarily to Paris. Ludger Lunier's vast survey of all of France turned up only twenty-seven cases related to the war and blockade and a mere three cases connected to the Commune,[22] but at Sainte-Anne in Paris itself—the heart of the battle—the registers were thick with allusions to the events.

Proportions are nevertheless hard to evaluate: What criteria should be employed? To keep things straightforward, I counted all delusional states that included terms directly and specifically related to current events (fear of shells, of Prussians, of the Versailles troops, or delusions involving food, firing squads, arson, etc.). The results came to 25 percent of total cases for men and 24 percent for women. The proportion is all the higher in that they include only delusions that were specifically *mentioned* or *detailed*—for all we know, a given patient suffering from "maniacal insanity with hallucinations" had visions of civil war that the doctor did not bother to report. By way of comparison—although perhaps unfair, given the difference in context—recall that Esquirol estimated that 2.3 percent of the patients at Charenton went mad owing to the "political events" of 1830.

Nothing better expresses the state of mind of these men and women caught in a nightmare of history than the long list of their delusions, one after the after. Take the registers for female patients: "visions of ghosts, flames, cats, insects"; "convinced she is . . . pursued by armed soldiers"; "thinks she will die, saw buildings burning all around her"; "hears voices at night, the cries of children, bugles—she is being magnetized, enervated, annihilated"; "snakes, smoke, fire"; "visions of animals, flames, and smoke"; "fits of political agitation, she wants to die for France"; "she saw ghosts and animals . . . she glimpsed wolves, lions, jackals, magpies and ravens"; "she burned the devil."[23] And on it goes: "runs, at night, in the gardens, and during the day in the church, armed with her husband's rifle, in order to show herself to her enemies"; "she is accused of being a Prussian, of betraying France"; "she is accused of being a Prussian spy"; "obsessed with mediating between the two sides in the civil war, with a mania for giving passersby letters recommending these ends"; "relapse caused by the civil war and the explosion of a shell on her home"; "apparitions of ghosts, cats, rats, spiders, and all kinds of animals. . . . *she can taste cat in her mouth*"; "she constantly repeats the pained phrase, 'Oh my God, they're still firing!'"; "she sees dogs, rats"; "she will be shot, guillotined, her son will be taken."[24]

An overwhelming majority of these delusions involved persecution related to a war that, for Parisians, was not yet over.[25] The burning buildings of the Commune revived memories of the siege with its appalling hardships. The unusually high presence of animals in hallucinations was obviously related to the scarcity caused by the blockade in the winter of 1870–71. Having quickly run out of meat, Paris began eating horses, dogs, cats, and rats, then turned to the animals in the zoo—hence the appearance of lions and jackals in patients' ravings. Lithographs publicized the deaths of two elephants, Castor and Pollux, butchered in late December; recipes were published on how to cook monkey, beaver, and raven. Psychological inhibitions had to be overcome in order to eat pets such as dogs or disgusting animals such as rats and snakes, not to mention apprehensions over ingesting the exotic meat of wild animals. All this supposed, of course, that people had the means to pay for meat: a chicken cost 60 francs, a cat 20 francs, and a rat 2 francs, while a sparrow cost 1.25—and a worker's daily wage was roughly 4 francs.[26] That the registers at Sainte-Anne should reflect the impact of such experiences is thus quite plausible. Several patients, on arriving at the asylum, admitted they had attempted suicide several times. One of them said she wanted "to escape the dreadful situation and poverty she experienced during the siege—she apparently went eleven days without food."[27]

Persecution complex with hallucinations involving animals was also predominant among male patients, although accompanied by maniacal delusions of grandeur: "he is accused of throwing fire bombs in order to destroy everything"; "he has been named a general, Flourens has put him in command, he is a millionaire, etc."; "he sees corpses, mutilated bodies, ruined weapons, is about to be engulfed by waves"; "he is generous and wants to make everyone happy, he will be promoted to every rank in the army, he knows everything about the events"; "believes he is surrounded by lions, jackals, and foxes who are determined to chase him"; "thinks he sees armed men who insult him, and insects in the food he is about to eat"; "people want to execute him"; "armed men are threatening him"; "speaks of a trip he took to the desert, and his discussions with a lion and various other animals"; "people accuse him of being a policeman, a papal soldier, and reproach is heaped upon him"; "he thought he was chased by men armed with knives; he saw birds, cats, and rats"; "the patient left his home [in the Seine-et-Oise region, north of Paris] with the conviction that he could put a stop to the civil war by coming and making the sign of the cross, an idea he got from God"; "is afflicted with inventive insanity, [having discovered] all kinds of ways to defend the cities"; "he will be promoted to colonel, marshal"; "he is called an informer, a spy, people are plotting against him, they are threatening to have him shot"; "he has written a history of the last religion, will be given a commission in the army, will head the moral movement of humanity."[28] Or again: "people insult him, constantly calling him an informer"; "people were threatening him, they wanted to arrest him and have him shot, he saw monkeys jump around and make faces."[29]

Apart from specific references to the civil war and to Gustave Flourens, the general in charge of defending revolutionary Paris, it is hard to determine whether the patients are referring to the Franco-Prussian war or to events associated with the Commune. No one knows whether the soldier, policeman, colonel, marshal, or general belonged to the regular army or the radical national guard. What such delusions primarily glorified was combat and confrontation with an idealism whose sole object seems to have been heroic virility, either exalted (by taking command) or found wanting (being taken for an informer), as strikingly summed up in the following comment: "He wants to be the head of the Republic; he is masculine and wants masculinity for all."[30]

In her memoirs, revolutionary activist Louise Michel reported that many Communards went mad in front of her eyes because of "the horror of the things they saw" during the fight to the death against the Versailles forces.[31] Meanwhile, the panic over being taken for an informer probably stemmed from the climate of denunciation encouraged by the Versailles authorities, who offered rewards for information on the whereabouts of members of the Commune and its central committee. To give a rough idea of the situation, the authorities received 379,823 anonymous written accusations between May 22 and June 13 alone.[32]

In the months that followed the "bloody week" of repression, Commune-related delusions decreased, falling from 25 percent to 12 percent of the patients at Sainte-Anne. Similarly, fewer people headed to the asylums, including Bicêtre and La Salpêtrière, which had just reopened. One of the reasons proposed for this drop is also the simplest—it has been estimated that 100,000 workers were killed, imprisoned, deported, or on the run when the Commune fell: one-quarter of the city's working-class population.[33]

Of the seventy female patients admitted to La Salpêtrière's first ward between September and December 1871, twenty-nine were diagnosed with melancholia accompanied by persecution complex, representing 41 percent.[34] The torment of the Prussian siege continued to haunt certain minds—one woman signed herself "Tom Thumb, general,"[35] while another claimed to be "the niece of a German countess, related to the duke of Saxony."[36] Joan of Arc was recalled to active duty: "she saw battles; voices told her she was destined to save France."[37] A spirit of revenge, combined with methods of denunciation, survived at Bicêtre: "he was promised one hundred thousand francs if he arrested Mr. von Bismarck."[38]

For the first time, however, the Commune was embodied in delusions. In other words, there was a delayed effect. During the Commune itself, delusions focused on war. After the Commune, delusion became insurrectional. Delusions? Maybe. What about a forty-eight-year-old seamstress who suffered from "enfeebled mental faculties" and was found wandering just outside Paris, whose persecution complex consisted of being called a *pétroleuse* (arsonist)? "They want to put her in prison, they douse her through the ceiling with vapors of sulfur and petrol [kerosene]."[39] For what should a twenty-three-year-old shirtmaker blame herself, her feverish state being due to "the probable distress at her husband's being sent to the [prison] hulks"?[40] Or how about a traveling female peddler who had been the object of slanderous comments and was accused of "having lit fires with kerosene?"[41]

The trade in cheap prints depicting the events of the Commune soon turned the *pétroleuses*—female arsonists—into a legend, largely fueled by a reactionary press that endlessly depicted tattered, unkempt women sowing destruction in their path as they tossed burning bottles of kerosene through basement windows. The fires that raged in Paris during the "bloody week" notably reduced to ashes the city hall, the Tuileries Palace, and the Cour des Comptes, helping to instill the somber myth of *pétroleuses* who were responsible for all the ills of Paris. It was they who ignited, fanned, and spread the disaster. They alone summed up the horror of "the Commune," the title of a Versailles-camp caricature that distorted Eugène Delacroix's *Liberty Leading the People* to portray a virago wearing a Phrygian cap and red classical-style tunic (from which spills a flabby breast), holding a torch in one hand and a watering can labeled *pétrole* in the other.

According to Prosper-Olivier Lissagaray—a participant in the uprising and one of its early historians—the myth of the *pétroleuses* was based on a rumor that resulted in hundreds of murders during the closing days of the bloody week. "Any woman poorly dressed or carrying a milk can, a flask, or an empty bottle was called a *pétroleuse*. With [her clothes] torn to shreds, she would be dragged to the nearest wall and finished off with a revolver."[42] Although a few of the approximately ten thousand women who participated in the uprising did take part in setting fires—usually in groups that included men—it has now been proved that *pétroleuses* were a fantasy (Louise Michel had always denied that they existed). The fantasy extended to all the women of the Commune, on whom partisans of "order" heaped abuse. Referring to the insurgents, Alexandre Dumas wrote, "We will say nothing of these animals out of respect for the women they resemble—once they are dead."[43] Edmond de Goncourt said they had the eyes of madwomen, while Maxime Du Camp, who admitted the falsity of the legend of *pétroleuses*, nevertheless felt that "nearly all the wretched women who fought for the Commune were what mental physicians would call 'ill.'"[44]

What the registers at Saint-Anne reflect is therefore not the impact of the deeds of the Commune but the powerful effect of political repression on the discourse of madness. First *pétroleuses* were compared to "madwomen"; then "madwomen," assuming their role of scapegoat, began accusing themselves of being *pétroleuses*. Internment therefore justified society's view of revolutionary women and made it official.

Politics entered the asylums. Octavie B., a servant, "tells soldiers to dig a hole in the ground and to shoot her on the spot, because she too wanted to die for the Commune!"[45] Forty-two-year-old Marie C. was "arrested for having been a Commune teacher in the first arrondissement" and suffered from maniacal insanity characterized by "emphatic tales, Latin quotations, prophecies, etc."[46] Eugène P., meanwhile, was committed to Charenton: "This patient was arrested for violent rebellion against policemen. He has already been treated in a mental home in Maréville. His mother had many fits of madness. His father has just been shot by the firing squad at La Roquette."[47] Contingents of Communards also filled private nursing homes. Madame Rivet, who ran the clinic founded by her father, Alexandre Brierre de Boismont, recounted the case of a wealthy widow, the well-educated owner of a manor, who was given to drinking absinthe and who had been arrested on a barricade with a "rifle still warm." She was taken to the Satory camp, where she was judged insane. Her declarations allegedly proved her "political madness": "I entered a wine shop, I sat at a table, I began to speak, and a circle gathered round. I warmed to my subject, the circle grew. Soon the enthusiasm was such that the room was packed;

La Femme, émancipée, repandant la lumière sur le monde.

FIGURE 33. Eugène Girard, *Emancipated Woman Lighting the World* (1871). Musée Carnavalet, Paris. Girard portrayed the Commune's *pétroleuses* (arsonists) as demented Furies, a view shared by the bourgeoisie and most psychiatrists. Photograph © Musée Carnavalet/Roger-Viollet/The Image Works.

people climbed on tables just to hear me. . . . I drew crowds all the more for being a Communard, true enough, but I was a convivial Communard. My phrases were well-turned, I electrified them, and there you have it."[48] This patient would later be transferred to an asylum in the provinces after having tried to win over to the feminist cause a woman committed by her husband.

Memories of 1848 were revived. At Bicêtre, the doctor hesitated over a patient who suffered from alcoholic fits and had escaped from Sainte-Anne, yet who "answered accurately" and "showed no sign of mental illness since his arrival"; an aggravating circumstance, however, was "an early bout [of madness] in 1848."[49] He would be discharged after three days. Similarly, Widow J., a sixty-two-year-old rag-and-bone woman suffering from chronic alcoholism and confused ideas of persecution, had already been treated in 1848 and "arrested for seditious cries."[50] Seditious cries, moreover, would change sides with the change in regime. Adolphe H., who went around shouting "Long live the emperor, long live the empress, and long live the crown prince!" was well aware of this. "He claims he is fulfilling a political role by shouting seditious statements; he just wants to get an idea of the mood of the people." Endowed with a talent for "raising apparitions for everyone" and an obvious sense of imagery, "he crisscrossed Paris to exhibit the imperial family, and at the Orient he made Hope appear in the form of an anchor."[51]

Such comments, which were too fragmentary to permit overall conclusions, called for further elucidation by psychiatric opinion. Physicians therefore played a key role—newspapers consulted them, and the government sought their expertise. Their opinions were all the more critical in that with a word they could prevent a deportation or a lifelong prison sentence. Thus starting in 1871 the *Annales Médico-psychologiques* regularly devoted some of its pages to the war and the Commune. This is the source we must turn to now in order to understand the stakes behind the debate.

HISTORY STUTTERS

Distinct yet linked, the Franco-Prussian War and the Commune were first addressed as early as the latter half of 1871 by Morel, who claimed he was performing "an act of patriotism" by challenging a book published by a German physician, Carl Stark.[52] Stark's book was titled *Die psychische Degeneration des französischen Volkes, ihr pathologischer Charakter, ihre Symptome und Ursachen* (The psychological degeneration of the French people, its pathological nature, its symptoms, and its causes). According to Stark, the brutality and horror of the war were to be attributed to a bastardized, decadent, and corrupt people whose native (and notorious) arrogance had become "a monomania, an *idée fixe*, a true delusion."[53] The French nation, always convinced that it was at the forefront of civilization, allegedly resembled a mental patient afflicted with "reasoning monomania" and suffering from "general paresis, lying on its pallet even as it proclaims that it is full of strength and health."[54] Crowning these humiliations, Stark expressed a physician's commiseration for a nation that had become a feeble organism. "The French," he wrote, "have a brain organized in a special fashion, and Huschke [another specialist] has shown that the weight of French brains is less than that of German brains; and, strangely, the brains of French horses are also lighter than those of German horses. Thus we should rejoice in the epithet of 'square heads' that the French inflict on us."[55]

Morel gagged at Stark's avalanche of insults. Born in Vienna in 1809, Morel felt true admiration for German science, which explains part of his obvious discomfort. The attack was all the more insufferable in that Stark employed a concept that Morel himself theorized—degeneracy—even as it exacerbated the rivalry between Berlin and Paris by taking aim at French scientific research, which Stark claimed was stricken with "intellectual degeneracy." Morel, his physician's honor wounded and his patriotism cut to the quick, mounted a pathetic defense that vaunted the talent of French artists compared with German philosophers, who had become impossible to understand. Alongside such arguments, which primarily served to underscore an inferiority complex, Morel also pointed out the absurdity of characterizing an entire nation as mentally ill when it was all of Europe and the times that were morally unwell.

Like all his compatriots, Morel had been humiliated by the military defeat. But above all he was ashamed of the spectacle presented to the world by the Commune, which prompted him to unearth a comment on 1848 by a German mental specialist, which Morel reported as though he agreed with it: "France, says Mr. Virchow, is an unruly nation that sparks revolutions, while Germany is a well-behaved nation that carries out reforms."[56] The Commune revived the endless debate over a convulsive, revolutionary France suffering from a chronic, endemic illness. That a new chapter in the tumultuous history of psychiatry's relation to revolution and nationalism had indeed opened was clear from the energy Morel devoted to challenging this unbearable picture: he insisted that Communards were not insane but were "monsters of a moral kind,"[57] lowlifes fully responsible for their acts. He even denounced, in coded language, the Marxist (hence German) origin of the Internationale: "You should be aware," thundered Morel in the direction of the enemy nation, "that when your soldiers watched with pleasure and satisfaction as the Vendôme column fell and Paris burned, millions of Frenchmen were ready to defend the civilization insulted and jeopardized by the revolutionary leaders from Europe who had gathered in our unfortunate capital. We know where they came from, which country gave birth to them, and which country harbors them. The mere names of the leaders of the Internationale reveal their roots. You will see them at work one day in your own cities and countrysides."[58]

This initial article could be considered, at least chronologically, the point of departure for a wider and more serious debate. In subsequent months that debate would try to decide—through studies and theoretical reasoning—what distinguishes mental illness from moral responsibility. In other words, it tried to answer the decidedly insoluble question, What is madness?

"History doesn't repeat itself—it stutters." This famous witticism, attributed to Karl Marx, might easily be applied to psychiatric debate following the events of the Commune. A polemic identical to the one in 1848 erupted, partly spurred by the same protagonists. In responding to the question of the impact that major political upheavals have on madness, psychiatrists roughly fell into two camps.

The first was illustrated by Morel, who challenged physicians to fit the "abominable crimes" the Communards were guilty of into a nosological framework. "Madness is an illness," he declared as early as June 6, 1871, in *Le Nouvelliste de Rouen*, "and a gulf separates it from crime and simple passion." The insurgents' "drunken faces" showed no trace of "the sacred stamp of disease, the *res sacra miser* of suffering, unaware beings."[59] By according them "awareness," Morel rehabilitated the rebels in terms of lucidity, the better to condemn them as dangerous delinquents.

The second camp considered Communards raving mad, suited only to be locked away without further ado. Brierre de Boismont was the loudest advocate of this position. His diagnosis did not stop with the "maniacs" who had led the Commune and were already rotting in the nation's prisons but extended to all their accomplices. "There are still fanatics who dream of remaking the world through workable schemes, these being the first elements of demagogic insanity; but there is above all a multitude of individuals who hold ideas about the family, property, individual freedom, intelligence, and the constitution of society that are so opposed to human nature that madness alone can explain them." That is why Brierre de Boismont argued for founding specialized institutions whose particular feature would ultimately be the abolition of the distinction between psychiatric asylum and political prison. "If this measure were adopted in France, as it has been in England, all those people who spread subversive ideas that might lead to the dreadful consequences we have just witnessed would be immediately taken to these asylums and subjected to mechanical treatments as soon as they have fits, make threats, or seek to escape."[60]

That Brierre de Boismont did not take the trouble to explain how Communards could be considered, clinically, to be mentally ill indicates how obvious this "diagnosis" seemed at the time. In fact, the "obviousness" was an idea shared by most of his colleagues, who stumbled over one specific point and hence subdivided the question: Were Communards afflicted with organic insanity or "moral" insanity? Dr. Jean-Baptiste Laborde, author of a book on the morbid psychology of "the men and deeds of the insurrection of Paris," believed the rebels suffered extensively from a hereditary defect that predisposed them to madness.[61] In the grand tradition of Esquirol, Laborde believed this dormant organic madness may have been awakened by political events, but he rejected any notion of collective insanity or a domino effect. On what did Laborde base his theory? On one simple supposition: unable to demonstrate the existence of hereditary antecedents among Communards, he relied on their behavior to provide proof of the innateness of the disease. The weakness of this analysis left his colleagues unconvinced, even though they gave a favorable reception to the principle behind his book. Some specialists expressed regret that Laborde had not informed himself better. "Among the Commune and its main proponents," asserted Lunier, "there were at least eight madmen whose hereditary antecedents were clearly established."[62] Others, such as Dr. Irénée-Célestin Baume, uncomfortable with the crude syllogism, criticized Laborde for overstating the influence of heredity when he proclaimed that "all morbid kinships are fecund"[63]—which experience hardly bears out, since many people have an insane relative without being insane themselves.

Furthermore, Laborde dodged the crucial question of moral responsibility, which Prosper Despine exploited to develop a different theory. The Communards' madness entailed moral insanity. The epidemic that cut through them even had a name—socialism. The goal of socialism was said to be the destruction of the basic values of civilization. Revolutionaries were presented as nihilists driven by covetousness and bitterness, by envy and laziness, with no agenda other than enjoying the harm they advocated and propagated.

> The specific nature of acts of madness could be seen in all the deeds of the men of the Commune. We saw that the specific property of mad actions is destruction, a total inability to organize and construct anything whatever. For what did the Commune produce? Decrees that lasted a day, an hour, overruled by new decrees constantly being reissued; authorities and committees that continually succeeded and replaced one another. What issued from the mouths of Communards? Words that advocated pillage, burning, death, the abolition of God, worship, the family, and all institutions based on the soul's higher instincts.[64]

Madness allegedly resided in an "anomalous psychological state" characterized by moral blindness. In other words, an individual endowed with reason inevitably desired, in all awareness, "the good," the definition of which resided solely in ideology—and religion. Now, through their speech and behavior, the Communards demonstrated their state of "moral or instinctive insanity." "These madmen are much more dangerous than [organically] ill madmen," wrote Despine, "and are convinced that they have acted wisely," which merely proved their incurability.[65] In this respect Despine did not agree with Morel, who considered the revolutionaries to be not madmen but criminals responsible for their acts.

From both perspectives, the insurrectionists lost out. Either they were considered criminals to be dealt with by the law or else they were lunatics to be locked away, whether their illness was hereditary or moral. They were thus guilty whether responsible or not, aware or unaware. Whatever the case, internment remained an indispensable public-health measure. The moralizing of the debate was accompanied by a depoliticizing. At no point did the physicians query the ideas behind the Commune or its motivations, characterized as pure blind instinct and savage destruction by a gang of drunkards. Here we perceive a huge shift with respect to 1848: the sufferers of "political delusions" and "communist monomania" whom Brierre de Boismont could still ridicule in June 1848 had become, in 1871, bloodthirsty animals.

Their ideas were thus automatically discredited at the source, even though, in the space of two months, the "emancipation of workers by workers themselves" had translated into decisive acts: the separation of church and state; free, mandatory public education; equal wages for men and women (which benefited schoolmistresses); free notarizing of documents; the abolition of night shifts for bakers. But such acts would never be discussed, any more than the barbaric acts of repression by the Versailles faction would ever be raised in terms of collective madness.

In this respect, psychiatrists reinforced the opinion of the bourgeoisie, quick to describe the Commune as an act of total insanity. Writers in particular accepted the obviousness of it—all, with just a few exceptions, condemned the uprising, as Paul Lidsky has shown.[66] Maxime Du Camp, the most vehement among them, blithely employed allusions to mental illness, as mentioned above. Du Camp, a doctor's son who was personally decorated by General Louis Eugène Cavaignac for his service to the counterrevolutionary militia in June 1848, could not find words harsh enough to stigmatize Communards in his large tome *Les convulsions de Paris*, which won him election to the Académie Française. In it he notably mentioned Jules Allix, a representative for the eighth arrondissement who was also an eccentric who had in fact spent time in an asylum on several occasions. Allix was a godsend for Du Camp, whose pen branded all leaders of the Commune with a diagnosis of mental illness, which he then embroidered for the fun of it.

> [Allix] was a prophetic, incoherent maniac, but a good and absolutely harmless man. He was not afflicted with homicidal monomania, as were Rigault, Ferré, G. Ranvier, and Urban; or pyromania, as was Pindy; or kleptomania, as was Eudes; or delusions of grandeur, as was J. Vallès; or reasoning monomania, as was Léo Meillet; or denunciatory monomania, as was Millière; or alcoholism, as were all the confederates; or lycanthropy with complications of cowardice, as was Félix Pyat; or chronic scatology, as was Vermersch; nor was he God, like Babick; no, Allix suffered from escargotomania, believing only in snails, a harmless belief that earned him a certain notoriety. He invented a mode of correspondence that relied on sympathetic snails.[67]

Du Camp—who neglected to mention that the Commune, worried about Allix's harebrained ideas, had him arrested—might have done better to dwell on the case of Jules Vallès. The author of the autobiographical *L'insurgé* (The insurgent), Vallès in fact constituted a singular case spanning the full range of relations between politics and mental illness in the nineteenth century. He started out as a victim of arbitrary internment, because when he joined the barricades that went up in Nantes in 1851 his father—a respected teacher who feared scandal—had him locked up in the Saint-Jacques asylum. His sister, traumatized by the incident, would join him there a few weeks later. Vallès owed his release in March 1852 to the energetic efforts of his friend Arthur Arnould. His sister would not be so lucky; she died in 1859 still interned as a madwoman.

Vallès was elected to the Commune and founded the newspaper *Le Cri du Peuple*. He miraculously escaped the crackdown and made his way to London. In 1881 the internment in Charenton of his friend André Gill prompted him to raise the issue that had always haunted him: the use of hospital internment as a form of political and familial censure. Gill, a mordant, highly popular caricaturist during the Second Empire, had refused to commit himself to the insurrectional movement in 1871. Once calm had returned, Gill devoted himself to painting, having decided that his role as a critic had played itself out. The death of a child and his frustration at seeing his painting *Madman* poorly hung at the Salon triggered several incidents of raving that led to the asylum. He died in Charenton in 1885. Vallès's interpretation of this tragedy, running counter to the psychological theories of degeneracy, was an expression of faith that cast the whole issue in a new light.

> Were he able, that headless man who was once my friend, were he able, despite whatever the doctors say, to recover his reason, I would tell him how not to go mad despite the pain and poverty—whereas in fortune and fame you can still lose your mind! . . .
>
> In any case, whether victims or executioners, all who are intensely involved in the public forum will survive a long time, keeping their brains fresh and spirits strong, whether they be named Dufaure or Blanqui, Senard or Raspail. The fever of struggle keeps them straight and upright until they topple like trees or are killed; the spears aimed at them nail them to life rather than prodding them toward death. . . .
>
> You have to take sides. Gill did not want to. He shunned every partisan cap and simply donned an artist's beret. Then the beret tightened

around his temples and became the headgear of a prisoner in Sainte-Anne![68]

Vallès inverted the terms of the equation: Gill went mad because he shunned political commitment, the guarantee of mental health and lucidity. Vallès concluded this text with a prophecy worth meditating upon. "We must begin pulling together, and not wait to go mad before storming the fortresses. Then perhaps one day we shall overturn them all, royal households and mental homes alike."

Postamble

Dedicated to three "raving madwomen"
in recollection of a trip to Charenton

On November 23, 2010, shortly after finishing this book, I paid my first visit to Charenton. I was already familiar with La Salpêtrière and its Pinel wing, just across from the Charcot lecture hall. I had also visited Saint-Anne, and I had seen Bicêtre with its ward devoted to "Neuroscience, Head and Neck" (most inspiring for anyone interested in the guillotine). Charenton was the only asylum whose archives I had consulted (and what archives they are!) without having set eyes on the buildings themselves. And what buildings they are!

Charenton, or the Esquirol Hospital, as it was renamed in 1973, is a layering of abstract surfaces: a wall of foliage around blind stone walls with landings at regular intervals, set on a promontory overlooking the Seine where the Marne River meets it. You can no longer see the rivers or appreciate the natural environment that ringed it in the days of Sade, but you can hear the eastern highway that creates an aural and physical barrier to all reverie. The surrounding trees, whose colors on that day bore the mark of damp, dull autumn, were thin. Beyond the branches, through sparse gaps in the groves, you could see housing projects and high-rises beneath an empty, watery sky—a dirty white like the horizon around greater Paris. The landscape was grim and monotonous. Like madness.

Esquirol felt that mental homes should be an "instrument of cure."[1] Walking across the grounds, passing the asylum buildings—erected between 1838 and 1886 to Esquirol's recommendations—now represents the best way to assess what a sign proudly posted at the entrance earnestly calls "the most brilliant period of French psychiatry."

Charenton is a blend of barracks and monastery. It is a bucolic prison, a strict haven that has all the advantages of a place of rest—

FIGURE 34. A view of Charenton. Now named Esquirol Hospital, the buildings at Charenton are still home to a psychiatric ward. Here the pediment of the chapel peeks over the wall. Photograph © Laure Murat.

enclosed and symmetrical in a neoclassical layout that reins in the imagination. The chapel is an ancient-style temple set, Valhalla-like, atop a straight double flight of stairs, crowning the collection of silent facades with their barred windows and column-lined courtyards. From up there you can enjoy the view, but no vistas open outward.

At the foot of this staircase, in a niche that draws the eye, is a statue of the great man. It is an allegory of science and experience, of progress and philanthropy showing a seated Esquirol, his right hand inscribing the future of psychiatry on a tablet while at his feet there crouches a wretched mental patient, whom the doctor shields with his enveloping cloak.

Charenton, between its insistence on conformity with the geometry of a rectilinear space representing order and reason and its invitation to honor the psychiatrist as a benefactor of humanity, embodies the triumph of nineteenth-century psychiatry: authoritarian and full of good intentions. Asylums modeled on this ideal plan, along with their accompanying coercive methods, survived until the therapeutic-community movement led by François Tosquelles, after World War II and the discovery of the concentration camps, realized that these places were themselves diseased. Asylums had grown with capitalism and industry, and they disintegrated with the revelation of totalitarian horror. Their historical trajectory reveals how far mental asylums were the special site of a confrontation between the individual and the collective, between the singular and the standardized. What could be more revealing, in fact, than this repetitive, regular architecture that induces patients to follow the norm, to stay on the straight and narrow? Whether here at Charenton or at Bicêtre, La Salpêtrière, or Saint-Anne, the clockmaker who had lost his head, the man who thought he was Napoleon, the unmarried communist woman, the hysterical *pétroleuse*, and all the insane revolutionaries had to stick to the rules and the boundaries imposed by the setting.

Things apparently change with time. Although Esquirol Hospital still provides the setting for psychiatric care, today's psychiatry—based on local treatment, outpatient care, day hospitalization, therapeutic apartments, and sheltered housing—obviously has nothing in

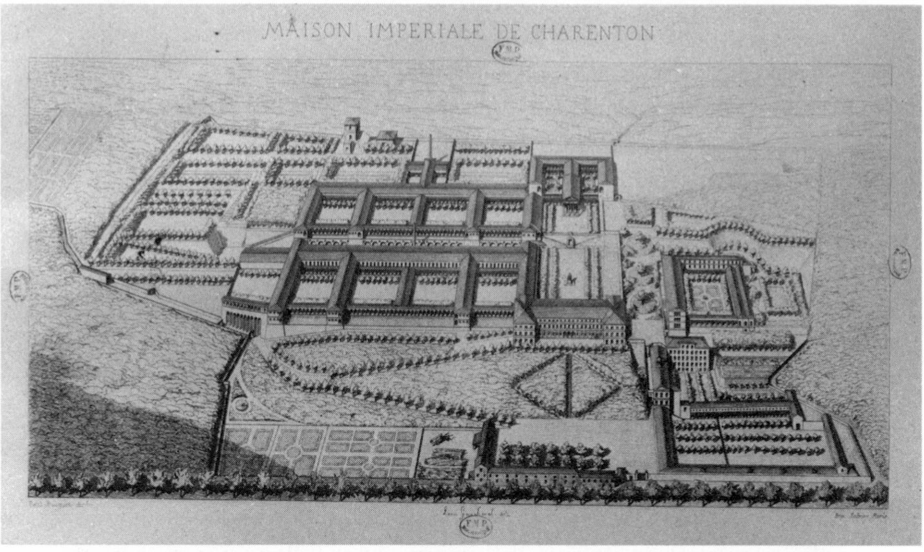

FIGURE 35. Léon Gaucherel, *The Imperial Mental Home at Charenton*. Lithograph. For the Marquis de La Vallette's *Établissements généraux de bienfaisance placés sous le patronage de l'Impératrice* (1866). According to Dr. Étienne Esquirol, the asylum itself was "an instrument of cure." Photograph © BIU Santé, Paris.

common with the mental care of yore. The walls of the asylum have indeed come down, as have the methods of a bygone era. In theory, at least. Because Charenton's physical obsolescence might in fact be matched, metaphorically, by a contemporary relevance.

"A society is judged by the way it treats its mental patients," said twentieth-century psychiatrist Lucien Bonnafé. Viewed from this angle, the twenty-first century clearly paints a grim picture. In 2003 the États Généraux de la Psychiatrie—a national conference attended by more than 1,500 doctors, nurses, and social workers—sounded the alarm over a deteriorating situation in France owing to lack of funds and a trend toward short-term profitability instead of a true policy of health care. Many things point to extremely serious regression regarding the accomplishments of psychiatry: a return to the obsession with security, psychological harassment by the authorities (echoed by the media) concerning the "danger" of schizophrenics, court-ordered compulsory internments, and profitability criteria promoted by the pharmaceutical industry and the cognitive behavioral sciences, not to mention wholesale attacks on psychoanalysis (the only system currently apt to establish a singular relationship in a singular time frame). The deliberate hardening of policies is creating greater exclusion. Patients are finding themselves more and more marginalized and abandoned, increasingly housed apart or placed in chemical straitjackets as a replacement for costly psychotherapeutic care that the national health service will no longer cover. They are being left on their own—or sometimes in jail.[2]

So have we truly left the nineteenth century behind, morally speaking? That question haunted me throughout the writing of this book. Sometimes it struck me as silly—the antipsychiatry movement and the counterculture events of 1968 saw to that—and sometimes it seemed relevant: Aren't we experiencing a "return to order" right now? Then I came across a comment on the current situation by Jean Oury: "Antipsychiatry now rules." Oury's assertion may seem surprising at a time of unbridled free-market thinking, globalization, and financial logic. Yet in fact it offers insight into a complex ideological collusion that occurred between the late 1960s and the early 1990s, and that I hope I will be excused for very broadly summing up as follows: By combating psychiatric authorities and a system of treatment similar to a system of subordination and colonization of the mind, antipsychiatry seems to have paved the way for a free-market economy that, in an inspired takeover operation, simply acquired and liquidated the costly heritage of asylums—we need merely recall America's Regan-era closure of psychiatric hospitals one after another, turning patients out onto the street and leaving them to their fate. Thus the radically opposed motives of an idealist, libertarian left and a pragmatic, cynical right in the end served the same goal—or at least produced the same result.

In a society that refers to a "mental health plan" and seeks to detect "delinquent and abnormal behavior" right from nursery school based on multiple-choice questionnaires,[3] the voice of madness—with all its insights, digressions, and pain—is having a harder and harder time making itself heard. Our globalized world has little time for listening and dialogue. Aggressive medication and "virtual therapy" in which image and simulation supplant speech have whittled down deluded stories until they become inaudible and illegible. Institutions are getting rid of cumbersome archives, and ever since files have been made accessible to patients' families, psychiatrists have been limiting their comments to a strict minimum, out of discretion and concern for medical privacy. Doctors now conform narrowly to the basic codes found in the all-powerful *Diagnostic and Statistical Manual of Mental Disorders*, fourth edition (DSM-IV), which has established itself as the sole authoritative nomenclature with respect to mental disorders. This means that a book like *The Man Who Thought He Was Napoleon* could not be written about the present day, for lack of available material. And yet merely questioning a few psychiatrists, psychoanalysts, and patients would soon reveal that history clearly supplies as much delusional material as it once did, and that Esquirol's venerable plan of using the discourse of madness to write the nation's history is as imaginable today as it was two centuries ago. But as patients are increasingly reduced to silence, and as their voices are decreasingly recorded, the murmur of madness is fading, smothered by indifference.

Not everywhere, of course. After a speech made by French president Nicolas Sarkozy on December 2, 2008, announcing a series of freedom-restricting measures (the geolocalizing of compulsorily interned patients, the establishment of closed institutions, the creation of two hundred solitary confinement rooms, mandatory outpatient care, attribution of full powers to the directors of hospitals, and so on), a collective came together to protest *la nuit sécuritaire* ("the dark days of law and order") and to circulate a petition that received nearly thirty thousand signatures. The "group of thirty-nine" who founded the collective and the signers of the petition included psychiatrists, psychoanalysts, and health workers who, in public and private practices, were committed to their patients and sought to develop a fertile approach that entertained diverse expressions of madness.

Those people not only were continuing the efforts of Freud and Lacan, they were pursuing Pinel's pioneering gesture of talking to madness, a breakthrough immediately blocked by the triumph of an asylum system that guaranteed the failure of mental therapy. In 1845 Dr. Jacques-Joseph Moreau de Tours made an admission that already sounded like a warning. "Although the patients sometimes spoke, we did not take sufficient account of what they said."[4] The nineteenth-century archives, of which I used just a tiny fraction, prove not only that insanity—an individual's rampart against personal collapse—has much to tell us about political violence, but that seeking to reduce it to silence and bury its traces actually threatens, rather than protects, society.

Acknowledgments

With every new book, I promise myself it will be the last to require so much archival research, obliging me to wrestle with France's huge administrative machinery: filling out forms, requesting authorizations and special permissions, sometimes waiting months for replies from civil servants or copyright holders. Yet the pleasure of discovery always gets the better of the nervous exhaustion triggered by the preliminary work, and I find myself beginning all over again. Indeed, I always seem to encounter individuals who resolve some deadlock with a word, who endorse and ultimately advance my research. Élise Lewartowski, head of the educational and cultural section of the Archives Départementales du Val-de-Marne, and Maïlys Mouginot, an official at the Archives de l'Assistance Publique–Hôpitaux de Paris, know why I wish to see their names at the head of this list.

This kind of research calls above all for long stretches of work that would be undermined by interruptions. From that standpoint a professor's job is demanding, and this book would not have seen the light of day without the generosity of the Academic Senate of the University of California, Los Angeles, which accorded me the means to pursue it. I would also like to express my warm gratitude to Professor Dominic Thomas, chair of the Department of French and Francophone Studies at UCLA, for demonstrating his faith in me.

Throughout this long project, I found Jean-Loup Champion to be an exceptionally fine editor. His demanding standards and attentive presence were a constant support. I also benefited greatly from Philippe Bernier's copyediting, for which I am grateful.

Some sections of the book served as the material for lectures and seminars where I profited from numerous comments. I would notably like to thank Gisèle Sapiro, Natania Meeker, and Béatrice Mousli, as well as Jonathan Strauss, who invited me to present my research at, respectively, the École des Hautes Études en Sciences Sociales in Paris on October 29, 2009, the University of Southern California on January 28, 2010, and Miami University, Ohio, on February 11, 2010. Such occasions resulted in improvements to the manuscript.

For their information, advice, or encouragement, I also thank Manuela Aranzabal, Michel Caire, Elena Rasi Caldogno, Laurence Camous, Patrick Chemla, and the patients at the Centre Antonin-Artaud, Clément Fromentin, Marie-Rose Guarniéri, Jean-Louis Jeanelle, Teresa Johnson, Annie Le Brun, Cécile Vargaftig, Jean-François Vincent, and Dora Weiner.

I thank Alan Thomas, who made this book happen in its American edition, and Alice Kaplan for her invaluable support; and my deepest gratitude also goes to Deke Dusinberre for his marvelous translation and to Randolph Petilos and Inés ter Horst for helping me navigate the publication process.

Finally, heartfelt thanks that I never weary of expressing go to Zrinka Stahuljak.

Notes

ABBREVIATIONS

AAP-HP: Archives de l'Assistance Publique-Hôpitaux de Paris
ADVDM: Archives Départementales du Val-de-Marne

PREAMBLE

1. By "history" I mean the events themselves—notably political—*not* the academic field that studies and recounts those events.

2. Étienne [fully, Jean-Étienne-Dominique] Esquirol, *Mental Maladies: A Treatise on Insanity*, trans. E. K. Hunt (Philadelphia: Lea and Blanchard, 1845), 44.

3. Charlotte Beradt, *The Third Reich of Dreams: The Nightmares of a Nation, 1933–1939*, trans. Adrienne Gottwald (Wellington, UK: Aquarian Press, 1985).

4. Frantz Fanon, *The Wretched of the Earth*, trans. Richard Philcox (New York: Grove, 2004). See notably the final chapter, "Colonial War and Mental Disorders," 181–234.

5. Françoise Davoine and Jean-Max Gaudillère, *History Beyond Trauma*, trans. Susan Fairfield (New York: Other Press, 2004).

6. Cathy Caruth, ed., *Trauma: Explorations in Memory* (Baltimore: Johns Hopkins University Press, 1995); Caruth, *Unclaimed Experience: Trauma, Narratives, and History* (Baltimore: Johns Hopkins University Press, 1996).

7. Gilles Deleuze and Félix Guattari, *Anti-Oedipus: Capitalism and Schizophrenia*, trans. Robert Hurley, Mark Seem, and Helen R. Lane (Minneapolis: University of Minnesota Press, 1983). This passage is taken from the dust jacket of the French edition.

8. The "runaway madness" characteristic of drapetomania, well known to southern planters, was described by Cartwright as a widespread mental disorder, but one that was easy to cure if the masters avoided becoming too familiar toward slaves and convinced them, Bible in hand, that their natural condition was one of servitude. Now considered to be an example of scientific racism, this "illness" was widely discussed within the American medical community of the day. I thank John McCumber for drawing my attention to this troubling syndrome. See Thomas Szasz, "The Sane Slave: An Historical Note on the Use of Medical Diagnosis as

Justificatory Rhetoric," *American Journal of Psychotherapy* 25 (1971): 228–39. On "chronic paranoia," see notably Vladimir Bukovsky, *Une nouvelle maladie mentale en URSS: L'opposition* (Paris: Seuil, 1971), and the account given by Victor X in Roger Dadoun, ed., *La folie politique* (Paris: Payot, 1971).

9. Esquirol, *Mental Maladies*, 210. Originally published as "De la lypémanie ou mélancolie" (1820).

10. See Pinel's "Tableau général des fous de Bicêtre," in Dora Weiner, *Comprendre et soigner: Philippe Pinel (1745–1826), la médecine de l'esprit* (Paris: Fayard, 1999), 143.

11. A comparative study of private or provincial institutions over the same period would probably have shed additional light, yet would have above all rendered this already highly ambitious project unwieldy. Similarly, extending what Eric Hobsbawm called "the long nineteenth century" up to 1914 would have confronted issues—European instability, World War I, mechanization, the invention of psychoanalysis—that would have altered the book's scale and thus called for a different conceptualization. To complete this picture, I might add that a very simple administrative and legal obstacle would have made such a task impossible: medical archives in France are not opened—except by special dispensation—until 150 years after the birth of the patient concerned.

12. Jan Goldstein, *Console and Classify: The French Psychiatric Profession in the Nineteenth Century* (Cambridge: Cambridge University Press, 1990).

13. The entire French text of the 1838 "law on the mentally ill" can be found at http://www.ch-charcot56.fr/textes/11838-7443.htm, accessed September 1, 2011.

14. Goldstein, *Console and Classify*, 291.

15. Archives Nationales, F15 2606–7. Debouteville's name is spelled de Bouteville.

16. Goldstein, *Console and Classify*, 158.

17. Laure Murat, "'Proust, Marcel, 46 ans, rentier,'" *La Revue Littéraire* 14 (May 2005): 82–92.

18. This name stems from the 1838 law on mental asylums in France, which obliged those establishments to keep and to archive ledgers containing every patient's identity, dates of admission and release, and diagnosis.

19. *Histoires Littéraires* 1 (2000), a quarterly review of nineteenth- and twentieth-century French literature.

20. Quoted in Pierre Nora, "Michelet, ou L'hystérie identitaire," *L'Esprit Créateur* 46, no. 3 (2006): 6.

21. Lucien Febvre, *Combats pour l'histoire* (1952; Paris: Armand Colin, 1992), 12.

22. Jules Michelet, "Préface de 1869," in *Histoire de France*, vol. 4 of *Œuvres complètes* (Paris: Flammarion, 1893–98), iv.

23. Jean-Marc Mandosio, *D'or et de sable* (Paris: Éditions de l'Encyclopédie des Nuisances, 2008), 181.

24. Charles-Augustin Sainte-Beuve, *Portraits littéraires* (Paris: Garnier Frères, 1964), 3:222.

25. Archives de l'Assistance Publique-Hôpitaux de Paris (hereafter AAP-HP), La

Salpêtrière, Registre d'observations médicales, 5th division, 4th section, 1870–73, 6R61, fol. 354.

26. AAP-HP, Bicêtre, Registre d'observations médicales, 5th division, 1st and 2nd sections, 1871–72, 6R34, fol. 85.

27. The term *candeur* ("ingenuousness") was used by Alain Corbin in "Ne rien refuser d'entendre," *Vacarme* 35 (Spring 2006), available at http://www.vacarme.org/article492.html, accessed September 2011. "Historians set off in search of those who have preceded them, trying to relive things with them, getting under their skin. And it is obvious that this approach calls for *ingenuousness*. Alphonse Dupront rightly said that 'faced with a document, wait and let the meaning surface by remaining *ingenuous*.' When they go to archives, historians should begin by emptying themselves of everything. Otherwise their work may turn out to be merely illustrative, leading them to discover only what supports their hypotheses."

28. See Michel Foucault, *History of Madness*, trans. Jonathan Murphy and Jean Khalfa (Oxford: Routledge, 2009), and Marcel Gauchet and Gladys Swain, *Madness and Democracy: The Modern Psychiatric Universe*, trans. Catherine Porter (Princeton, NJ: Princeton University Press, 2012).

29. Foucault, *History of Madness*, 44 (translation slightly modified) and 45.

30. Ibid., 47.

31. Ibid., xxviii. The quotation is drawn from the introduction to the 1961 edition of *Histoire de la folie*, which Foucault removed from subsequent French editions. It nevertheless survives in recent English translations.

32. Jacques Derrida, "Cogito et histoire de la folie," in *L'écriture et la différence* (Paris: Seuil, 1967), 51–97. Derrida's text was a slightly modified version of a lecture given at the Collège Philosophique on March 4, 1963, and published that same year in the *Revue de Métaphysique et de Morale*. His critique targeted above all Foucault's interpretation of Descartes's first meditation. Foucault responded in 1972 in an article titled "Mon corps, ce papier, ce feu," appended to the second edition of *Histoire de la folie à l'âge classique*, reprinted in *Dits et écrits* (Paris: Gallimard, 1994), 2:245–68. See Jacques Derrida, "Cogito and the History of Madness," in *Writing and Difference*, trans. Alan Bass (New York: Routledge, 2001), and Michel Foucault, "My Body, This Paper, This Fire," trans. Geoff Bennington, in *Aesthetics, Method, and Epistemology* (New York: New Press, 1999).

33. This assertion is equally true of the history of sexuality, notably homosexuality, which is partly (but not exclusively) forged *in relation* to medical discourse, that is, along the fault lines of such discourse, *against* and *alongside* that discourse. In the past twenty years, gay and lesbian studies have shown that medicine did not introduce or organize this knowledge, but rather catalyzed a certain number of concerns, which are more complex than generally believed. See notably Jonathan Ned Katz, *The Invention of Heterosexuality* (New York: Dutton, 1995), and George Chauncey, *Gay New York* (New York: Basic Books, 1995).

34. François Rabelais, *Five Books of the Lives: Heroic Deeds and Sayings of Gargantua and His Son Pantagruel*, trans. Sir Thomas Urquhart of Cromarty and Peter Anthony Motteux (1708; Hong Kong: Forgotten Books, 1952), 352.

35. Philippe Pinel, *Traité médico-philosophique sur l'aliénation mentale ou la manie* (Paris: Richard, Caile et Ravier, Year IX [1800]), 231. Hereafter Pinel, *Traité médico-philosophique* (1800). [This first edition of Pinel's famous treatise, which was followed by an expanded edition in 1809, was rendered into English by Dr. D. D. Davis in 1806 in an extremely uneven translation as *A Treatise on Insanity* (Sheffield, UK: W. Todd, 1806). Passages quoted here from Pinel's first edition have been translated directly from the French, but with an eye on the Davis translation—Trans.]

36. This is the French definition of *historiette* as given in *Le Trésor de la langue française*, http://atilf.atilf.fr/tlf.htm, accessed September 2011. The term *historiette* is also associated with the volume *Historiettes* by Gédéon Tallemant des Réaux. [Davis quite reasonably rendered Pinel's *historiettes* as "anecdotes" in his translation of *A Treatise on Insanity*, 222. Another possibility is "vignette," which Merriam-Webster's Unabridged Dictionary defines as "a short literary sketch chiefly descriptive and characterized usually by delicacy, wit, and subtlety"—Trans.]

37. Once Bicêtre and La Salpêtrière, formerly attached to the Département de la Seine, no longer sufficed to house the mentally ill, the government of the Second Empire launched a major campaign to build new asylums. One of them was Sainte-Anne (opened in 1867), the central institution charged with dispatching patients to other hospitals; later openings included Perray-Vaucluse (1869), Ville-Evrard (1875), Villejuif (1884), Maison Blanche (1900), Moisselles (1905), and Chezal-Benoît (1910). Charenton, the former almshouse of the Hospitaller Brothers of St. John of God, had a special status; closed during the Revolution when the religious orders were suppressed, it was taken over by the government and reopened in 1797 as the Maison Nationale [i.e., National Mental Home] de Charenton.

38. Archives Départementales du Val-de-Marne (hereafter ADVDM), Maison Royale de Charenton, Registre d'observation medicales "femmes," 1818, 4X677, fol. 1. In 1817, La Salpêtrière took in almost double its usual number of patients owing to food shortages, according to Alexandre Brierre de Boismont, "De la loi sur les aliénés," *Revue Universelle* 4 (Year VI, 1839): 189.

39. Call number 6R1; yet the subsequent volume, 6R2, begins in 1847.

40. Jules Michelet, *Nos fils*, quoted by Paul Viallaneix in his foreword to Michelet's *Le peuple* (Paris: G. F. Flammarion, 1974), 33.

41. François Leuret, *Du traitement moral de la folie* (Paris: J.-B. Baillière, 1840), 185.

42. Maxime Du Camp, *Paris, ses organes, ses fonctions et sa vie dans la seconde moitié du XIXe siècle* (Paris: Hachette, 1875), 4:385.

43. [Pinel's concept of *traitement moral* was unfortunately translated by Davis in 1806 as "moral treatment," which was then picked up by Samuel Tuke, grandson of William Tuke, an early pioneer of asylum reform in England. The term moral treatment thus found its way into much nineteenth- and twentieth-century literature on the subject, even though it is far more "moralizing" than the more nuanced connotations of *moral* (mental) in French. This translation therefore follows Pinel expert Dora B. Weiner and the recent translators of the second edition of Pinel's treatise in

rejecting "moral treatment" in favor of terms such as "mental therapy" and "treating the mind"—Trans.]

CHAPTER ONE

1. Letter sent by Charles-Henri Sanson to Jacques-Antoine Dulaure, editor of *Le Thermomètre du Jour*, on February 20, 1793, to refute comments published in that paper on February 13. Quoted in Georges Lenôtre, *La guillotine et les exécuteurs des arrêts criminels pendant la Révolution d'après des documents inédits tirés des Archives de l'état* (Paris: Perrin, 1910), 4n. This letter was also published in a key source for the first part of this chapter, Daniel Arasse's *La guillotine et l'imaginaire de la Terreur* (Paris: Flammarion, 1987), 77.

2. *Révolutions de Paris* 185 (January 19–26, 1793): 202. *Le Moniteur Universal* stated that Louis XVI's head fell at 10:20; see *La Gazette National, ou Le Moniteur Universel* 23 (January 23, 1793): 242.

3. *Mémoires de Cléry, de M. le duc de Montpensier, de Riouffe*, with foreword and notes by François Barrière (Paris: Firmin Didot, 1864), 14.

4. Although at the time of his death he was styled "king of the French," Louis XVI was the last "king of France" in the sense of being heir to a monarchy based on divine right. On the king's two bodies, see Ernst Kantorowicz, *The King's Two Bodies: A Study in Mediaeval Political Theology* (Princeton, NJ: Princeton University Press, 1997).

5. Quoted by Pierre-Édouard Lemontey, "Essai sur l'établissement monarchique de Louis XIV," in Lemontey, *Œuvres* (Paris: Sautelet, 1839), 5:15, based on the manuscript of a course of instruction on public law that Louis XIV had drawn up for his grandson, the duc de Bourgogne.

6. François-René de Chateaubriand, *Mémoires d'outre-tombe* (Paris: Gallimard, 1951), 1:184.

7. Louis Sébastien Mercier, *Le nouveau Paris* (Paris: Brunswick, 1800), 1:43.

8. Camille Desmoulins, *Le Vieux Cordelier* 4 (December 20, 1793), reprinted in Desmoulins, *Œuvres* (Paris: Charpentier, 1874), 2:185.

9. The verses go: Je vais monter sur l'échafaud; / Ce n'est que changer de théâtre; / Vous pouvez, citoyen bourreau / M'assassiner, mais non m'abattre. / Ainsi finit la Royauté, / La valeur, la grâce enfantine . . . Le niveau de l'égalité,/ C'est le fer de la guillotine. (On the scaffold shall I appear, / for 'tis just another stage. / Oh, Citizen executioner / you may slay, yet will not humble, me. / Thus end royalty, simple grace, and valor . . . / the level of equality / is the guillotine's razor.) Quoted in Paul d'Estrées, *Le théâtre sous la Terreur (théâtre de la peur), 1793–1794* (Paris: Émile Paul Frères, 1913), 302.

10. *Révolutions de Paris* 185 (January 19–26, 1793): 206.

11. Eugène Fontenay, *Les bijoux anciens et modernes* (Paris: Compagnie Générale d'Impression et d'Édition, 1887), 128. A similar pair of earrings is held by the Musée Carnavalet in Paris.

12. Victor Hugo, *Ninety-Three* (New York: Mondial, 2008), 78.

13. Joseph Clarke, *Commemorating the Dead in Revolutionary France: Revolution and Remembrance, 1789–1799* (Cambridge: Cambridge University Press, 2007).

14. See, among others, Donald Greer, *The Incidence of the Terror during the Revolution: A Statistical Interpretation* (Cambridge, MA: Harvard University Press, 1935); Jean Tulard, Jean-François Fayard, and Alfred Fierro, *Histoire et dictionnaire de la Révolution française* (Paris: Robert Laffont, 1987); François Furet, Mona Ozouf, and Bronislaw Baczko, *Dictionnaire critique de la Révolution française* (Paris: Flammarion, 1992); and the excellent website *Portail sur l'histoire de la justice, des crimes et des peines*, http://www.criminocorpus.cnrs.fr, accessed October 2012. These figures concern only executions carried out by guillotine. In addition, it is estimated that there were 25,000 summary executions and 500,000 cases of imprisonment.

15. Antoine Louis, *Avis motivé sur le mode de décollation*, quoted in Arasse, *La guillotine*, 209.

16. Quoted in Arasse, *La guillotine*, 35–36.

17. "Lettre de M. Soemmering à M. Oelsner sur le supplice de la guillotine," *Gazette Nationale, ou Le Moniteur Universel*, 18 Brumaire Year IV (November 9, 1795), 378. For a more thorough analysis of this debate, see Ludmilla Jordanova, "Medical Meditations: Mind, Body and the Guillotine," *History Workshop* 28 (Autumn 1989): 39–52.

18. Conrad E. Ölsner, "Sur le supplice de la guillotine, par le professeur Soemmering," *Magasin Encyclopédique* 3 (1795): 464–65; Jean-Joseph Sue, *Opinion du chirugien Sue, professeur de médecine et de botanique, sur le supplice de la guillotine*, (n.p., Brumaire Year IV (November 1795).

19. Pierre Jean Georges Cabanis, *Notes sur le supplice de la guillotine*, 1796 (Orléans: Orient, 2007), 60; emphasis added.

20. I am using the term psychiatry here for convenience, fully aware of the anachronism—the term is attested in French only from 1842 onward—since at the time there was no fixed term for the treatment of the insane.

21. Philippe Pinel, *Lettres de Pinel précédées d'une notice plus étendue sur sa vie, par son neveu le Dr. Casimir Pinel* (Paris: Victor Masson, 1859), 10.

22. François-Joseph Talma, *Mémoire de J.-F. Talma, écrit par lui-même et mis en ordre sur les papiers de sa famille par Alexandre Dumas*, 1849 (Montreal: Joyeux Roger, 2006), 219. See also Paul Bru, *Histoire de Bicêtre* (Paris: Lecrosnié et Babé, 1890), 87.

23. In French the semantic link is even tighter, because *perdre la tête* means both "to lose your head" and "to lose your mind," a double meaning already common during the Revolution, as witnessed by Rivarol's famous quip about the governor of the Bastille: "Monsieur de Launay lost his head before they cut it off." Antoine de Rivarol, *Journal Politique-National* 16 (1789): 4. The semantic and phantasmal connections between guillotine and madness gave birth to a strange anecdote, well known to typographers, which is worth reporting here as a curiosity. "Monsieur X. had written two volumes on the treatment of the mentally ill. The second

volume ended with a quotation from Dr. Pinel. Monsieur X., having noticed on the proofs that this passage lacked proper quotation marks, wrote at the bottom of the final page, *Il faut guillemetter tous les alinéas.* [All line breaks must have quotation marks.] Imagine his consternation a few days later on reading the closing lines of his book, printed in fine italics: *Il faut guillotiner tous les aliénés* [All lunatics must be guillotined]. He paled, leaped up, and remained nearly insane for twenty-four hours." L. Grange, "Les coquilles," *L'Ouvrier* 397 (December 5, 1868): 256.

24. Robert Castel, *L'orde psychiatrique: L'âge d'or de l'aliénisme* (Paris: Éditions de Minuit, 1976), 9.

25. Jean Colombier and François Doublet, *Instructions sur la manière de gouverner les insensés et de travailler à leur guérison dans les asyles qui leur sont destinés* (Paris: Imprimerie Royale, 1785); Jacques Tenon, *Mémoires sur les hôpitaux de Paris* (Paris: Pierres, 1788), 211–20.

26. Pinel, letter to his brother dated December 8, 1778, *Lettres de Pinel*, 37.

27. These details were revealed by his nephew, Casimir Pinel, in Pinel, *Lettres de Pinel*, 29. The nephew greatly admired his uncle and can hardly be suspected of willfully denigrating him.

28. Pierre Basile Bailly, *Souvenir d'un élève des écoles de santé de Strasbourg et de Paris* (Strasbourg: René-Simon Bailly, 1924), 16.

29. Pinel, *Traité médico-philosophique sur l'aliénation mentale ou la manie* (Paris: Richard, Caille et Ravier, Year IX [1800]), 50–51. (Cf. Pinel, *Treatise on Insanity*, trans. D. D. Davis [London: Cadell and Davies, 1806], 52.)

30. Constant Saucerotte, *Les médecins pendant la Révolution* (Paris: Perrin, 1887).

31. Philippe Pinel, "Variété," *Journal de Paris*, January 18, 1790, 70–72.

32. Philippe Pinel, "Réflexions médicales sur l'état monastique," *Journal Gratuit* 9, no. 6 (1790): 80–93.

33. Ibid., 85.

34. Philippe Pinel, "Observation sur les suites funestes d'une vie sédentaire et d'une contention d'esprit trop forte et trop longtemps retenue," *Gazette de Santé* 7 (1788): 25–26.

35. Ibid., 91.

36. On this subject see Dora B. Weiner, "Philippe Pinel (1745–1826), clerc tonsuré," *Annales Médico-psychologiques* 149, no. 2 (1991): 169–73. Weiner states that in this context being a "tonsured cleric" did not mean being a monk but only being a prebend. Pinel later decorated his house at Torfou, in the Maine-et-Loire region, with a set of paintings depicting the life of Saint Bruno. See Thierry Gineste, *Le lion de Florence: Sur l'imaginaire des fondateurs de la psychiatrie—Pinel, 1745–1826, et Itard, 1774–1838* (Paris: Albin Michel, 2004).

37. Pinel, letter to his brother dated July 7, 1792, *Lettres de Pinel*, 53.

38. Ibid., 56.

39. Pinel, letter of January 21, 1793, *Lettres de Pinel*, 12.

40. G. W. F. Hegel, *Hegel's Philosophy of Mind, Translated from the Encyclopedia of the Philosophical Sciences*, trans. William Wallace (Oxford: Clarendon Press,

1894), 38. In the same passage Hegel pays tribute to the pioneer of "treating the mind": "This humane treatment, no less benevolent than reasonable (the services of Pinel toward which deserve the highest acknowledgment), presupposes the patient's rationality, and in that assumption has the sound basis for dealing with him on this side—just as in the case of bodily disease the physician bases his treatment on the vitality which as such still contains health." Michel Foucault cited this passage in his *History of Madness* (485) but eliminated the phrase in parentheses. See also Gladys Swain, *Dialogue avec l'insensé* (Paris: Gallimard, 1994), 1–28.

41. Philippe Pinel, "Observations sur la manie pour servir l'histoire naturelle de l'homme," quoted in Jacques Postel, *Genèse de la psychiatrie: Les premiers écrits de Philippe Pinel* (Paris: Institut Synthélabo/Empêcheurs de Penser en Rond, 1998), 235. Postel was the first to publish this document by Pinel in its entirety, with variants. The English translation used here was first published in Dora B. Weiner, "Philippe Pinel's 'Memoir on Madness' of December 11, 1794: A Fundamental Text of Modern Psychiatry," *American Journal of Psychiatry* 149, no. 6 (June 1992): 725–32.

42. Pinel, "Observations sur la manie," 245, emphasis added; Weiner, "Philippe Pinel's 'Memoir on Madness,'" 732. In the second decade of the nineteenth century Esquirol would point out that "people thought that applying mental therapy to maniacs involved reasoning and arguing with them—that is a pipe dream. . . . Mental therapy involves capturing their attention. Although such patients can be bold and rash, they allow themselves to be dominated easily." Étienne Esquirol, "Manie," in *Dictionnaire des sciences médicales* (Paris: Panckoucke, 1818), 30:464.

43. See Jacques Guilhaumou, "La erreur à l'ordre du jour (juillet 1793–mars 1794)," *Dictionnaire des usages socio-politique, 1770–1815* (Paris: Champion, 1987), section 2. An extended version can be found at http://revolution-francaise.net/2007/01/06/94-la-terreur-a-lordre-du-jour-un-parcours-en-revolution-juillet-1793-mars-1794, accessed August 2012.

44. Philippe Pinel, "Observations sur l'hospice des insensés de Bicêtre," quoted in Postel, *Genèse de la psychiatrie*, 232; emphasis added.

45. Philippe Pinel, *Traité médico-philosophique sur l'aliénation mentale*, 2nd French edition, completely revamped and expanded (1809), reprinted with annotations by Jean Garrabé and Dora B. Weiner (Paris: Empêcheurs de Penser en Rond, 2005), 243. Translated into English by Gordon Hickish, David Healy, and Louis C. Charland as *Medico-philosophical Treatise on Mental Alienation* (Chichester, UK: Wiley–Blackwell, 2008), 95 (§215). Hereafter Pinel, *Medico-philosophical Treatise* (1809).

46. The rehabilitation of Pussin's role is relatively recent. See, among others, Dora B. Weiner, "The Apprenticeship of Philippe Pinel: A New Document, 'Observations of Citizen Pussin on the Insane,'" *American Journal of Psychiatry* 136, no. 9 (September 1979): 1128–34. Also see Jack Juchet, "Jean-Baptiste Pussin, 'médecin des folles,'" *Soins Psychiatrie* 142/143 (August/September 1992): 46–54; Michel Claire, "Pussin avant Pinel," *L'Information Psychiatrique* 69, no. 6 (1993): 529–38l; and Marie Didier, *Dans la nuit de Bicêtre* (Paris: Gallimard, 2006).

47. Louis Sébastien Mercier, Le *tableau de Paris* (1788; Paris: La Découverte, 1998), 79–80.

48. Victor Hugo, *Le dernier jour d'un condamné* (1829; Paris: Gallimard, 2000), 102.

49. See Bru, *Histoire de Bicêtre*, 157 ff. On visitors to Bicêtre, see Honoré-Gabriel Riquetti Mirabeau, *Observations d'un voyageur anglais sur la maison de force appellée Bicêtre* ([Paris], 1788), 6–9.

50. "Réponses aux questions de M. de Jussieu, lieutenant de maire au département des hôpiteaux, jointes à sa letter, en date du 12 avril 1790, concernant la maison de Bicêtre," quoted in Alexandre Tuetey, *Les hôpitaux et hospices*, vol. 1 of *L'assistance publique à Paris pendant la Révolution* (Paris: Imprimerie Nationale, 1845), 237. Pussin's influence had begun to make itself felt by this time, however, since the steward added, "Any time a madman is not furious or dangerous, he is free to stroll all day long in the courtyards of the ward. They are all treated with the greatest gentleness, even in their fits of fury." When the same question ("Is there any method of cure used for madness?") was posed at La Salpêtrière, the answer was, "There are very few who recover their senses naturally, and none at all through the help of [pharmaceutical] remedies, since no remedies are administered at La Salpêtrière" (ibid., 275). Useful details can be found in Michel Caire, "Pussin, avant Pinel," *L'Information Psychiatrique* 69, no. 6 (1993): 529–38, notably including five unpublished records between 1786 and 1788, which show that Pussin acted as an adviser to the legal authorities about releasing patients who had recovered their reason.

51. Philippe Pinel, "Tableau général des fous de Bicêtre au nombre d'environ 200," quoted in Dora B. Weiner, *Comprendre et soigner: Philippe Pinel (1745–1826), la médecine de l'esprit* (Paris: Fayard, 1999), 143.

52. I have drawn up this chart from the following information in Pinel's *Traité* (1800), 106: "In the census of madmen that I carried out at Bicêtre in Year III of the Republic, I observed that the determining causes of their illness were usually highly vivid affections of the mind. . . . Of the 113 madmen on whom I could obtain accurate information, 34 were reduced to that state owing to domestic misfortunes, 24 by obstacles to a strongly desired marriage, 30 by events connected with the Revolution, and 25 by religious fanaticism or terror of the afterlife." (Cf. Davis translation, *Treatise on Insanity*, 113.)

53. Pinel, *Traité* (1800), 9. (Cf. Davis translation, *Treatise on Insanity*, 9.)

54. "Observations du citoyen Pussin sur les fous," Archives Nationales, 27, Archives de Paris, 8, published in Weiner, "Apprenticeship of Philippe Pinel."

55. See Dominique Godineau, "Pratiques du suicide à Paris pendant la Révolution française," *French History and Civilization: Papers from the Georges Rudé Seminar* 1 (2005): 126–40.

56. P.-J.-B. Buchez and P.-C. Roux, *Histoire de la Révolution française, ou Journal des Assemblées nationales depuis 1789 jusqu'en 1815*, vol. 25 (Paris: Paulin, 1836), 135.

57. *Voyage du diable et de la folie comme causes des révolutions de France, Brabant, Liège et autres*, "printed on the Moon, May 1793, in the fourth year of the Reign of the Cannibals, and found in most booksellers in Europe."

58. *Collection de Vinck: Inventaire analytique* (Paris: Imprimerie Nationale, 1914), vol. 2, *La constituante* (1914), 513, and vol. 3, *La législative et la convention* (1921), 681.

59. Pinel, *Medico-philosophical Treatise* (1809), xxiiin2.

60. Philippe Pinel and Isidore Bricheteau, "Observation," in *Dictionnaire des sciences médicales* (Paris: Panckoucke, 1819), 37:33.

61. AAP-HP, La Salpêtrière, Registre des mutations (1791–Year XIII).

62. Philippe Pinel, *Nosographie philosophique* (Paris: J. A. Brosson, 1818), 3:52–53.

63. Pinel, *Medico-philosophical Treatise* (1809), 91 (§209).

64. Pinel, *Traité* (1800), 239. (Cf. Davis translation, *Treatise on Insanity*, 230.)

65. Pinel, *Traité* (1800), 168. (Cf. Davis translation, *Treatise on Insanity*, 166–67.)

66. Laurence Mall, "Révolution, traumatisme et non-savoir: La 'longue surprise' dans *Le nouveau Paris* de Mercier," *Études Littéraires* 38, no. 1 (Autumn 2006): 11–23. When the Girondin faction fell, Louis Sébastien Mercier was thrown into prison, where he remained from October 8, 1793, to October 28, 1794.

67. Victor Hugo, *Les Misérables*, trans. Isabel F. Hapgood (New York: Thomas Y. Crowell, 1887), 15.

68. Letter from Sade to his lawyer, January 21, 1795, quoted in Gilbert Lely, *Vie du marquis de Sade* (Paris: Jean-Jacques Pauvert, 1965), 539.

69. *Révolutions de Paris* (published by L. Prudhomme) 185 (January 19–26, 1793): 203.

70. "Alleged suspects include former nobles and their relatives, persons who have been refused a certificate of civic behavior, and all persons who, 'by their behavior, relations, comments, or writings show themselves to be advocates of federalism and enemies of freedom.'" Tulard, Fayard, and Fierro, *Histoire et dictionnaire de la Révolution française*, 1105. According to an estimate by Albert Mathiez, just before Robespierre fell there were 300,000 suspects in all of France, 8,000 of whom lived in Paris.

71. Pinel, *Traité* (1800), 141–42. (Cf. Davis translation, *Treatise on Insanity*, 141–42.)

72. Pinel, *Medico-philosophical treatise* (1809), 63 (§164) and 84 (§198).

73. This and the following quotations are drawn from Pinel, *Traité* (1800), 235–37. (Cf. Davis translation, *Treatise on Insanity*, 224–28.)

74. Jean Starobinski, *Histoire du traitement de la mélancolie des origines à 1900* (Basel: Laboratoires Geigy, 1960), 55. An English version was published as "History of the Treatment of Melancholy from the Earliest Times to 1900," *Acta Psychosomatica* 4 (1962): 9–100.

75. Pinel, *Medico-philosophical Treatise* [1809], 132–33 (§283).

76. Joseph Daquin, *La philosophie de la folie* (Paris: Chez Née de la Rochelle, 1792), 52. Daquin campaigned for better hygiene in asylums, advocated therapeutic work, and promoted the benefits of music, summing up his "philosophy" this way: "Success is infinitely greater and more certain . . . through patience, a good deal of gentleness, enlightened caution, kind attentions and considerations, good reasons and consoling comments" (97). Daquin was wary of pharmaceuticals and

suggested that electrical "commotion"—electroshock therapy—might one day be used to treat the brain. Pinel must have been aware of Daquin, who in 1804 dedicated the second edition of his book to him in a resounding tribute that also discreetly stressed the primacy of Daquin's own work. Yet even if willfully ignored, Daquin is perhaps not an inspired, unjustly overlooked discoverer. His theory of the humors, other archaic aspects of his ideas, and his conviction that the moon influences mental patients all place him behind the great—if ungenerous—clinician that was Pinel. On this subject see Swain, *Dialogue avec l'insensé*, 131–47, and Marcel Gauchet and Gladys Swain, *Madness and Democracy: The Modern Psychiatric Universe*, trans. Catherine Porter (Princeton, NJ: Princeton University Press, 1999), 195 ff.

77. This quotation and the next are drawn from Pinel, *Traité* (1800), 66–70. (Cf. Davis translation, *Treatise on Insanity*, 69–72.) "Witty jests" like the one mentioned in the second passage did not always work. When a religious fanatic claimed he was "the fourth person of the Trinity," Pinel sent another patient who was an elegant orator and who had memorized a poem by Voltaire on "natural religion" to recite the provocative verse to the zealot. The fanatic became furious and broke into dreadful epithets. Pinel did not repeat the experiment. *Traité* (1800), 73–74. (Cf. Davis translation, *Treatise on Insanity*, 76.)

78. AAP-HP, La Salpêtrière, Registre des mutations (1791-Year XIII), fols. 70, 216, and 225.

79. Archives Départementales du Val de Marne (hereafter ADVM), Charenton, Registres médicaux hommes et femmes, 1798–1826, 4X682 (2Mi60), unfoliated register.

80. ADVM, Charenton, Registre d'observations médicales, hommes et femmes, 1819, 4X678, fol. 31. Admitted September 14, 1819, died November 27, 1819.

81. ADVM, Charenton, Registres d'observations médicales, hommes et femmes (cas particuliers), 1827, 2 Mi 62, fol. 217. This ledger sums up the cases admitted between 1798 and 1827 and includes some later annotations. The female patient in question was born in 1775, was admitted to Charenton on July 26, 1820, and was still there in July 1827.

82. *Mémoires de Mlle Fore*, vol. 2, quoted in Annie Le Brun, *Petits et grands théâtres du marquis de Sade* (Paris: Paris Art Center, 1989), 90.

83. ADVM, Charenton, Registres d'observations médicales, hommes et femmes (cas particuliers), 1827, 2 Mi 62, fol. 13. The minutes of an executive committee meeting on 27 Fructidor Year VI (September 3, 1798) state that Laujon apparently emigrated in 1792 and claimed to be a "merchant" at the time of his arrest (see Archives Nationales, AF/III/543).

84. ADVM, Charenton, Registres d'observations médicales, hommes et femmes (cas particuliers), 1827, 2 Mi 62, fol. 36.

85. AAP-HP, Bicêtre, Registre d'observations médicales, 5th division, 1st and 2nd sections, 1855–56, 6R8, fol. 97.

86. AAP-HP, Bicêtre, Registre d'observations médicales, 5th division, 1st and 2nd sections, 1856–58, 6R10, fol. 111.

87. Alexandre Dumas, *Les mille et un fantômes*, preceded by *La femme au collier de velours*, ed. Anne-Marie Callet-Bianco (Paris: Gallimard, 2006), 243. *One Thousand and One Ghosts* has been translated from French by Andrew Brown (London: Hesperus Press, 2004), without the introduction quoted above.

88. Alexandre Dumas, "The Woman with the Velvet Necklace," in *Chauvelin's Will, a Romance of the Last Days of Louis XV, and Stories of the French Revolution: The Woman with the Velvet Necklace and Blanche de Beaulieu* (Boston: Little, Brown, 1897), 239.

89. Ibid., 281.

90. Ibid., 351.

91. Ibid., 351. Dumas based his story on a tale originally published by Washington Irving, which Pétrus Borel had already borrowed under the title *Gottfried Wolfgang* (1843). For a study of the Dumas novel and its sexual implications, see Catherine Nesci, "Talking Heads: Violence and Desire in Dumas Père's (Post-)Terrorist Society," *SubStance* 27, no. 2 (1998): 73–91.

CHAPTER TWO

1. Dora B. Weiner, *Comprendre et soigner: Philippe Pinel (1745–1826), la médecine de l'esprit* (Paris: Fayard, 1999), 76.

2. Decree dated August 16–24, title XI, article 3. See Michel Caire's website devoted to L'histoire de la psychiatrie en France; the menu "Législation," followed by submenu "Internements," describes the evolution in conditions of detention for the mentally ill from the ancien régime up to a law passed on July 5, 2011. http://psychiatrie.histoire.free.fr/index.htm, accessed September 2012.

3. Mona Ozouf, "Saint Just," *Dictionnaire critique de la Révolution française*, vol. 2, *Acteurs* (Paris: Flammarion, 2007), 273–93.

4. Philippe Pinel, *Traité médico-philosophique sur l'aliénation mentale ou la manie* (Paris: Richard, Caille et Ravier, Year IX [1800]), 51. (Cf. Davis translation, *Treatise on Insanity*, trans. D. D. Davis [London: Cadell and Davies, 1806], 52.)

5. Archives Nationales, DV5, no. 58. I established these statistics from ledgers in which one case (2 percent of the total) was not specified. On Pinel's years at the Belhomme home, see in particular André Ferroni, "Une maison de santé pour le traitement des aliénés à la fin du XVIIIe siècle: La maison Belhomme" (MD thesis, Faculté de Medecine, Université de Paris, 1954), and Jacques Postel, "Les premières expériences psychiatriques de Philippe Pinel à la maison de santé Belhomme," *Revue Canadienne de Psychiatrie* 28, no. 7 (November 1983): 571–75.

6. Archives Nationales, F7 4592. The full name of the Breteuil family was Le Tonnelier de Breteuil, so "the Tonnelier woman" probably thought it safer to go by just the first—non-noble—part of her name.

7. Jean-Charles Sournia, *La médecine révolutionnaire, 1789–1799* (Paris: Payot, 1989), 210.

8. On Belhomme's nursing home, see Olivier Vincienne, "La maison de santé Belhomme: Légende et réalité," *Paris et Île-de-France, Mémoires Publiés par la Fédé-*

ration des Sociétés Historiques et Archéologiques de Paris et de l'Île-de-France 36 (1985): 135–208. This article refutes the legend spread by Georges Lenôtre in *Paris révolutionnaire: Vieilles maisons, vieux papiers* (Paris: Perrin, 1922), 119–41. It is true, though, that Belhomme's story is the stuff of fiction. In Richard Pottier's 1951 film *Caroline chérie*, Cécil Saint-Laurent (played by Jacques Laurent) would save his "dear Caroline" (Martine Carole) from the guillotine by housing her with the cynical "Doctor" Belhomme (Raymond Souplex).

9. See Jean Tulard, "1800–1815, l'organisation de la police," in *Histoire et dictionnaire de la police du Moyen-Âge à nos jours* (Paris: Robert Laffont, 2005), 268–305.

10. Archives Nationales, F7 8752. Letter of September 9, 1807, from the prefect of Puy-de-Dôme to the state counselor in charge of the second division of the Police Générale de l'Empire.

11. Weiner, *Comprendre et soigner*, 246.

12. Maison Belhomme ledger (1775–1810), fols. 23 and 24. This register is now held by the Louise M. Darling Biomedical Library, UCLA (call number MS. Coll. 96).

13. Ibid., fol. 25. The order by Dubois is dated April 13, 1809.

14. Dubuisson's nursing home became a government jail in 1810. That same year Dr. Claude-Henri Jacquelin Dubuisson (1739–1812) turned management of the establishment over to his nephew, Dr. Jean-Baptiste-Rémy Jacquelin Dubuisson (1770–1836).

15. Victor-Claude-Alexandre Fanneau de Horie (or Lahorie) was the lover of Victor Hugo's mother. Having long lived clandestinely in a house at the back of the grounds of the former Feuillantine convent where the Hugos resided, he was Victor's godfather and tutor.

16. Quoted in Tulard, "1800–1815," 301.

17. That, at any rate, is the version reported by Alexandre Brierre de Boismont, who bought the Dubuisson establishment from a Dr. Pressat in 1847. See Alexandre Brierre de Boismont, *Des hallucinations, ou Histoire raisonnée des apparitions, des visions, des songes, de l'extase, du magnétisme et du somnambulisme* (Paris: Germer-Baillière, 1862), 88n2. Dubuisson's credentials as a specialist in mental illness were confirmed by his publication of a dissertation ("Dissertation sur la manie," 1812) and a book on the subject (*Des vésanies, ou Maladies mentales*, 1816).

18. César Cantu, *Histoire universelle* (Brussels: Vanbuggenhoud, 1849), 10:137.

19. Adolphe Thiers, *Histoire du Consulat et de l'Empire* (Paris: Paulin, 1856), 14:524. Thiers's opinion was hotly challenged by Ernest Hamel in *Histoire des deux conspirations du Général Malet* (Paris: Librairie de la Société des Gens de Lettres, 1873).

20. Max Billard, *La conspiration de Malet* (Paris: Perrin, 1907), 37.

21. Henri Gaubert, *Conspirateurs au temps de Napoléon Ier* (Paris: Flammarion, 1962), 291.

22. Letter from Ferdinand Bascans to his mother, March 12, 1832. Quoted in Georges d'Heylli, *La fille de George Sand* (Paris: A. Davy, 1900), 123. Casimir Pinel opened his home on 76 rue de Chaillot in 1820. In 1845 he transferred it to Château Saint-James in Neuilly, where he died in 1866. See Émile Gilbrin, "La lignée médi-

cale des Pinel, leur aide aux prisonniers politiques sous la Terreur et pendant la Restauration," *Histoire des Sciences Médicales* 11 (1977): 29–34.

23. Letter of May 29, 1832, in Heylli, *La fille de George Sand*, 125.

24. Once the siege was lifted, Bascans promised to turn himself in, and he did so. In January 1833, when he still had a year and a half to serve, he dropped all his journalistic activities. He then mused, "And now what will I do upon leaving my gentle prison of Chaillot?" Letter to his mother, January 18, 1883, in Heylli, *La fille de George Sand*, 131.

25. Pinel, *Traité* (1800), 299–300. (Cf. Davis translation, *Treatise on Insanity*, 283–84.)

26. Letter from Pussin (erroneously spelled Piersin) to the members of the Commission des Administrations Civiles, Police et Tribunaux at Place des Piques in Paris, 19 Frimaire Year III (December 9, 1794), reproduced in Alexandre Tuetey, *L'assistance publique à Paris pendant la Révolution* (Paris: Imprimerie Nationale, 1897), 3:373.

27. On the relationship between science and ideology, I know of no better book than Anne Fausto-Sterling's *Sexing the Body: Gender Politics and the Construction of Sexuality* (New York: Basic Books, 2000).

28. Michael Sibalis, "Un aspect de la légende noire de Napoléon: Le mythe de l'enfermement des opposants comme fous," *Revue de l'Institut Napoléon* 156, no. 1 (1991): 9–24.

29. Marc-Antoine Baudot, *Notes historiques sur la Convention Nationale, le Directoire, l'Empire et l'exil des votants* (Paris: D. Jouaust, 1893), 62–64. See also Michel Vovelle, "Notes complémentaires sur le poète Théodore Desorgues, ou Quand les inconnus se font connaître," *Annales Historiques de la Révolution Française* 265 (1986): 341–45.

30. Michael Sibalis, "L'enfermement de Théodore Desorgues: Documents inédits," *Annales Historiques de la Révolution Française* 284 (1991): 243–46. My thanks to Gisèle Sapiro for bringing this article to my attention.

31. ADVDM, Charenton, Registres d'observations hommes et femmes, 1799–1814, 4X681, unfoliated.

32. *Gazette Nationale, ou Le Moniteur Universel* 351 (December 16, 1792): 744.

33. ADVDM, Charenton, Registres d'observations hommes et femmes, 1799–1814, 4X681.

34. Louis Sébastien Mercier, *Le tableau de Paris* (1788; Paris: La Découverte, 1998), 260.

35. Auguste Kuscinski, *Dictionnaire des conventionnels* (Paris: F. Rieder, 1916).

36. Archives Nationales, F15, 2604–5. Copy of a letter from Dr. Lanefranque to M. Desportes, a member of the hospital commission, Bicêtre, September 23, 1807.

37. Philippe Pinel, *Traité médico-philosophique sur l'aliénation mentale*, 2nd French edition, completely revamped and expanded (1809), reprinted with annotations by Jean Garrabé and Dora B. Weiner (Paris: Empêcheurs de Penser en Rond, 2005). Translated into English by Gordon Hickish, David Healy, and Louis C. Char-

land as *Medico-philosophical Treatise on Mental Alienation* (Chichester, UK: Wiley-Blackwell, 2008), 101 (§228). Hereafter Pinel, *Medico-philosophical Treatise* (1809).

38. Psalms 14:1.

39. Three authoritative biographies are Gilbert Lely, *Vie du marquis de Sade*, rev. ed. (Paris: Jean-Jacques Pauvert, 1965); Maurice Lever, *Donatien Alphonse François, marquis de Sade* (Paris: Fayard, 1991); and Jean-Jacques Pauvert, *Sade vivant*, 3 vols. (Paris: Robert Laffont, 1986–90). Studies focusing on Sade's stay in Charenton include J. F. Reverzy, "Sade à Charenton: Une scène primitive de l'aliénisme," *L'Information Psychiatrique* 53, no. 10 (December 1977): 1169–81, and Michel Gourévitch, "Le théâtre des fous: Avec Sade, sans sadisme," in *Petits et grands théâtres du marquis de Sade*, ed. Annie Le Brun (Paris: Paris Art Center, 1989).

40. Lettre from Sade to Gaufridy, 1790, quoted in Lely, *Vie du marquis de Sade*, 399.

41. Archives Nationales, DVI, no. 7, quoted by Tuetey, *Assistance publique*, 1:455.

42. Marcel Gauchet and Gladys Swain, *Madness and Democracy* (Paris: Gallimard, 2007), 172. Various sources spell the name of the director of Charenton in two ways: Coulmier and Coulmiers; I adopt the former, which is faithful to his signature as found in the archives.

43. Charles Nodier, "Souvenirs et portraits," in *Œuvres complètes* (Paris: Eugène Renduel, 1833), 8:166.

44. "My manner of thinking, so you say, cannot be approved. Do you suppose I care? A poor fool indeed is he who adopts a manner of thinking to suit other people! My manner of thinking stems straight from my considered reflections; it holds with my existence, with the way I am made. It is not in my power to alter it; and if it were, I'd not do so. This manner of thinking you find fault with is my sole consolation in life; it alleviates all my sufferings in prison, it composes all my pleasures in the world outside, it is dearer to me than life itself. Not my manner of thinking but the manner of thinking of others has been the source of my unhappiness." Letter from Sade to his wife, early November 1783, translated by Richard Seaver in Marquis de Sade, *Letters from Prison* (New York: Arcade, 1999), 327.

45. Letter from Sade to Coulmier, 27 Messidor Year II (July 16, 1803), published in D. A. F. de Sade, *Lettres inédites et documents*, introduced and annotated by Jean-Louis Debauve (Paris: Ramsay, 1990) 488–90.

46. Ibid., 494. "Plainte contre M. de Coulmiers," Charenton, 1804.

47. Quoted by Lely, *Vie du marquis de Sade*, 634.

48. Hippolyte de Colins, "Notice sur l'établissement consacré au traitement de l'aliénation mentale, établi à Charenton près Paris, 1812," published as an appendix to D. A. F. Sade, *Journal inédit* (Paris: Gallimard, 1994), 116.

49. Archives Nationales, F15 2606–7. Letter from Eu. de Gaillion to the minister of the interior, Charenton, August 1, 1807. Gaillion was admitted to Charenton on October 15, 1806, at government expense.

50. Quoted in Sade, *Journal inédit*, 116.

51. August Friedrich Schweigger, "Une visite des établissements d'aliénés pari-

siens en 1808," translated from German to French and uploaded by Michel Caire to his website, Histoire de la Psychiatrie en France, http://psychiatrie.histoire.free.fr/index.htm, accessed September 2012.

52. Charles François Giraudy, *Mémoire sur la maison nationale de Charenton* (Paris: Société de Médecine, 1804), 7.

53. The marquis de Sade presented Marie-Constance Quesnet as his illegitimate daughter so she could stay with him. Coulmier was probably aware of this subterfuge.

54. This and the two following passages are excerpted from Royer-Collard's letter of August 2, 1808, to the minister of police, Joseph Fouché, quoted in Lely, *Vie du marquis de Sade*, 640–41.

55. Quoted in Lely, *Vie du marquis de Sade*, 642.

56. Letter from Coulmier to the minister of the interior, December 24, 1810, quoted in Marquis de Sade, *Correspondance* (Geneva: Slatkine, 1997), 25:332.

57. Archives Nationales, F15 1946. Letter from Coulmier to Emperor Napoleon, 1811.

58. Quoted in Lely, *Vie du marquis de Sade*, 647.

59. Sade, *Journal inédit*. Some of this material has been translated into English by John Philips in *Ghosts of Sodom: The Secret Journals of the Marquis de Sade* (Clerkenwell, UK: Creation Books, 2003).

60. Chapron is identified in the archives as Coulmier's "secretary," but his poor spelling leads me to think that, technically unable to fulfill that role, he acted instead as the director's factotum.

61. Archives Nationales, F15 2608. All the testimony is filed under this call number. The italics imitate the original documents.

62. Archives Nationales, F15 2609–2609B. Letter dated April 5, 1813. This alcoholic veteran was at that moment being investigated for stealing from other inmates. His accusations may therefore have been a way out of his predicament, according to the old principle that the best defense is an attack.

63. Archives Nationales, F15 2608. Letter dated April 21, 1812. Coulmier would next enter into dispute with Rivet, a surgical student at Charenton.

64. Archives Nationales, F15 2608.

65. Archives Nationales, F15 2606–7. Undated letter from Coulmier to the minister of the interior.

66. Annie Le Brun, *On n'enchaîne pas les volcans* (Paris: Gallimard, 2006), 69 ff. On the notion of theatricality in Sade's oeuvre, see Annie Le Brun's other publications, notably *Soudain, un bloc d'abîme, Sade* (Paris: Jean-Jacques Pauvert, 1986), and *Petits et grands théâtres du marquis de Sade* (Paris: Paris Art Center, 1989).

67. Antoine-Athanase Royer-Collard, "État sommaire de la maison de Charenton sous le rapport du service médical et aperçu des réformes qui y sont nécessaires," reprinted in Thierry Haustgen, "Les débuts difficiles du Dr Royer-Collard à Charenton," *Synapse* 58 (November 1989): 57–66.

68. Pinel, *Medico-philosophical Treatise* (1809), 91 (§209). Hippolyte de Colins quoted this passage in his "Notice sur l'établissement," 147–48.

CHAPTER THREE

1. Alphonse Esquiros, *Paris, ou Les sciences, les institutions et les mœurs au XIXe siècle* (Paris: Au comptoir des Imprimeurs Unis, 1847), 2:118.

2. See notably "Esquirol et la nosographie," in *Nouvelle histoire de la psychiatrie*, ed. Jacques Postel and Claude Quétel (Paris: Dunod, 1994), as well Esquirol's entry "Monomanie," in *Dictionnaire des sciences médicales*, vol. 34 (Paris: Panckoucke, 1819). [*The Physiognomy of Mental Diseases* (London: Longman, 1840), by Sir Alexander Morison, MD, included a chapter titled "Monomania with Elated Ideas," which repeatedly refers to "delusions of grandeur"; Morison, a physician at Bethlem Hospital and the Surrey Asylum, also described other monomanias with various "propensities"—a propensity to "homicide," to "burn," to "drunkenness"—as well as "erotomania" and "nymphomania."—Trans.]

3. Charles Duveyrier, *Le monomane*, a play in five acts (Paris: Bufquin-Desessart, 1835), 32.

4. Eugène Scribe, *Une monomanie*, a comedy in one act, performed at the Théâtre du Gymnase, Paris, August 31 1832, published in Eugène Scribe, *Œuvres complètes* (Paris: E. Dentu, 1876–85), 24:123–24.

5. Jean-Étienne-Dominique Esquirol, *Mental Maladies: A Treatise on Insanity*, trans. E. K. Hunt (Philadelphia: Lea and Blanchard, 1845), 320.

6. Ibid., 333.

7. Ibid., 334.

8. Philippe Pinel, *Traité médico-philosophique sur l'aliénation mentale*, 2nd French edition, completely revamped and expanded (1809), reprinted with annotations by Jean Garrabé and Dora B. Weiner (Paris: Empêcheurs de Penser en Rond, 2005). Translated into English by Gordon Hickish, David Healy, and Louis C. Charland as *Medico-philosophical Treatise on Mental Alienation* (Chichester, UK: Wiley–Blackwell, 2008), 84 (§198). Hereafter Pinel, *Medico-philosophical Treatise* (1809).

9. François-Josephe-Victor Broussais, *De l'irritation et de la folie* (Paris: J.-B. Baillière, 1839), 2:368.

10. Ulysse Trélat, *La folie lucide* (Paris: Adrien Delahaye, 1861), 178–223.

11. ADVDM, Charenton, Registre d'observations médicales hommes et femmes, 1819, 4X678, fol. 19. Entry dated June 2, 1819.

12. L. F. Calmeil, "Paralysie générale des aliénés," *Dictionnaire de médecine, ou Répertoire général des sciences médicales considérées sous le rapport théorique et pratique*, ed. Adelon, Béclard, Bérard et al. (1841), 23:141. See also the chapter on general paresis in Postel and Quétel, *Nouvelle histoire de la psychiatrie*, 203–14.

13. Ibid., 134.

14. Ibid., 135–36.

15. Jan Goldstein, *Console and Classify: The French Psychiatric Profession in the Nineteenth Century* (Cambridge: Cambridge University Press, 1990), 161. In 1841 psychiatrists were still learning to differentiate cases of general paresis from certain patients with delusions of grandeur, so it is very risky to combine figures that may partly overlap. Motor disorders caused by dysfunction of the nervous system

nevertheless ultimately identify the former with certainty, the main symptoms of progressive paralysis being uneven pupils, staggering gait, and trembling tongue. Twenty years later, Louis Victor Macé, then a physician at Bicêtre, would write: "Distinguishing delusions of grandeur from general paresis should not pose serious difficulties. The very different gait displayed in monomania and general paresis, plus the presence or absence of problems of mobility, serves as the basis for diagnosis; as to the delusions themselves, they display distinct differences. Monomaniacs claim to be prophets, sons of kings, generals, or ministers and say they have a vast fortune or great power; they are often maniacs who, despite their deluded ideas, retain vigor and logic in their thinking. Their appearance, dress, and speech rigorously conform to their pretensions; they are proud, disdainful, hypersensitive, and demand that they be treated with honor; and with respect to their own birth and social position they recount stories that, despite being implausible, are logical enough and do not diverge from the order of general possibility; furthermore, they are consistent with themselves, and there are no internal contradictions to the titles they claim. As we have seen, there is nothing of the sort among paralytics, whose ideas are basically flitting and absurd; they are simultaneously pope and emperor; even as they speak of their wealth and millions, they acknowledge their trade, however humble it may be, and admit that they earn forty sous a day. Finally, monomaniacs with elated ideas cling to their organized, systematic delusions for years, whereas among paralytics ideas fall apart and lose coherence from day to day." Louis Victor Macé, *Traite pratique des maladies mentales* (Paris: J.-B. Baillière, 1862), 477–78.

16. Alfred de Musset, *La confession d'un enfant du siècle* (1836; Paris: Gallimard, 1973), 35.

17. François Leuret, *Fragments psychologiques sur la folie* (Paris: Crochard, 1834), 307.

18. François Fabre, *Maladies de l'encéphale, maladies mentales, maladies nerveuses*, vol. 9 of *Bibliothèque du médecin-praticien, ou Résumé général de tous les ouvrages de clinique médicale et chirurgicale etc.* (Paris: J.-B. Baillière, 1849), 494–95. This publication was written by a group of doctors; individual entries are not signed.

19. Hugo had this motto carved in wood over the doors of Hauteville House. Of all writers, Hugo was the most susceptible to a diagnosis of delusions of grandeur. Following the events of the Commune, when a journalist ridiculed Hugo's oracular pretensions and called for a Charenton worthy of him, Dr. Prosper Despine replied, "It can hardly be contested that V. Hugo has been in a psychological state that constitutes madness through ideas of grandeur and other passions: his blindness with regard to the irrational ideas he preaches has been demonstrated more than once; yet it remains certain that you could not find one doctor who would sign a document of admission to the asylum for this poet with the goal of making him submit to medical treatment." Prosper Despine, *De la folie du point de vue philosophique, ou Plus spécialement psychologique, étudiée chez le malade et l'homme de santé* (Paris: Savy, 1875), 788. There is also Jean Cocteau's well-known quip, "Victor Hugo was a madman who thought he was Victor Hugo."

20. ADVDM, Charenton, Registre médical, 1818, fol. 21. Patient admitted on May 18, 1818, discharged as cured on March 13, 1819.

21. Esquiros, *Paris, ou Les Sciences*, 119–20.

22. Gérard de Nerval, "Le roi de Bicêtre (XVIe siècle): Raoul Spifame," in *Les Illuminés*, vol. 2 of *Œuvres complètes* (Paris: Gallimard, 1984), 891–92. This text was first published in the September 17–18, 1830, issue of *La Presse* under the title "Biographie singulière de Raoul Spifame, seigneur des Granges," pseudonymously signed "Aloysius." It was reprinted in 1845 in *La Revue Pittoresque* with the title "Le meilleur roi de France," under Nerval's name. According to the scholars who edited the Pléiade collection, this story may be the work not of Nerval, but rather of Auguste Maquet, Alexandre Dumas's famous ghostwriter.

23. Ibid., 892. Note that Nerval himself experienced this doppelgänger effect throughout his life. Under one of the few extant photographs of himself he wrote, "I am the other." On two occasions he was admitted to Dr. Blanche's nursing home, where in 1853 he began the manuscript of *Aurelia*, an attempt to understand what society termed "madness" and what he described as "the overflowing of dreams into real life." Raoul Spifame should be viewed in this light.

24. AAP-HP, La Salpêtrière, Registre d'observations médicales, 5th division, 1st section, (1820–51), 6R1, fol. 26. This patient's fate is worth mentioning. Virginie Devaux was admitted to La Salpêtrière on September 23, 1833, and died there on December 12, 1851. For many years she remained motionless beside her bed, repeatedly stating that she was the king of France. Dr. Ulysse Trélat, who recorded the comment quoted in the text, added, "It was impossible to draw other words from her. One day we managed to take her to the singing session, where she underwent a remarkable change. We discovered that she could sing, and she was soon displaying one of the most pleasant voices to charm the ear. One day Meyerbeer, Geraldi, and Liszt paid an unscheduled visit to La Salpêtrière, and they immediately compared Mademoiselle Devaux's flowing voice to 'that of Mademoiselle Persiani.' Today she has sunk into total dejection, no longer recalls anything, is absolutely unable to sing, no longer has good health, and is swiftly declining both physically and mentally."

25. Victor Hugo, *Les Misérables*, trans. Isabel F. Hapgood (New York: Thomas Y. Crowell, 1887), 234.

26. ADVDM, Charenton, Registre d'observations médicales hommes et femmes, 1831, 4X699, fol. 69. Patient admitted on May 2, 1831. At that time Charenton was headed by Esquirol, who replaced Royer-Collard upon the latter's death in 1825.

27. ADVDM, Charenton, Registre d'observations médicales hommes et femmes (cas particulier) 1812–44, 2Mi63, unfoliated. Patient admitted on August 21, 1839.

28. ADVDM, Charenton, Registre d'observations médicales femmes, 1848–49, 4X723, fol. 63. Patient admitted on May 27, 1848, transferred to La Salpêtrière on September 30, 1849.

29. AAP-HP, Bicêtre, Registres d'observation médicales, 5th division, 1st and 2nd sections, 6R18 (1860–61), fol. 307. Patient admitted on February 15, 1861.

30. François-René de Chateaubriand, *Mémoires d'outre-tombe* (Paris: Gallimard, 1951), 1:1008.

31. ADVDM, Charenton, Registre médical hommes et femmes, 1818, 4X677, fols. 35, 39 and 47.

32. Hugo, *Les Misérables*, 111.

33. Thierry Haustgen, *Observations et certificats psychiatriques au XIXe siècle* (Rueil-Malmaison: Ciba, 1985), 238–39.

34. In the early twentieth century, Anna Anderson (among other candidates) claimed to be the Grand Duchess Anastasia, daughter of Czar Nicholas II, who was murdered by the Bolsheviks along with her entire family. The hoax has subsequently been confirmed by DNA testing on the remains of the imperial family. Binjamin Wilkormiski, meanwhile, was the name under which Bruno Grosjean wrote an earth-shattering account of his time in the Majdenak concentration camp as a four-year-old boy. His alleged memoirs turned out to be pure fiction—which has not prevented Wilkormiski from claiming to be Jewish and having been sent to the camp even though he spent his childhood in a Swiss orphanage. See Claude Arnaud, *Qui dit je en nous? Une histoire subjective de l'identité* (Paris: Grasset, 2006).

35. That I came across no other references to Louis XVII in the registers does not necessarily mean there were no other claimants to the title of dauphin; diagnoses sometimes merely indicate that the patient "thinks he is an important person" without mentioning a specific identity. The general absence is nevertheless striking, if only statistically. Note, however, that Esquirol claimed to have treated numerous patients who thought they were the dauphin.

36. ADVDM, Charenton, Registre d'observations médicales hommes et femmes, 1831, 4X699, fol. 77. Patient admitted on June 10, 1831, discharged not entirely cured, September 7, 1831.

37. Fabre, *Bibliothèque du médecin-praticien*, 9:496.

38. Esprit Blanche, *Du danger des rigueurs corporelles dans le traitement de la folie* (Paris: A. Gardembas, 1839), 21.

39. Leuret, *Fragments psychologiques*, 321. See also Leuret's *Du traitement moral de la folie* (Paris: J.-B. Baillière, 1840), 418–62, where he recounts the story of a former soldier who thought he was Napoleon for fifteen years but who was allegedly cured in a matter of months thanks to a combination of ruse and harsh therapies.

40. Leuret, *Du traitement moral*, 424. See also François Leuret, "Du traitement des idées ou conceptions délirantes," *Gazette Médicale de Paris* 37 (September 10, 1837): 577–81, where the physician cites several other cases of Napoleons cured by showers.

41. ADVDM, Charenton, Registre d'observations médicales, cas particuliers, 1812–44, 2Mi63, unfoliated. This case is dated July 3, 1836.

42. ADVDM, Charenton, Registre médical hommes et femmes, 1818, 4X677, fol. 21. Patient admitted on May 18, 1818, discharged as cured on March 13, 1819.

43. AAP-HP, La Salpêtrière, Registre d'observations médicales, 5th division, 2nd section, call number (1851–54), 6R24, fol. 108. Patient admitted on June 16, 1852, transferred on July 20, 1856.

44. The strange thing is that the very conservative *Journal des Débats* reported this information in its issue of December 16, 1840. It was mathematically impossible, since horses live thirty-five years at most, and the battle of Marengo took place on June 14, 1800, that is to say forty years earlier. See also Victor Hugo's account in *Choses vues, 1838–1840* (Paris: Gallimard, 1972), 154.

45. Alexandre Dumas, *Mes mémoires* (Paris: Alexandre Cadot, 1853), 15:213.

46. ADVDM, Charenton, Registre d'observations médicales hommes, 1841–42, 4X708, fol. 83. Patient admitted early June 1841, discharged on August 31, 1842, "having fallen into a kind of imbecility."

47. ADVDM, Charenton, Registre d'observations médicales, June 1841 to October 1843, 4X721, fol. 51. Patient admitted April 29, 1841, discharged as cured on October 30, 1841.

48. AAP-HP, La Salpêtrière, Registre d'observations médicales, 5th division, 1st section, 1820–51, 6R1, fol. 298. Patient admitted February 14, 1851, transferred on February 11, 1852.

49. ADVDM, Charenton, Registre d'observations médicales hommes, 1847–48, fol. 201. Patient admitted on October 25, 1848, transferred to Bicêtre on May 10, 1849.

50. Karl Marx, *The Eighteenth Brumaire of Louis Bonaparte* (Sydney: Objective Systems Pty, 2006), 1.

51. AAP-HP, Bicêtre, Registres d'observations médicales, 5th division, 1st and 2nd sections, 1847–53, 6R2, fol. 297.

52. Ibid., 1858–59, 6R13, fol. 353.

53. Ibid., 1863–64, 6R23, fol. 314.

54. Ibid., 1867–69, 6R31, fol. 319.

55. Ibid., 1853–56, 6R6, fol. 133.

56. Ibid., 1858–59, 6R13, fol. 479.

57. Ibid., 1859–60, 6R15, fol. 268.

58. Ibid., 1862–63, 6R21, fol. 208.

59. Ibid., 1864–65, 6R25, fol. 314.

60. Benjamin Constant, *Œuvres politiques*, with an introduction, notes and index by Charles Louandre (Paris: Charpentier, 1874), 47.

61. Honoré de Balzac, *Autre étude de femme*, *La comédie humaine* (Paris: Gallimard, 1993), 700–701.

62. ADVDM, Charenton, Registre médical hommes et femmes, 1818, 4X677, fol. 35.

63. Casimir Pinel, ed., *Lettres de Pinel précédées d'une notice plus étendue sur sa vie, par son neveu le Dr. Casimir Pinel* (Paris: Victor Masson, 1859), 33. Casimir, the nephew of Philippe Pinel, asserted that this anecdote came straight from his uncle.

64. Scipion Pinel, *Physionomie de l'homme aliéné* (Paris: Librairie des Sciences Médicales, 1833), 40–41n. Scipion was the son of Philippe Pinel and was responsible for spreading the legend that his father freed the mentally ill from their chains in a startling move, despite warnings by Georges Couthon, who had visited Bicêtre in 1792 (whereas Pinel was not appointed there until 1793). Philippe Pinel himself

never claimed credit for this act, and the legend has subsequently been debunked. Scipion was also a physician who specialized in mental illness, and he is largely responsible for creating the myth of the inspired, philanthropic Pinel. Was he perhaps trying to establish a parallel between the emperor and the founder of psychiatry? Whatever the case, his assertions are open to doubt.

65. Emmanuel de Las Cases, *Mémorial de Sainte-Hélène* (Paris: Garnier Frères, 1961), 2:58, quoted in Marc Renneville, *Le langage des crânes: Une histoire de la phrénologie* (Paris: Institut d'Édition Sanofi-Synthélabo/Empêcheurs de Penser en Rond, 2000), 82. Renneville's book, notably pages 165–73, is the main source on the history of phrenology in this chapter.

66. David Richard, *La phrénologie et Napoléon* (Paris: Pihan Delaforest, 1835), 3.

67. Franz Gall and J. G. Spurzheim, *Anatomie et physiologie du système nerveux en général, et du cerveau en particulier* (Paris: Haussmann et d'Hautel, 1810–19), 3:184–85, quoted in Renneville, *Le langage des crânes*, 67.

68. The list of "organs" that Antommarchi noted on Napoleon's skull included those for dissimulation, conquest, benevolence, imagination, and ambition or thirst for glory. See François Antommarchi, *Derniers moments de Napoléon* (Brussels, H. Tarlier, 1825), 156–60. The story of Napoleon's death mask has given rise to extensive literature; for a bibliographic overview, see Chantal Lheureux-Prévot, "L'affaire des masques mortuaires de Napoléon," *Napoleonica: La Revue* 3 (2008): 60–75. It is worth pointing out that a cast of the back part of Napoleon's skull was also taken on Saint Helena, with the intention of combining it with the mask to make a complete head. But Dr. Francis Burton, the English physician who was involved in the process and intended to carry out the operation, imprudently gave the "Antommarchi" mask (the face and front part of the skull) to the wife of Maréchal Bertrand, who slipped it into her luggage and left for France. After several unsuccessful attempts to recover what he considered his property, Burton destroyed the rear section in his possession.

69. "Commentaire phrénologique sur la tête de Napoléon," *Gazette Médicale de Paris* 2, no. 28 (July 12, 1834): 435.

70. Ibid., 436.

71. Commentaire phrénologique sur la tête de Napoléon," *Gazette Médicale de Paris* 2, no. 29 (July 19, 1834): 453.

72. Dr. Louis Peisse was journalist, translator, and specialist in the history of science and philosophy as well as a regular popularizer of medical subjects. He ended his career as a curator at the École des Beaux-Arts in Paris.

73. Louis-Francisque Lélut, *Du démon de Socrate* (Paris: Trinquart, 1836), and *L'amulette de Pascal* (Paris; J.-B. Baillière, 1846).

74. Jacques-Joseph Moreau de Tours, *La psychologie morbide dans ses rapports avec la philosophie de l'histoire, ou De l'influence des névropathies sur le dynamisme intellectuel* (Paris: Victor Masson, 1859), 559–60. Moreau de Tours was following the lead of his colleague Alexandre Brierre de Boismont; see Brierre de Boismont's *Des hallucinations, ou Histoire raisonnée des apparitions, des visions, des songes, de l'extase, du magnétisme et du somnambulisme*, 2nd ed. (Paris: Germer-Baillière, 1852), 60–61.

75. Mirko D. Grmek, "Histoire des recherches sur les relations entre le génie et la maladie," *Revue d'Histoire des Sciences et de Leurs Applications* 15, no. 1 (1962): 51–68.

76. In a letter to Nietzsche written in Geneva on July 12, 1887, Taine wrote, "I am most pleased that my articles on Napoleon struck you as authentic, and nothing can sum up my impression more accurately than the two German terms that you use, *Unmensch* und *Uebermensch*." As is well known, Nietzsche drew inspiration from Napoleon for his theory of the superman.

77. Cesare Lombroso, *The Man of Genius*, trans. anonymous (New York: Walter Scott, 1917).

78. The rumors of Napoleon's epilepsy were triggered by an anecdote recounted by Talleyrand. The incident took place in 1805 when the emperor took Talleyrand by the arm and led him into his bedroom. "Scarcely were we there than the emperor fell to the floor; he had only enough time to tell me to shut the door. I removed his cravat, because he appeared to be suffocating. He did not vomit, but groaned and drooled. Monsieur de Rémusat gave him some water, I doused him in eau de cologne. He had these kinds of convulsions that would end after fifteen minutes; we set him in a chair; he began to speak, dressed himself, enjoined us to secrecy, and half an hour later was on the road to Karlsruhe." Charles Maurice de Talleyrand, *Mémoires du prince de Talleyrand*, with a preface and notes by the duc de Broglie (Paris: Calmann Lévy, 1891), 1:295–96. Benjamin Constant's memoirs refute Talleyrand: "Never had the emperor been subject to epileptic fits. That is another one of those tales bandied at his expense." Benjamin Constant, *Mémoires de Constant, premier valet de chambre de l'empereur, sur la vie privée de Napoléon, sa famille et sa cour* (Paris: Ladvocat, 1830), 3:17n.

79. Louis Proal, "Napoléon était-il épileptique?" *Archives d'Anthropologie Criminelle* 101 (1902): 261.

80. Dr. Augustin Cabanès, *Au chevet de l'empereur* (Paris: Albin Michel, 1958), 279. Concerning Napoleon's mental state, Cabanès followed the opinion of Dr. Gabriel Ravarit, former head of the mental illness clinic at the Poitiers hospital, who delivered a paper on the subject at the Société Médico-historique and published an article in *La Chronique Médicale* 16, no. 3 (February 1, 1909): 66 ff.

81. Maurice Beaujeu, *Psychologie des premiers Césars: Une étude de médecine légale dans l'histoire* (Lyon: A. Storck, 1893), 52.

82. Adolphe Thiers, *Histoire du Consulat et de l'Empire*, 21 vols. (Paris: Paulin, Lheureux, 1845–69).

83. Jules Michelet, *Ma jeunesse* (Paris: Calmann-Lévy, 1884), 148.

84. Jules Michelet, *Histoire du XIXe siècle* (Paris: Michel Lévy Frères, 1875), 3:347.

85. Pierre Larousse, "Napoléon," in *Grand dictionnaire universel du XIXe siècle* (Paris: Larousse, 1866–88), 16:809.

86. Pierre Larousse, "Bonaparte," in *Grand dictionnaire universel du XIXe siècle* (Paris: Larousse, 1866–88), 3:920. Alfred de Vigny underscored the divorce between the two men making up Napoleon Bonaparte in a different fashion. "Bona-

parte was the man, Napoleon was the role. The first wore a frock coat and a hat, the latter a laurel wreath and a toga." *Journal d'un poète* (Paris: Michel Lévy, 1867), 82.

87. Jacques Lacan, *Écrits: The First Complete Edition in English*, trans. Bruce Fink (New York: W. W. Norton, 2007), 139; the subsequent quotation is found on page 140.

88. François Leuret, "Du traitement des idées ou conceptions délirantes," *Gazette Médicale de Paris* 37 (September 10, 1837): 579.

CHAPTER FOUR

1. François-René de Chateaubriand, *Œuvres complètes* (Paris: Pourrat Frères, 1834), 4:84.

2. Ernest Jones, *Sigmund Freud: Life and Work* (London: Hogarth Press, 1953–57), 1:201.

3. Dr. Augustin Cabanès wrote an entire book on "revolutionary neurosis," while "*paranoia reformatoria*" (induced by ideas of social reform) was, along with hysteria and an overinflated sense of self, one of the pathologies ascribed to Olympe de Gouges by Dr. Alfred Guillois, who devoted a study to her. See Augustin Cabanès and Lucien Nass, *La névrose révolutionnaire* (Paris: Albin Michel, 1925), and Alfred Guillois, *Étude médico-psychologique sur Olympe de Gouges* (Lyon, 1904).

4. Jacques Postel, *Éléments pour une histoire de la psychiatrie occidentale* (Paris: Harmattan, 2007), 189. Postel argues that this tragedy "explains the loyalty of [Esquirol's] family toward Louis XVIII and the future political and administrative favor that he would enjoy during successive Restoration governments."

5. An early version of the case had already been published in the *Journal Général de Médecine*, 2nd ser., 1 (1818): 341–47.

6. Entry "Théroigne de Méricourt," in Alphonse de Beauchamps and Étienne Psaume, *Biographie moderne, ou Galerie historique, civile, militaire, politique, littéraire et judiciaire* (Paris: Mme Ve Jeunhomme, 1816), 3:287. [The corresponding passages from Hunt's translation of Esquirol's *Mental Maladies*, 218, have been adapted here to underscore the similarity of wording—Trans.]

7. Esquirol, *Mental Maladies*, 219.

8. Cabanès and Nass, *La névrose révolutionnaire*, 525.

9. Nor, for that matter, did the *Biographie moderne* mention this incident.

10. Esquirol, *Mental Maladies*, 219–20; translation slightly adapted here.

11. Ibid., 220.

12. Both sets of drawings by Gabriel can be consulted at the Bibliothèque Nationale de France in Paris. The series devoted to mental patients contains ninety-five drawings, call number Res-JF-29–4. In 1818 Esquirol wrote that "studying the physiognomy of madmen is not an object of pointless curiosity; this study helps to unravel the nature of the ideas and emotions that sustain the delusions in these patients. . . . I had over two hundred madmen drawn with this idea in mind; perhaps someday I will publish my observations on this interesting subject." Étienne Esquirol, *Des maladies mentales* (Paris: Frénésie, 1989), 2:19. [This part of volume 2 was

not included in Hunt's 1845 translation of *Mental Maladies*—Trans.] The BNF's set of portraits is not part of the two hundred commissioned in 1818, however. That set must have been done later, because it includes "Eugène Hugo, brother of the poet, idiot," who was institutionalized only in 1822 and did not arrive in Esquirol's ward until 1823. Hugo would end up in Charenton, where Esquirol was appointed in 1825. The conclusion is that the physician commissioned at least 295 portraits and also collected casts of the skulls of mental patients. I thank Annie Le Brun for bringing this remarkable sketchbook to my attention.

13. Esquirol, *Mental Maladies*, 217.

14. Elisabeth Roudinesco, *Théroigne de Méricourt: A Melancholic Woman during the French Revolution*, trans. Martin Thom (London: Verso, 1991), 150–51.

15. Félix Voisin, *Des causes morales et physiques des maladies mentales* (Paris: J.-B. Baillière, 1826), 28–29.

16. Esquirol, *Mental Maladies*, 44.

17. Étienne Esquirol, *Des passions considérées comme causes, symptômes et moyens curatifs de l'aliénation mentale* (Paris: Didot Jeune, [1805]), 15.

18. Esquirol, *Maladies mentales*, 2:303. [This part of volume 2 was not included in Hunt's 1845 translation of *Mental Maladies*—Trans.]

19. Ibid., 2:304.

20. Esquirol, *Mental Maladies*, 219.

21. Ibid., 42 and 43.

22. Ibid., 200.

23. Ibid., 43.

24. Paul Jacoby, *Études sur la sélection dans ses rapports avec l'hérédité chez l'homme* (Paris: Germer-Baillière, 1881), 440. Dr. Jacoby included mental patients who were treated at home, which explains his high figures (analysis of which led to a computational error on his part, since he calculated the increase as 530.87 percent instead of 363.35 percent).

25. The first set of figures is taken from Esquirol, *Des maladies mentales*, 2:280 [not translated by Hunt—Trans.], the second set is found in the English translation, *Mental Maladies*, 47. For the two years 1811–12 Esquirol reported that fourteen patients were admitted to La Salpêtrière for insanity owing to political events, representing 4.3 percent of the total. The difference in percentages between Esquirol's private establishment and La Salpêtrière can be explained by the fact that the latter admitted only women, who in theory were less exposed to political madness.

26. Étienne Esquirol, "Aliénation mentale," *Encyclopédie du dix-neuvième siècle* (Paris, 1838), 192.

27. Esquirol, *Des maladies mentales*, 2:280.

28. Alexandre Brierre de Boismont, "De l'influence de la civilisation sur le développement de la folie," *Annales d'Hygiène Publique et de Médecine Légale*, 1st ser., 21 (1839): 261.

29. ADVDM, Charenton, Registre d'observations médicales hommes et femmes, 1830, 4X698, fol. 99. Patient admitted on August 12, 1830.

30. Ibid., fol. 103. Patient admitted on August 8, 1830.

31. Ibid., fol. 105. Patient admitted on August 15, 1830.

32. Ibid., fol. 130. Patient admitted in September 1830, discharged on July 1, 1832.

33. Ibid., fol. 146. Patient admitted in October 1830, discharged on May 8, 1831.

34. Ibid., fol. 100. Patient admitted on August 5, 1830.

35. Ibid., fol. 26. Patient admitted on February 21, 1831, died on May 31, 1831.

36. Ibid., fol. 30. Patient admitted on February 27, 1831, died in January 1832.

37. B[enjamin] Desportes, *Compte rendu au conseil général des hospices et hôpitaux civils de Paris sur le service des aliénés traités dans les hospices de la vieillesse (hommes et femmes)* [Bicêtre et La Salpêtrière] *pendant les années 1825, 1826, 1827, 1828, 1829, 1830, 1831, 1832, 1833* (Paris: Mme Huzard, 1835), part 2, 3. The cholera epidemic caused 100,000 deaths—20,000 in Paris alone—and sparked panic among the population.

38. Jacques-Étienne Belhomme, *Influence des événements et des commotions politiques sur le développement de la folie*, paper read at the Académie de Médecine on May 2, 1848, followed by a report by M. Londe, delivered on March 6, 1849 (Paris: Germer-Baillière, 1849), 4.

39. Ludger Lunier, *De l'influence des grandes commotions politiques et sociales sur le développement des maladies mentales* (Paris: F. Savy, 1874), 14.

40. Ibid., 24. Baillarger addressed the Académie de Médecine on March 13, 1849.

41. Benedict-Augustin Morel, *Traité des maladies mentales* (1852; Paris: Victor Masson, 1860), 88.

42. Ibid., 86.

43. Alexandre Brierre de Boismont, "Influence des derniers événements sur le développement de la folie," *L'Union Médicale*, July 20, 1848.

44. Philippe Pinel, *Medico-philosophical Treatise* [1809], 62 (§161). Note that the massacres took place in September 1792, whereas Pinel was not appointed to Bicêtre until 1793. The anecdote must therefore have been told by Pussin to Pinel, who put it in writing.

45. Alexandre Brierre de Boismont, *Des hallucinations, ou Histoire raisonnée des apparitions, des visions, des songes, de l'extase, du magnétisme et du somnambulisme*, 2nd ed. (Paris: Germer-Baillière, 1852), 370. [This passage, like that cited in note 47, does not appear to be included in the abridged English translation, *On Hallucinations: A History and Explanation of Apparitions, Visions, Dreams, Ecstasy, Magnetism and Somnabulism*, trans. Robert T. Hulme (Columbus, OH: Joseph H. Riley, 1860)—Trans.]

46. Alexandre Brierre de Boismont, *Annales Médico-psychologiques*, 2nd ser., 4 (January 1852): 100.

47. Brierre de Boismont, *Des hallucinations*, 369–70; emphasis added. Brierre de Boismont was a prolific author who became a mental specialist fairly late by founding two nursing homes, one in Paris and the other in the nearby suburb of Saint-Mandé, which had a reputation that rivaled Dr. Jaques-Émile Blanche's famous clinic on Montmartre. These duties did not prevent Brierre de Boismont from applying for the post of director of Charenton when Esquirol died in 1840, but that eminently political appointment went instead to an Orléans supporter, Achille Fo-

ville (who was fired in 1848 when the monarchy fell). It might be added that Brierre de Boismont was one of the founders, along with Baillarger and Laurent Cerise, of the Société Médico-psychologique in 1843.

48. Wilhelm Griesinger, *Mental Pathology and Therapeutics*, trans. C. Lockhart Robertson and James Rutherford (New York: William Wood, 1882), 98.

49. ADVDM, Charenton, Registre d'observations médicales hommes, 1847–48, 4X711, fol. 114. Patient admitted on May 20, 1847.

50. Ibid., 4X712, fol. 157. Patient admitted on July 20, 1848, discharged on November 9, 1848.

51. For an overview of this issue, see Michelle Perrot, "1848: La révolution des femmes," *L'Histoire* 218 (1998). See also studies by Michèle Riot-Sarcey, notably "Parcours des femmes dans l'apprentissage de la démocratie: Désirée Gay, Jeanne Deroin, Eugénie Niboyet, 1830–1870" (PhD diss., Université de Paris I, 1990), and, with Maurizio Gribaudi, *1848, La révolution oubliée* (Paris: Découverte, 2008).

52. Alexandre Dumas, in *Le Mois, Revue Historique et Politique Jour par Jour de Tous les Événements Qui Se Produisent en France et à l'Étranger depuis Février 1848*, 2nd ser., 17 (May 1, 1849): 141.

53. ADVDM, Registre d'observations médicales femmes, 1848–49, 4X723, fol. 65. Patient admitted on May 30, 1848, discharged as cured on July 27, 1848.

54. Ibid., fol. 136. Patient admitted on October 22, 1848. Lamartine's name recurs several times in the archive. He "appeared" in the asylum in men's cells and in women's speech. One woman, for example, traumatized when the insurgents invaded her home, subsequently became convinced that she was the wife of the poet: "She believes herself to be Madame de Lamartine, so she protects her children from poverty. / She want to address the people in order to tell them about her generous ideas. She wants to improve the condition of workers. / She wants to go to the National Assembly and plead for mercy for the insurgents. / Menstruation regular." Ibid., fol. 78. Patient admitted on July 2, 1848, died of pneumonia on November 18, 1848.

55. Louis Bergeret, "Cas nombreux d'aliénation mentale d'une forme particulière ayant pour cause la perturbation politique et sociale de February 1848," *Annales d'Hygiène Publique et de Médecine Légale*, 2nd ser., 20 (1863): 145.

56. Ibid., 148.

57. Ibid., 164.

58. An aside: It is striking to note that archive registers generally offer diagnoses that are more balanced and dispassionate than published material, as though publication called for exaggerating or dramatizing cases. I make this comment in passing, aware that a substantiated analysis would be required to elucidate the reasons for, and conditions behind, the exaggerated assessments.

59. ADVDM, Charenton, Registre d'observations médicales hommes, 1848, 4X712, fol. 123. Patient admitted late May, transferred to Bicêtre on July 9, 1848.

60. Archives Nationales, F15, 3917–19. This file contains correspondence between ministers, police headquarters, and the prefect with respect to the internment of various mental patients, 1843–48.

61. ADVDM, Charenton, Registre d'observations médicales hommes, 1848, 4X712, fol. 63. Patient admitted on March 27, 1848, escaped on September 6 by scrambling over the wall using an overlooked fence. Brought back by the police on September 14, he escaped again on September 21 with another inmate, using a set of keys misplaced by a nurse. His family brought him back on October 3, but he managed to flee once again on April 3, 1849, leaving a letter that is illegible because letters and syllables are missing in every word. There is no further trace of him.

62. Ibid., fol. 209. Patient admitted on November 18, 1848, transferred to Bicêtre on July 12 in a state of complete insanity—in addition to visions of the Virgin and Christ, the patient said he was a child of the sun and moon.

63. Victor Hugo, *Choses vues (1830–1848)* (Paris: Gallimard, 1972), 668.

64. As reported by Georges Duveau, *1848* (Paris: Gallimard, 1965), 124.

65. Alexis de Tocqueville, *Recollections*, trans. Alexander Teixeira de Mattos (New York: Macmillan, 1896), 168–69.

66. The Ateliers Nationaux, or National Workshops, were designed to provide government work for unemployed laborers. Trélat was very hostile to the scheme. He resigned his post as minister on June 18, 1848, but his inaction and mistakes helped to trigger the crisis that ended in the bloody events of June 22–26. These biographical details on Trélat are based on two sources: Jean Maintron, ed., *Dictionnaire biographique du mouvement ouvrier francais* (Paris: Éditions Ouvrières, 1966), and Pierre Morel's introduction to Ulysse Trélat, *La folie lucide* (Paris: Frénésie éditions, 1988), v–xxi. A useful source on Trélat's links to the Charbonnerie (Carbonari) movement is his own article "La Charbonnerie," in *Paris révolutionnaire*, by Godefroy Cavaignac et al. (Paris: Guillaumin, 1848), 217–60.

67. Tocqueville, *Recollections*, 163.

68. Ibid., 164.

69. Quoted in Maurice Dommanget, *Les idées politiques et sociales d'Auguste Blanqui* (Paris: Marcel Rivière, 1957), 15.

70. Letter from Sand to Barbès, dated March 14, 1849. George Sand and Armand Barbès, *Correspondance d'une amitié républicaine: 1848–1870*, with notes and an introduction by Michelle Perrot (Paris: Capucin, 1999), 33.

71. Bergeret, "Cas nombreux d'aliénation mentale," 141.

72. Alphonse de Lamartine, *History of the French Revolution of 1848*, trans. Francis Durivage and William Chase (Boston: Phillips, Samson, 1851), 1:127.

73. Daniel Stern [Marie d'Agoult], *Histoire de la révolution de 1848* (Paris: Gustave Sandré, 1850–53), 3:33; emphasis added.

74. Tocqueville, *Recollections*, 164; emphasis added.

75. Eugène Ionesco, *Journal en miettes* (Paris: Mercure de France, 1967), 223.

76. François Pardigon, *Épisodes des journées de juin 1848*, with an introduction by Alix Héricord (Paris: Fabrique, 2008), 191.

77. Paul Briquet, *Traité clinique et thérapeutique de l'hystérie* (Paris: J.-B. Baillière, 1859), 21–23.

78. Stern, *Histoire de la révolution de 1848*, 2:357.

79. Alfred de Vigny, *Œuvres* (Paris: Gallimard, 1948), 2:969.

80. Alexis de Tocqueville, *Œuvres complètes* (Paris: Michel Lévy Frères, 1866), 9:518.

81. Carl Theodor Groddeck, *De la maladie démocratique, nouvelle espèce de folie*, anonymous trans. from German (Paris: Germer-Baillière, 1850), 50–51.

82. Ibid., 56.

83. Ibid., 59.

84. Alain Chevrier, "Psychiatrie et politique: Sur la réception en France de *La maladie démocratique* de Carl Groddeck," *L'Évolution Psychiatrique* 58, no. 3 (July–September 1993): 605. See also the article by Jacquy Chemouni, "Psychopathologie de la démocratie," *Frénésie* 2, no. 10 (1992): 265–82.

85. An anonymous correspondent in Berlin wrote a lively, ironic account in French of Groddeck's dissertation defense, published in *La Liberté de Penser: Revue Philosophique et Littéraire* 3 (1849): 515–18.

86. Alexandre Brierre de Boismont, "Die demokratische Krankheit, eine neue Wahnsinns Form, ou *De morbo democratico*, nova insaniae *forma* par le Dr C.-Th. Groddeck," *Annales Médico-psychologiques* 2 (1850): 519.

87. Ibid., 520–21.

88. Ibid., 521.

89. Étienne Cabet, *Voyage en Icarie* (Paris: Bureau du Populaire, 1848). See also Yolaine Dilas-Rocherieux, "Utopie et communisme: Étienne Cabet, de la théorie à la pratique," *Revue d'Histoire Moderne et Contemporaine* 40, no. 2 (April–June 1993): 256–71. [The first half of *Voyage en Icarie* has been translated into English (without the title page cited above) as *Travels in Icaria*, trans. Leslie J. Roberts (Syracuse, NY: Syracuse University Press, 2003)—Trans.]

90. In his introduction to the 1888 English edition of the Manifesto of the Communist Party (1847), Engels pointed out that in 1847 "Socialism was a middle-class movement, Communism a working-class movement." He argued that "whatever portion of the working class had become convinced of the insufficiency of mere political revolutions, and had proclaimed the necessity of total social change, called itself Communist. It was a crude, rough-hewn, purely instinctive sort of Communism; still, it touched the cardinal point and was powerful enough amongst the working class to produce the Utopian Communism, in France, of Cabet and, in Germany, of Weitling." Karl Marx and Friedrich Engels, *Manifesto of the Communist Party* (Chicago: Charles H. Kerr, 1910), 7.

91. Jacques Bouchet, "Du travail appliqué aux aliénés," *Annales Médico-psychologiques* 12 (1848): 307–8. In "Des maisons d'aliénés," Esquirol cites Bouchet as an example of "the admirable order [he] established" in the asylum of Saint-Jacques in Nantes. See Esquirol, *Des maladies mentales*, 2:175 [Passage not included in Hunt's 1845 translation of *Mental Maladies*—Trans.]

92. Brierre de Boismont, "Die demokratische Krankheit," 521–22.

93. Ibid., 523.

94. Alexandre Brierre de Boismont, in *Revue Médicale*, July 31, 1871, quoted in

Prosper Despine, *De la folie au point de vue philosophique, ou Plus spécialement psychologique étudiée chez le malade et chez l'homme en santé* (Paris: Savy, 1875), 785–86, cited in Chevrier, "Psychiatrie et politique," 609.

95. Louis Chevalier, *Classes laborieuses et classes dangereuses à Paris pendant la première moitié du XIXe siècle* (1958; Paris: Perrin, 2007), 518.

96. All these figures are taken from the entry "Ouvriers" in Jean Tulard, ed., *Dictionnaire du Second Empire* (Paris: Fayard, 1995). See also Stéphane Rials, *Nouvelle histoire de Paris: De Trochu à Thiers, 1870–1873* (Paris: Hachette, 1985), 22–33. Being registered on a charity list was a privilege—not everyone had the opportunity. For that matter, during the Second Empire there were some 250,000 beggars in France.

97. Frédéric Le Play, *Les ouvriers des deux mondes: Études sur les travaux, la vie domestique et la condition morale des populations ouvrières des diverses contrées et sur les rapports qui les unissent aux autres classes* (Paris: Société Internationale des Études Pratiques d'Économie Sociale, 1857–85), 1:30–31.

98. AAP-HP, La Salpêtrière, Registre d'observations médicales, 5th division, 1st section, 1820–51, 6R1, fol. 2.

99. Ibid., fol. 8.

100. Ibid., fol. 10.

101. Étienne Esquirol, "Maison d'aliénés," in *Dictionnaire des sciences médicales* (Paris: Panckoucke, 1818), 30:84.

102. Auguste Voisin, *Leçons cliniques sur les maladies mentales et sur les maladies nerveuses* (Paris: J.-B. Baillière, 1883), 428.

103. AAP-HP, La Salpêtrière, Registre d'observations médicales, 5th division, 5th section, 1852–55, 6R76, fol. 92. Patient admitted on May 18, 1853, discharged on May 6, 1854.

104. AAP-HP, La Salpêtrière, Registre d'observations médicales, 5th division, 2nd section, 1856–57, 6R26, fol. 262. Patient admitted on February 15, 1857, died on April 4, 1857.

105. Ibid., 1860–61, 6R29, fol. 36. Patient admitted on March 28, 1860, died on April 20, 1860.

106. Ibid., 1864–69, 6R33, fol. 138. Patient admitted on January 7, 1868, died on January 16, 1868.

107. Ibid., 5th division, 1st section, 1868–71, 6R8, fol. 81. Patient admitted on March 21, 1869, died on July 1, 1869.

108. Ibid., fol. 324. Patient admitted on September 25, 1871. This quotation is drawn from a transfer report dated September 24, 1871, signed by Dr. Prosper Lucas, physician at Sainte-Anne Hospital.

109. Ibid., 5th division, 3rd section, 1862–63, 6R45, fol. 332. Patient admitted on March 31, 1863, discharged on April 17, 1863.

110. Ibid., 5th division, 2nd section, 1863–65, 6R31, fol. 171. Patient admitted on May 13, 1864, returned to her mother on February 16, 1865.

111. Ibid., 5th division, 4th section, 1870–73, 6R61, fol. 119. Patient admitted on September 8, 1870, transferred to Ville Evrard at unspecified date.

112. Ibid., 5th division, 4th section, 1870–73, 6R61, fol. 138. Patient arrived from the fifth ward (*section*) on September 8, 1870, discharged on October 30, 1870.

113. Ibid., 5th division, 2nd section, 1863–65, 6R31, fol. 252. Patient admitted on August 5, 1864, returned to her husband on November 6, 1864.

114. Ibid., 5th division, 4th section, 1866–67, 6R59, fol. 69. Patient admitted on June 20, 1866, died on June 21, 1866.

115. Archives de Paris, Sainte-Anne, Registre de placements hommes et femmes, May 1 to June 10, 1867, D3X^{3}75.

116. AAP-HP, La Salpêtrière, Registre d'observations médicales, 5th division, 2nd section, 1868–69, 6R36, fol. 8. See also ibid., 5th division, 1st section, 1868–71, 6R8, fol. 18 and fol. 24.

117. Ibid., 5th division, 4th section, 1852–54, 6R57, fol. 389. Patient admitted on April 7, 1854, transferred on November 22, 1856.

118. Ibid., 5th division, 2nd section, 1860–62, 6R30, fol. 63. Patient admitted on March 30, 1861, discharged on May 8, 1861.

119. Ibid., fol. 256. Patient admitted on January 29, 1862, transferred to Orléans on July 5, 1862.

120. Ibid., 5th division, 3rd section, 1857–65, 6R44, fol. 103. Patient admitted on March 28, 1861, discharged on June 11, 1861.

121. Ibid., 5th division, 2nd section, 1860–62, 6R30, fol. 166. Patient admitted on August 9, 1861, discharged on February 18, 1862.

122. AAP-HP, Bicêtre, Registre d'observations médicales, 5th division, 1st and 2nd sections, 1858–59, 6R12, fol. 192. Patient admitted on July 3, 1858.

123. Ibid., 1860–61, 6R17, fol. 108. Patient admitted on September 17, 1860.

124. Ibid., 1859–60, 6R16, fol. 448. Patient admitted on April 15, 1860.

125. Ibid., 1860–61, 6R18, fol. 215. Patient admitted on November 15, 1860.

126. Ibid., 1868–69, 6R32, fol. 55. Patient admitted on February 23, 1868, died on April 15, 1868.

127. Ibid., 1853–56, 6R6, fol. 138. Patient admitted on February 3, 1854.

128. Ibid., 1856–58, 6R10, fol. 309. Patient admitted on August 1, 1857.

129. Ibid., 1863–64, 6R24, fol. 277. Patient admitted on May 15, 1864, transferred on July 4, 1865.

130. Ibid., 1856–58, 6R10, fol. 275. Patient admitted on June 26, 1857, discharged on August 12, 1857.

131. Ibid., 1861–62, 6R20, fol. 51. Patient admitted on September 18, 1861, discharged on February 13, 1862.

132. Ibid., 1861–62, 6R20, fol. 160. Patient admitted on January 16, 1862, transferred on April 26, 1862.

133. Ibid., 1864–65, 6R26, fol. 51. Patient admitted on December 3, 1864.

134. Ibid., 1865–66, 6R28, fol. 243. Patient admitted on April 20, 1866, discharged on July 16, 1866.

135. Nicolas Veysset, "La fin des dépôts de mendicité sous la IIIe République," in *Les exclus de l'Europe, 1830–1930*, ed. André Guesclin and Dominique Kalifa (Paris: Éditions de l'Atelier, 1999), 113.

136. AAP-HP, Bicêtre, Registre d'observations médicales, 5th division, 1st and 2nd sections, 1865–66, 6R28, fol. 5.

CHAPTER FIVE

1. For further details on the situation at La Salpêtrière and Bicêtre, see AAP-HP, Fossoyeux collection, "Évacuations d'établissements hospitaliers sous la Commune," 542 FOSS 78, and "Admissions dans les hôpitaux des blessés militaires," 542 FOSS 112. Sainte-Anne was originally a hospital founded by the French queen, Anne of Austria, in the seventeenth century, becoming the site of an experimental farm devised by Dr. Guillaume Ferrus in 1833 so mental patients from Bicêtre could perform agricultural labor. During the Second Empire it was chosen as the location for the modern mental asylum that Paris so needed. See Michel Caire's dissertation, "Contribution à l'histoire de l'hôpital Sainte-Anne (Paris): Des origines au début du XXe siècle (MD thesis, Université de Paris V, 1981, no. 20). Available on Caire's invaluable website, http://psychiatrie.histoire.free.fr/index.htm, accessed October 2012.

2. Louis Gustave Bouchereau and Valentin Magnan, "Statistiques des malades entrés en 1870 et 1871 au bureau d'admission des aliénés de la Seine," *Annales Médico-psychologiques*, 5th ser., 8 (1872): 385.

3. Michel de Clercq and François Lebigot, *Les traumatismes psychiques* (Paris: Masson, 2001), 28. See also Louis Crocq, *Les traumatismes psychiques de guerre* (Paris: Odile Jacob, 1999), 35, and Philippe Birmes, Leah Hatton, Alain Brunet, and Laurent Schmitt, "Early Historical Literature for Post-traumatic Symptomatology," *Stress and Health* 19 (2003): 17–26.

4. The term *fièvre obsidionale* was notably used by Alphonse Daudet in *Souvenir d'un homme de lettres* and by Victor Hugo in his famous speech seeking amnesty for the Communards: "Paris, after a deadly, five-month-long assault, suffered from that dreadful fever the soldiers call 'obsidional fever.'"

5. Benedict-Augustin Morel, "Du délire panophobique des aliénés gémisseurs: Influence des événements de guerre sur la manifestation de cette forme de folie," *Annales Médico-psychologiques*, 5th ser., 6 (1871): 345.

6. Bouchereau and Magnan, "Statistiques des malades," 385.

7. AAP-HP, La Salpêtrière, Registre d'observations médicales, 5th division, 4th section, 1870–73, 6R61, fol. 218. Patient admitted on October 31, 1871, discharged on January 10, 1872.

8. Bouchereau and Magnan, "Statistiques des malades," 359–60.

9. ADVDM, Charenton, Registre matricules hommes, 1870–74, 4X523, fols. 76, 80, and 97.

10. Archives de Paris, Sainte-Anne, Registre de suivi mensuel hommes, September 13, 1870, to October 18, 1870, D3X3 150, fol. 1. Patient admitted on September 13, 1870, discharged on November 23, 1870.

11. Ibid., fol. 65. Patient admitted on September 20, 1870, discharged on July 19, 1871.

12. Archives de Paris, Sainte-Anne, Registre de suivi mensuel femmes, April 19, 1870, to August 17, 1870, fol. 116. Patient admitted on July 28, 1870, transferred to Pont l'Abbé on July 18, 1871.

13. Archives de Paris, Sainte-Anne, Registre de suivi mensuel femmes, April 19, 1870, to August 17, 1870, fol. 126. Patient admitted on August 8, 1870, transferred to Bourg on September 5, 1870.

14. Bouchereau and Magnan, "Statistiques des malades," 378. Magnan would republish this passage in his book *Recherches sur les centres nerveux: Pathologie et physiologie* (Paris: Masson, 1876), 212. The comment by Magnan merits comparison with one of Pinel's anecdotes about a mental patient who thought he was the prophet Mohammed. Both entailed a similar confusion between madwoman and witch or between madman and oracle. "One day, when there was a heavy cannonade in Paris in celebration of some political event, he seemed firmly convinced that it was intended as a tribute of homage to himself. He enjoined silence all around, could not contain his joy, and had I not been retained by other considerations I would have been tempted *to see this sight as the truest picture of the supernatural inspiration of the ancient prophets*." Pinel, *Traité médico-philosophique* [1800], 28–29; emphasis added. [Cf. Davis's translation of Pinel, *Treatise on Insanity*, 30—Trans.]

15. "Communications relatives à l'influence exercée par la guerre sur l'aliénation mentale et le service des aliénés," *Annales Médico-psychologiques*, 5th ser., 6 (1871): 229.

16. Henri Legrand du Saulle, *Le délire de persécutions* (Paris: Plon, 1871), 503–4. See also "Communications relatives à l'influence exercée par la guerre," 229.

17. Legrand du Saulle, *Le délire de persécutions*, 502–3.

18. This analysis is based on the following registers, in which I focused on the period from March 18 to May 28, 1871: Archives de Paris, Sainte-Anne, Registre de suivi mensuel hommes, D3X3 172 (March 15 to May 1, 1871) and D3X3 173 (May 7 to July 17, 1871) as well as Registre de suivi mensuel femmes (February 15 to March 31, 1871), D3X3 176, (March 31 to June 6, 1871), D3X3 177 (March 31 to June 6, 1871).

19. Bouchereau and Magnan, "Statistiques des malades." In the Sainte-Anne registers, only three broad categories are strictly identical across the two genders and can therefore be assessed for the specific period of the Commune. They partly confirm Bouchereau and Magnan's figures: "enfeebled mental faculties" afflicted 15.9 percent of the women and 1.7 percent of the men, while "general paresis" was diagnosed in 7.4 percent of the women and 18.6 percent of the men, and "senile dementia" concerned 6.2 percent of the women and 2.3 percent of the men.

20. Claude Quétel and Jean-Yves Simon, "L'aliénation alcoolique en France (XIXe siècle et 1ere moitié du XXe siècle)," *Histoire, Économie et Société* 7, no. 4 (1988): 507–33.

21. Valentin Magnan and Louis Gustave Bouchereau, "Statistiques des alcooliques entrés au bureau d'admission à Sainte-Anne, pendant les mois de mars, avril, mai, juin 1870 et les mois correspondants de 1871," *Annales Médico-psychologiques*, 5th ser., 7 (1872): 52–57. See also Michel Caire, "Du *morbus democraticus* à l'idéalisme passionné: Quelques réactions des aliénistes français aux lendemains de la

Commune de Paris," *Annales Médico-psychologiques* 4 (1990): 379–86, also available at http://psychiatrie.histoire.free.fr/index.htm, accessed October 2012.

22. Ludger Lunier, *De l'influence des grandes commotions politiques et sociales sur le développement des maladies mentales* (Paris: Savy, 1874).

23. Archives de Paris, Sainte-Anne, Registre de suivi mensuel femmes (February 15 to March 31, 1871), D3X3 176, fols. 112, 113, 117, 127, 132, 133, 139, 140, 142.

24. Ibid., Registre de suivie mensuel femmes (March 31 to June 6, 1871), D3X3 177, fols. 19, 28, 53, 66, 78, 81, 100, 117, 129.

25. In his survey, Lunier found that war-related delusions affected 59 percent of the 133 male patients admitted to Charenton and 40 percent of the 53 women, but he made no mention of Commune-related events. It therefore seems that, in Paris and the surrounding region, the siege was much more damaging to mental health than was the Commune. See Lunier, *De l'influence des grandes commotions politiques*.

26. Charles Simond, *Paris de 1800 à 1900* (Paris: Plon, 1901), 3:25.

27. Archives de Paris, Sainte-Anne, Registre de suivi mensuel femmes, (March 31 to June 6, 1871), D3X3 177, fol. 42.

28. Ibid., Registre de suivi mensuel hommes, (March 15 to May 1, 1871), D3X3 172, fols. 23, 39, 42, 62, 70, 72, 73, 75, 77, 81, 87, 88, 93, 120, 136, 142.

29. Ibid., Registre de suivi mensuel hommes, (May 1 to July 17, 1871), D3X3 173, fols. 7, 28.

30. Ibid., Registre de suivi mensuel hommes, (May 1 to July 17, 1871), D3X3 173, fol. 32.

31. Louise Michel, *La Commune* (1898; Paris: Stock, 1978), 403.

32. Maurice Garçon, *Histoire de la justice sous la Troisième République* (Paris: Fayard, 1957), quoted by Jean-Paul Doucet, entry "Dénonciation anonyme," in the online *Dictionnaire de droit criminel*, http://ledroitcriminel.free.fr/dictionnaire/lettre_d/lettre_d_denonciation.htm, accessed October 2012.

33. Stéphane Rials, *Nouvelle histoire de Paris: De Trochu à Thiers, 1870–1873* (Paris: Hachette, 1985), 207. In general there was a drop in the number of admissions to mental homes throughout France (11,655 between July 1, 1869, and July 1, 1870, as against 10,243 between July 1, 1870, and July 1, 1871), alongside an increase in delusions linked to political upheaval, the latter basically involving the war and the siege. It was only in 1873 that asylum populations began to rise. According to Lunier, political dissension, unemployment, bankruptcy, and poverty "were so many causes that were not fleeting but permanent—or, at least, lasting—which contributed to the rise in the number of admissions to asylums, perhaps even more than war-related events." Lunier, *De l'influence des grandes commotions politiques*," 275.

34. These statistics are based on AAP-HP, La Salpêtrière, Registre d'observations médicales, 5th division, 1st section, 1868–71, 6R8. This percentage is consistent with the figures at Sainte-Anne, where 42 percent suffered from melancholia.

35. Ibid., fol. 361. Patient admitted on November 15, 1871, transferred on March 25, 1872.

36. Ibid., fol. 335. Patient admitted on September 30, 1871.

37. AAP-HP, La Salpêtrière, Registre d'observations médicales, 5th division, 4th section, 1870–73, 6R61, fol. 353. Patient admitted on November 8, 1872, discharged on April 3, 1873.

38. AAP-HP, Bicêtre, Registre d'observations médicales, 5th division, 1st and 2nd sections, 1871–72, 6R34, fol. 37. Patient admitted on September 25, 1871, discharged on March 15, 1872.

39. AAP-HP, La Salpêtrière, Registre d'observations médicales, 5th division, 1st section, 1868–71, 6R8, fol. 368. Patient admitted on November 28, 1871.

40. Ibid., fol. 370. Patient admitted on November 30, 1871, discharged on December 23, 1871.

41. Archives de Paris, Sainte-Anne, Registre de suivi mensuel femmes (March 31 to June 6, 1871), D3X3 177, fol. 134.

42. Prosper-Olivier Lissagaray, *Histoire de la Commune de 1871* (Brussels: Librairie Contemporaine de Henri Kistemaeckers, 1876), 387. See also Gay L. Gullickson, "La Pétroleuse: Representing Revolution," *Feminist Studies* 17, no. 2 (Summer 1991): 240–65, and Gullickson, *Unruly Woman of Paris: Images of the Commune* (Ithaca, NY: Cornell University Press, 1996).

43. Alexandre Dumas fils, *Une lettre sur les choses du jour* (Paris: Michel Lévy Frères, 1871), 16–17.

44. Maxime Du Camp, *Les convulsions de Paris*, 5th ed. (Paris: Hachette, 1881), 2:62. In this book Du Camp copied almost word for word the passage by Lissagaray quoted above on the repression of the so-called *pétroleuses*, adding, "More than one mistake was made, and more than one misfortune occurred. Where is the blame to be laid? On the gullibility of the people, certainly, but above all on those who overstimulated that gullibility through a series of incomprehensible crimes. If the Commune hadn't burned down half of Paris, it would never have been considered capable of burning the other half" (287).

45. Archives de Paris, Sainte-Anne, Registre de suivi mensuel femmes, (June 7 to August 5, 1871), D3X3 178, fol. 48. Patient admitted on June 26, 1871, discharged on March 28, 1872.

46. AAP-HP, La Salpêtrière, Registre d'observations médicales, 5th division, 4th section, 1870–73, 6R61, fol. 198. Patient admitted on August 24, 1871.

47. ADVDM, Charenton, Registres de la loi, placements d'office et volontaires, fol. 134. Patient committed on June 10, 1871, discharged as cured on August 31, 1871.

48. Mme M. Rivet, *Les aliénés dans la famille et dans la maison de santé: Étude pour les gens du monde* (Paris: Masson, 1875), 243.

49. AAP-HP, Bicêtre, Registres d'observations médicales, 5th division, 1st and 2nd sections, 1871–72, 6R34, fol. 54.

50. AAP-HP, La Salpêtrière, Registre d'observations médicales, 5th division, 4th section, 1870–73, 6R61, fol. 324. Patient admitted on July 9, 1872, discharged on October 23, 1872.

51. AAP-HP, Bicêtre, Registres d'observations médicales, 5th division, 1st and 2nd sections, 1871–72, 6R34, fol. 140.

52. Benedict-Augustin Morel, "La dégénérescence du peuple français, son carac-

tère pathologique, ses symptômes et ses causes: Contribution de médecine mentale à l'histoire médicale des peuples," *Annales Médico-psychologiques*, 5th ser., 6 (1871): 291.

53. Ibid., 292.

54. Ibid., 293.

55. Ibid., 296.

56. Ibid., 298.

57. Ibid., 299.

58. Ibid., 293–94.

59. Bénedict-Augustin Morel, in *Le Nouvelliste de Rouen*, June 6, 1871, quoted by Prosper Despine, *De la folie du point de vue philosophique, ou Plus spécialement psychologique, étudiée chez le malade et l'homme de santé* (Paris: Savy, 1875), 791–92.

60. Alexandre Brierre de Boismont, in *Annales Médico-psychologiques*, 5th ser., 6 (1871): 124. Quoted in Michel Landry, *L'état dangereux: Un jugement déguisé en diagnostic* (Paris: Harmattan, 2002), 32n. During this same period Achille Foville proposed a study of asylums for alcoholics in *Annales d'Hygiène Publique et de Médecine Légale*, 2nd ser., 37 (1872): 299–379.

61. Jean-Baptiste Laborde, *Les hommes et les actes de l'insurrection de Paris devant la psychologie morbide* (Paris: Germer-Baillière, 1872).

62. "Séance du January 15, 1872," *Annales Médico-psychologiques*, 5th ser., 7 (1872): 257.

63. Irénée-Célestin Baume, "Les hommes et les actes de l'insurrection de Paris devant la psychologie morbide, par le Dr Laborde," *Annales Médico-psychologiques*, 5th ser., 7 (1872): 304.

64. Despine, *De la folie du point de vue philosophique*, 779.

65. Ibid., 794.

66. Paul Lidsky, *Les écrivains contre la Commune* (Paris: Maspero, 1970).

67. Du Camp, *Les convulsions de Paris*, 2:245. Du Camp explained Allix's invention of correspondence via snails: "Given two snails who have a sympathy for one another, he established a kind of synchronicity in their movements; at any distance whatever, the movement of one is imitated and reproduced by the other at the same moment. This discovery had incalculable consequences: no more postal correspondence, no more electric telegraph—sympathic snails could replace everything. Here is the recipe: take forty-eight snails whose degree of sympathy has been scientifically established; divide them into two groups of equal size, twenty-four in one, twenty-four in the other. On each shell write one letter of the alphabet; keep one alphabet in Paris, send the other to Constantinople. When you move snail A in Paris, snail A in Constantinople will instantly jiggle, being in sympathy. This yields a simple mode of correspondence safe from prying eyes."

68. Jules Vallès, in *Le Réveil*, October 23, 1881. Quoted by Aude Fauvel, "Punition, dégénérescence ou malheur?" *Revue d'Histoire du XIXe Siècle* 26/27 (2003): 285.

POSTAMBLE

1. Jean-Étienne-Dominique Esquirol, *Des maladies mentales, considérées sous les rapports médical, hygiénique et médico-légal* (Paris: J.-B. Baillière, 1838), 2:144. [This part of volume 2 was not included in Hunt's 1845 translation of *Mental Maladies*—Trans.]

2. A remarkable overview of the current state of psychiatry in France was presented in a sixty-seven-minute film by Philippe Borel, *Un monde sans fous*, coproduced by Cinetévé and Forum des Images, broadcast on France 5 television station on April 13, 2010. The entire film, plus additional outtakes from the interviews, is available online on the Mediapart website, http://www.mediapart.fr/content/un-monde-sans-fous-ou-les-derives-de-la-psychiatrie, accessed October 2012.

3. Multiple-choice questionnaires designed to detect potential psychological problems in children (depression, phobia, anxiety, etc.) are based on the *Diagnostic and Statistical Manual* of Mental Disorders, 4th ed. (DSM-IV). The child usually has to answer yes or no to computer-displayed questions such as "Are you always sad?" "Do you sometimes want to die?" "Would you like to stay home with your parents rather than go to school?"

4. Jacques Moreau de Tours, *Du haschisch et de l'aliénation mentale* (Paris: Fortin, Masson, 1845), 133.

Selected Bibliography

ARCHIVAL SOURCES

Archives de l'Assistance Publique—Hôpitaux de Paris, Paris
Series R: Registers of medical observations at La Salpêtrière and Bicêtre
Series Q: Registers of admissions to La Salpêtrière and Bicêtre
Fossoyeux Collection

Archives Départementales du Val-de-Marne, Créteil
Series X: Registers of medical observations at Charenton
Series Q: Registers of admissions

Archives Nationales, Paris
Series F: subseries F^7 (Police) and F^{15} (Asylums and Aid)

Archives de Paris, Paris
Series X: Registers of medical observations at Sainte-Anne

Archives de la Préfecture de Police, Paris
Series B, subseries B^A: Communard
Series C, subseries C^A: Analytical listings and registers of personal files and internments

Bibliothèque de l'Académie de Médecine, Paris
Collection of observations made on Dr. Ulysse Trélat's ward in La Salpêtrière by J. A. Fort, intern

Bibliothèque Nationale, Cabinet des Estampes, Paris
Sketchbook of drawings by Georges-François-Marie Gabriel

Louise M. Darling Biomedical Library, Special Collections, UCLA, Los Angeles
Registers of the Belhomme and Esquirol nursing homes

PRIMARY SOURCES

Annales d'hygiène publique et de médecine légale, 1829–1922.

Annales médico-psychologiques, 1843–2011.

Antommarchi, François. *Derniers moments de Napoléon*. Brussels: H. Tarlier, 1825.

Archives d'anthropologie criminelle, 1886–1914.

Baillarger, Jules. *Essai de classification des maladies mentales*. Paris: Victor Masson, 1854.

Beaujeu, Maurice. *Psychologie des premiers Césars: Une étude de médecine légale dans l'histoire*. Lyons: A. Storck, 1893.

Belhomme, Jacques Étienne. *Influence des événements et des commotions politiques sur le développement de la folie*. Paper read at the Académie de Médecine on May 2, 1848, followed by a report by M. Londe, delivered on March 6, 1849. Paris: Librairie Germer-Baillière, 1849.

Bertier de Sauvigny, Ferdinand. *Souvenirs inédits d'un conspirateur*. Paris: Tallendier, 1990.

Blanche, Esprit. *Du danger des rigueurs corporelles dans le traitement de la folie*. Paris: A. Gardembas, 1839.

Bloch, C. *L'assistance publique: Instruction. Notes sur la législation et l'administration de l'assistance de 1789 à l'an VIII. Recueil des principaux textes. Notes sur les sources aux Archives nationales*. 1909.

Bourdin, C. E. *Études médico-psychologiques: De l'influence des événements politiques sur la production de la folie*. Paris: Adrien Delahaye, 1873.

Brierre de Boismont, Alexandre. *Des hallucinations, ou Histoire raisonnée des apparitions, des visions, des songes, de l'extase, du magnétisme et du somnambulisme*. 1845. Paris: Germer-Baillière, 1852, 1862.

Briquet, Paul. *Traité clinique et thérapeutique de l'hystérie*. Paris: J.-B. Baillière, 1859.

Broussais, François-Josephe-Victor. *De l'irritation et de la folie*. Paris: J.-B. Baillière, 1839.

Bru, Paul. *Histoire de Bicêtre*. Paris: Lecrosnié et Babé, 1890.

Buchez, P.-J.-B., and P.-C. Roux. *Histoire de la Révolution française, ou Journal des Assemblées nationales depuis 1789 jusqu'en 1815*. Vol. 25. Paris: Paulin Libraire, 1836.

Cabanès, Augustin. *Au chevet de l'empereur*. Paris: Albin Michel, 1958.

———. *L'histoire éclairée par la clinique*. Paris: Albin Michel, 1921.

Cabanès, Augustin, and L. Nass. *La névrose révolutionnaire*. Paris: Albin Michel, 1925.

Cabanis, Pierre Jean Georges. *Note sur le supplice de la guillotine*. 1796. Orléans: Orient, 2007.

———. *Rapports du physique et du moral de l'homme*. Paris: Crapart, Caille et Ravier, Year X (1802).

Calmeil, L. F. *De la folie considérée sous le point de vue pathologique, philosophique, historique et judiciaire*. 2 vols. Paris: J.-B. Baillière, 1845.

Chateaubriand, François-René de. *Mémoires d'outre-tombe*. Paris: Gallimard, 1951.

Colins, Hippolyte de. Notice sur l'établissement consacré au traitement de l'aliénation mentale, établi à Charenton près Paris, juin 1812. In D. A. F. de Sade, *Journal inédit*. Paris: Gallimard, 1994.

Colombier, Jean, and François Doublet. "Instruction sur la manière de gouverner les insensés et de travailler à leur guérison dans les asyles qui leur sont destinés." In *Observations faites dans le département des hôpitaux civils*, 339–92. Paris: Imprimerie Royale, 1785.

Constant-Rebecque, Benjamin de. *De l'esprit de conquête et de l'usurpation dans ses rapports avec la civilisation*. Hanover: Hahn, 1814.

Daquin, Joseph. *La philosophie de la folie, ou Essai philosophique sur le Traitement des personnes attaquées de folie*. Chambéry: Gorrin Père et Fils, 1791; Paris: Chez Née de la Rochelle, 1792.

———. *La philosophie de la folie, où l'on prouve que cette maladie doit plutôt être traitée par les secours moraux que par les secours physiques; et que ceux qui en sont atteints, éprouvent d'une manière non équivoque l'influence de la lune*. 2nd ed. Chambéry: P. Cléaz, Year XII (1804).

Descuret, J. B. F. *La médecine des passions*. Paris: Labé, 1844.

Despine, Prosper. *De la folie du point de vue philosophique, ou Plus spécialement psychologique, étudiée chez le malade et l'homme de santé*. Paris: Savy, 1875.

Desportes, B[enjamin]. *Compte rendu au conseil général des hospices et hôpitaux civils de Paris sur le service des aliénés traités dans les hospices de la vieillesse (hommes et femmes) [Bicêtre et la Salpêtrière] pendant les années 1825, 1826, 1827, 1828, 1829, 1830, 1831, 1832, 1833*. Paris: Mme Huzard, 1835.

Dictionnaire des sciences médicales. 60 vols. Paris: Panckoucke, 1812–22.

Dictionnaire encyclopédique des sciences médicales. Edited by M. A. Dechambre. 100 vols. Paris: Asselin et Masson, 1864–89.

Du Camp, Maxime. *Les convulsions de Paris*. 5th ed., 4 vols. Paris: Hachette, 1881.

———. *Paris, ses organes, ses fonctions et sa vie dans la seconde moitié du XIXe siècle*. Paris: Hachette, 1869–76.

Dumas, Alexandre. *Les mille et un fantômes*, preceded by *La femme au collier de velours*. Edited by Anne-Marie Callet-Bianco. Paris: Gallimard, 2006.

———. "The Woman with the Velvet Necklace." In *Chauvelin's Will, a Romance of the Last Days of Louis XV, and Stories of the French Revolution: The Woman with the Velvet Necklace and Blanche de Beaulieu*. Anonymous translation from the French. Boston: Little, Brown, 1897.

Ellis, W. C. *Traité de l'aliénation mentale*. Translated by T. Archambauld and annoted by Étienne Esquirol. Paris: De Just Rouvier, 1840.

Encyclopédie du XIXe siècle, répertoire universel des sciences, des lettres et des arts. 25 vols. Paris, 1838.

Esquirol, Jean-Étienne-Dominique. *De la lypémanie ou mélancolie*. Edited by P. Fedida and J. Postel. Toulouse: Privat, 1977.

———. *Des établissements des aliénés en France et des moyens d'améliorer le sort de ces infortunés*. Paris: Mme Huzard, 1819.

———. *Des maladies mentales, considérées sous les rapports médical, hygiénique et médico-légal.* 2 vols. Paris: J.-B. Baillière, 1838; Paris: Frénésie, 1989.

———. *Des passions considérées comme causes, symptômes et moyens curatifs de l'aliénation mentale.* Paris: Didot Jeune, [1805].

———. "Introduction à l'étude des aliénations mentales (Fragments de la première leçon du cours clinique fait à la Salpêtrière sur ces maladies)." *Revue Médicale Française et Étrangère* 8 (1822).

———. *Mental Maladies: A Treatise on Insanity.* Translated by E. K. Hunt. Philadelphia: Lea and Blanchard, 1845.

Esquiros, Alphonse. *Paris, ou Les sciences, les institutions et les mœurs au XIXe siècle.* Paris: Comptoir des Imprimeurs Unis, 1847.

Estrées, Paul de. *Le théâtre sous la Terreur (théâtre de la peur), 1793–1794.* Paris: Émile-Paul Frères, 1913.

Eymard, Sylvain. *La politicomanie, ou Coup d'œil critique sur la folie révolutionnaire qui a régné en Europe depuis 1789 jusqu'au 2 décembre 1851.* Paris: Garnier Frères, 1853.

Fabre, François. *Maladies de l'encéphale, maladies mentales, maladies nerveuses.* Vol. 9 of *Bibliothèque du médecin-praticien, ou Résumé général de tous les ouvrages de clinique médicale et chirurgicale etc.* Paris: J.-B. Baillière, 1849.

Falret, Jean-Pierre. *Des maladies mentales et des asiles d'aliénés.* Paris: J.-B. Baillière, 1864.

Flore, Mlle. *Mémoires de Mlle Flore.* 3 vols. Paris: Comptoir des Imprimeurs Unis, 1845.

Fodéré, François Emmanuel. *Traité du délire.* Paris: Croullebois, 1817.

Girard de Cailleux, J. H. *Études pratiques sur les maladies nerveuses et mentales.* Paris: J.-B. Baillière, 1863.

Giraudy, Charles François. *Mémoire sur la maison nationale de Charenton.* Paris: Imprimerie de la Société de Médecine, Year XII (1804).

Grand dictionnaire universel du XIXe siècle. Edited by Pierre Larousse. 17 vols. Paris: Administration du Grande Dictionnaire, 1866–88.

Griesinger, Wilhelm. *Traité des maladies mentales.* Translated by Adrien Doumic. Paris: Delahaye, 1865.

Groddeck, Carl Theodor. *De la maladie démocratique, nouvelle espèce de folie.* Anonymous translation from the German. Paris: Germer-Baillière, 1850.

Guillois, Alfred. *Étude médico-psychologique sur Olympe de Gouges.* Lyon, 1904.

Hamel, Ernest. *Histoire des deux conspirations du Général Malet.* Paris: Librairie de la Société des Gens de Lettres, 1873.

Hugo, Victor. *Choses vues (1830–1848).* Paris: Gallimard, 1972.

———. *Les Misérables.* Translated by Isabel F. Hapgood. New York: Thomas Y. Crowell, 1887.

———. *Quatrevingt-treize.* Paris: Gallimard, 1979.

Jacoby, Paul. *Étude sur la sélection dans ses rapports avec l'hérédité chez l'homme.* Paris: Germer-Baillière, 1881.

Laborde, Jean-Baptiste-Vincent. *Fragments médico-psychologiques: Les hommes et les actes de l'insurrection de Paris devant la psychologie morbide*. Paris: G. Baillière, 1872.

Lamartine, Alphonse de. *Histoire de la révolution de 1848*. 2 vols. Paris: Perrotin, 1849. Translated by Francis Durivage and William Chase as *History of the French Revolution of 1848*. Boston: Phillips, Samson, 1851.

La Rochefoucauld-Liancourt, Duc de. *Rapport, fait au nom du Comité de mendicité, des visites faites dans divers hôpitaux, hospices et maisons de charité de Paris*. Paris: Imprimerie Nationale, 1790.

Legrand du Saulle, Henri. *Le délire de persécution*. Paris: Plon, 1871.

Lélut, Louis-Francisque. *L'amulette de Pascal*. Paris: J.-B. Baillière, 1846.

———. *Du démon de Socrate*. Paris: Trinquart, 1836.

Le Play, Frédéric. *Les ouvriers des deux mondes: Études sur les travaux, la vie domestique et la condition morale des populations ouvrières des diverses contrées et sur les rapports qui les unissent aux autres classes*. Paris: Société Internationale des Études Pratiques d'Économie Sociale, 1857–85.

Leuret, François. *Du traitement moral de la folie*. Paris: J.-B. Baillière, 1840.

———. *Fragments psychologiques sur la folie*. Paris: Crochard, 1834.

Lissagaray, Prosper-Olivier. *Histoire de la Commune de 1871*. Brussels: Librairie Contemporaine de Henri Kistemaeckers, 1876.

Lombroso, Cesare. *Le crime politique et les révolutions par rapport au droit, à l'anthropologie criminelle et à la science du gouvernement*. Translated by A. Bouchard, 2 vols. Paris: Félix Alcan, 1892.

———. *The Man of Genius*. Anonymous translation from the Italian. New York: Walter Scott, 1917.

Lunier, Ludger. *De l'influence des grandes commotions politiques et sociales sur le développement des maladies mentales*. Paris: Savy, 1874.

Macé, Louis Victor. *Traité pratique des maladies mentales*. Paris: J.-B. Baillière, 1862.

Mercier, Louis Sébastien. *Le nouveau Paris*. Paris: Brunswick, 1800.

———. *Le tableau de Paris*. 1788. Paris: La Découverte, 1998.

Michel, Louise. *La Commune*. 1898. Paris: Stock, 1978.

Michelet, Jules. *Histoire du XIXe siècle*. Paris: Michel Lévy Frères, 1875.

———. *Ma jeunesse*. Paris: Calmann-Lévy, 1884.

Mirabeau, Honoré-Gabriel Riquetti, comte de. *Observations d'un voyageur anglais sur la maison de force appellée Bicêtre*. [Paris], 1788.

Moreau de Tours, Jacques-Joseph. *La psychologie morbide dans ses rapports avec la philosophie de l'histoire, ou De l'influence des névropathies sur le dynamisme intellectuel*. Paris: Victor Masson, 1859.

Morel, Benedict-Augustin. *Traité des maladies mentales*. 1852. Paris: Victor Masson, 1860.

Mullois, Isidore. *La charité et la misère à Paris*. Paris: 1856.

Nerval, Gérard de. *Les illuminés*. Vol. 2 of *Œuvres complètes*. Paris: Gallimard, 1984.

Nodier, Charles. *Souvenirs, épisodes et portraits pour servir à l'histoire de la Révolution et de l'Empire*. Paris: Alphonse Levasseur, 1831.

Pardigon, François. *Épisodes des journées de juin 1848*. With an introduction by Alix Héricord. Paris: Fabrique, 2008.

Pigeaud, Jackie. *Théroigne de Méricourt: La lettre-mélancolie*. Paris: Lagrasse, Verdier/L'Éther Vague, 2005.

Pinel, Casimir, ed. *Lettres de Pinel précédées d'une notice plus étendue sur sa vie, par son neveu le Dr. Casimir Pinel*. Paris: Victor Masson, 1859.

Pinel, Philippe. *Nosographie philosophique, ou La méthode de l'analyse appliquée à la médecine*. 2 vols. Paris: Maradan, Year VI (1797).

———. "Réflexions médicales sur l'état monastique." *Journal Gratuit* 9, no. 6 (1790): 81–93.

———. *Traité médico-philosophique sur l'aliénation mentale ou la manie*. Paris: Richard, Caille et Ravier, Year IX (1800).

———. *Traité médico-philosophique sur l'aliénation mentale*. 2nd ed. (1809). Introduced and annotated by Jean Garrabé and Dora B. Weiner. Paris: Empêcheurs de Penser en Rond, 2005. Translated by Gordon Hickish, David Healy, and Louis C. Charland as *Medico-philosophical Treatise on Mental Alienation* (Chichester, UK: Wiley–Blackwell, 2008).

———. *Treatise on Insanity*, trans. D. D. Davis. London: Cadell and Davies, 1806.

———. "Variété." *Journal de Paris*, January 18, 1790, 70–72.

Pinel, Scipion. *Physionomie de l'homme aliéné*. Paris: Librairie des Sciences Médicales, 1833.

Potter, Agathon de. "La peste démocratique (*morbus democraticus*): Contribution à l'étude des maladies mentales." *Philosophie de l'Avenir, Revue du Socialisme Rationnel* 10 (1885–86): 1–99.

Richard, David. *La phrénologie et Napoléon*. Paris: Pihan Delaforest, 1835.

Rivet, Mme M. *Les aliénés dans la famille et dans la maison de santé: Étude pour les gens du monde*. Paris: Masson, 1875.

Sachaile, Claude. *Les médecins de Paris jugés par leurs œuvres, ou Statistique scientifique morale des médecins de Paris*. Paris: De la Barre, 1845.

Sade, D. A. F. de. *Journal inédit*. Paris: Gallimard, 1994.

———. *Lettres inédites et documents*. Introduced and annotated by Jean-Louis Debauve (1900). Paris: Ramsay, 1990.

Sanson, Charles Henry. *Mémoires de Sanson (1739–1806), exécuteur des jugements criminels*. Paris: Albin Michel, 1911.

Stern, Daniel [Marie d'Agoult]. *Histoire de la révolution de 1848*. 3 vols. Paris: Gustave Sandré, 1850–53.

Sue, Jean-Joseph. *Essai sur le supplice de la guillotine et sur la douleur qui survit à la décollation*. 1796.

Talma, François-Joseph. *Mémoire de J.-F. Talma, écrit par lui-même et mis en ordre sur les papiers de sa famille par Alexandre Dumas*. 1849. Montreal: Joyeux Roger, 2006.

Tenon, Jacques. *Mémoire sur les hôpitaux de Paris*. Paris: Pierres, 1788.
Thiers, Adolphe. *Histoire du Consulat et de l'Empire*. 21 vols. Paris: Paulin [later Paulin, Lheureux, then Lheureux], 1845–69.
Tocqueville, Alexis de. *Souvenirs*. Paris: Calmann-Lévy, 1893.
Trélat, Ulysse. *La folie lucide*. Paris: Adrien Delahaye, 1861.
Tuetey, Alexandre. *Les hôpitaux et hospices*. Vol. 1 of *L'assistance publique à Paris pendant la Révolution*. Paris: Imprimerie Nationale, 1845.
Voisin, Auguste. *Leçons cliniques sur les maladies mentales et sur les maladies nerveuses*. Paris: J.-B. Baillière, 1883.
———. *Traité de paralysie générale des aliénés*. Paris: J.-B. Baillière, 1879.
Voisin, Félix. *Des causes morales et physiques des maladies mentales*. Paris: J.-B. Baillière, 1826.

SECONDARY SOURCES

Ackerknecht, Erwin H. *La médecine hospitalière à Paris (1794–1848)*. Translated by Françoise Blateau. Paris: Payot, 1986.
———. "Political Prisoners in French Mental Institutions before 1789, during the Revolution, and under Napoleon I." *Medical History* 19, no. 3 (July 1975): 250–55.
Adhémar, Jean. "Un dessinateur passionné par le visage humain: Georges-François-Marie Gabriel (1775–1836)." In *Omagiu lui George Oprescu*. Bucharest, 1961.
Arasse, Daniel. *La guillotine et l'imaginaire de la Terreur*. Paris: Flammarion, 1987.
Auboin, Michel, Arnaud Teyssier, and Jean Tulard. *Histoire et dictionnaire de la police, du Moyen Âge à nos jours*. Paris: Robert Laffont, 2005.
Beauvois, Delphine. "La criminalité féminine enregistrée au Dépôt de la Préfecture de Police de Paris sous le Second Empire (1853–1869)." Master's thesis, Université de Paris VII, 1999.
Bernard, Anne-Marie, and Jacques Houdaille. "Les internés de Charenton: 1800–1854." *Population* 49, no. 2 (March/April 1994): 500–515.
Bessette, Jean-Michel. *Il était une fois . . . la guillotine*. Paris: Éditions Alternatives, 1982.
Bigorre, Alain, and Gabriel Bollotte. "L'assistance aux malades mentaux à Paris de 1789 à 1838." *Annales médico-psychologiques* 124, no. 4 (1966): 463–74.
Billard, Max. *La conspiration de Malet*. Paris: Perrin, 1907.
Bing, François, Georges Canguilhem, Jacques Derrida, Arlette Farge, René Major, Agostino Pirella, Jacques Postel, Claude Quétel, and Élisabeth Roudinesco. *Penser la folie: Essais sur Michel Foucault*. Paris: Galilée, 1992.
Birmes, Philippe, Leah Hatton, Alain Brunet, and Laurent Schmitt. "Early Historical Literature for Post-traumatic Symptomatology." *Stress and Health* 19 (2003): 17–26.
Bonnat, Jean-Louis. "Gérard de Nerval, un précurseur du 'stade du miroir' (ou

L'irraison de la psychose, au service du gouvernement politique, 'Le roi de Bicêtre')." *Cliniques Méditerranéennes* 64 (2001): 273–84.

Boukovsky, Vladimir. *Une nouvelle maladie mentale en URSS: L'opposition*. Paris: Seuil, 1971.

Caire, Michel. "Contribution à l'histoire de l'hôpital Sainte-Anne (Paris): Des origines au début du XXe siècle." MD thesis, Université de Paris V, Cochin-Port-Royal, 1981, no. 20.

———. "Du *morbus democraticus* à l'idéalisme passionné: Quelques réactions des aliénistes français aux lendemains de la Commune de Paris." *Annales Médico-psychologiques* 4 (1990): 379–86.

———. "Un état des fous de Bicêtre en 1792." *Nervure* 7 (1993): 62–67.

———. "Pussin, avant Pinel." *L'information Psychiatrique* 69, no. 6 (1993): 529–38.

Caruth, Cathy, ed. *Trauma: Explorations in Memory*. Baltimore: Johns Hopkins University Press, 1995.

———. *Unclaimed Experience: Trauma, Narratives, and History*. Baltimore: Johns Hopkins University Press, 1996.

Castel, Pierre-Henri. *L'esprit malade: Cerveaux, folies, individus*. Paris: Ithaque, 2009.

Castel, Robert. *L'ordre psychiatrique: L'âge d'or de l'aliénisme*. Paris: Éditions de Minuit, 1976.

Chemla, Patrick, ed. *Asile?* Ramonville Sainte-Agne: Érès, 1999.

Chemouni, Jacquy. "Psychopathologie de la démocratie." *Frénésie* 2, no. 10 (1992): 265–82.

Chevalier, Louis. *Classes laborieuses et classes dangereuses à Paris pendant la première moitié du XIXe siècle*. 1958. Paris: Perrin, 2007.

Chevrier, Alain. "Psychiatrie et politique: Sur la réception en France de *La maladie démocratique* de Carl Groddeck." *L'Évolution Psychiatrique* 58, no. 3 (1993): 605–17.

Clarke, Joseph. *Commemorating the Dead in Revolutionary France: Revolution and Remembrance, 1789–1799*. Cambridge: Cambridge University Press, 2007.

Clercq, Michel de, and François Lebigot. *Les traumatismes psychiques*. Paris: Masson, 2001.

Coffin, Jean-Christophe. *La transmission de la folie: 1850–1914*. Paris: Harmattan, 2003.

Crocq, Louis. *Les traumatismes psychiques de guerre*. Paris: Odile Jacob, 1999.

Dadoun, Roger, ed. *La folie politique*. Paris: Payot, 1971.

Davoine, Françoise, and Jean-Max Gaudillière. *Histoire et trauma: La folie des guerres*. Paris: Stock, 2006.

Deleuze, Gilles, and Félix Guattari. *L'anti-Œdipe: Capitalisme et schizophrénie 1*. Paris: Minuit, 1972. Translated by Robert Hurley, Mark Seem, and Helen R. Lane as *Anti-Oedipus: Capitalism and Schizophrenia* (Minneapolis: University of Minnesota Press, 1983).

Didier, Marie. *Dans la nuit de Bicêtre*. Paris: Gallimard, 2006.

Fanon, Frantz. *Les damnés de la terre*. Paris: Maspero, 1961.

Fauvel, Aude. "Punition, dégénérescence ou malheur?" *Revue d'Histoire du XIXe Siècle* 26/27 (2003): 277–304.

Fau-Vincenti, Véronique. "De la maladie démocratique." *Le Monde Diplomatique*, September 2010, 28.

Ferroni, André. "Une maison de santé pour le traitement des aliénés à la fin du XVIIIe siècle: La maison Belhomme." MD thesis, Université de Paris, 1954.

Fleishmann, Hector. *La guillotine en 1793*. Paris: Librairie des Publications Modernes, 1908.

Forzinetti-Motet, Mme. "L'hôtel Colbert et les débuts de la maison Belhomme." *Histoire de la Médecine*, December 1952, 27–34.

———. "La maison Belhomme." *Histoire de la Médecine*, January 1953, 47–64.

Foucault, Michel. *Les anormaux: Cours au Collège de France, 1974–1975*. Paris: Gallimard/Seuil, 1999.

———. *Dits et écrits*. 2 vols. Paris: Gallimard, 2001.

———. *History of Madness*. Translated by Jonathan Murphy and Jean Khalfa. Oxford: Routledge, 2009.

———. *Le pouvoir psychiatrique: Cours au Collège de France, 1973–1974*. Paris: Gallimard/Seuil, 2003.

Freud, Sigmund. *Essais de psychanalyse*. Paris: Payot, 1968.

Fromentin, Clément. "Qu'est-ce qui s'écrit de la psychiatrie? Du 'secrétaire de l'aliéné' aux archives de l'asile Sainte-Anne—une approche de la littératie en psychiatrie." *Psychiatrie, Sciences Humaines, Neurosciences* 6 (2008): 215–24.

Garrabé, Jean, ed. *Philippe Pinel*. Le Plessis-Robinson: Synthélabo/Les Empêcheurs de Penser en Rond, 1994.

Gaubert, Henri. *Conspirateurs au temps de Napoléon Ier*. Paris: Flammarion, 1962.

Gauchet, Marcel, and Gladys Swain. *La pratique de l'esprit humain: L'institution asilaire et la révolution démocratique*. Paris: Gallimard, 1980.

Gilbrin, Émile. "La lignée médicale des Pinel, leur aide aux prisonniers politiques sous la Terreur et pendant la Restauration." *Histoire des Sciences Médicales* 11 (1977): 69–79.

Gineste, Thierry. *Le lion de Florence: Sur l'imaginaire des fondateurs de la psychiatrie, Pinel (1745–1826) et Itard (1774–1838)*. Paris: Albin Michel, 2004.

Glazer, Catherine. "De la Commune comme maladie mentale." *Romantisme* 48 (1985): 63–70.

Godineau, Dominique. "Pratiques du suicide à Paris pendant la Révolution française." *French History and Civilization: Papers from the Georges Rudé Seminar* 1 (2005): 126–40.

Goffman, Erving. *Asiles*. Paris: Minuit, 1968.

Goldstein, Jan. *Console and Classify: The French Psychiatric Profession in the Nineteenth Century*. Cambridge: Cambridge University Press, 1990.

Gourévitch, Michel. "Qui soignera le divin marquis? Documents inédits sur les conflits de pouvoirs entre directeur et médecin à Charenton en 1812." *Perspectives Psychiatriques* 2, no. 96 (1984): 85–91.

Greer, Donald. *The Incidence of the Terror during the Revolution: A Statistical Interpretation*. Cambridge, MA: Harvard University Press, 1935.

Grmek, Mirko D. "Histoire des recherches sur les relations entre le génie et la maladie." *Revue d'Histoire des Sciences et de Leurs Applications* 15, no. 1 (1962): 51–68.

———. *Les maladies à l'aube de la civilisation occidentale*. Paris: Payot, 1983.

Guérin, J.-L., F. Collet, and P. Hostiou. "Ulysse Trélat, ou La tentation eugéniste." *Revue Française de Psychiatrie et de Psychologie Médicale*, January 2002.

Gueslin, André, and Dominique Kalifa, eds. *Les exclus en Europe: 1830–1930*. Paris: Éditions de l'Atelier, 1999.

Gullickson, Gay L. "La Pétroleuse: Representing Revolution." *Feminist Studies* 17, no. 2 (Summer 1991): 240–65.

———. *Unruly Woman of Paris: Images of the Commune*. Ithaca, NY: Cornell University Press, 1996.

Haustgen, Thierry. "Les débuts difficiles du Dr Royer-Collard à Charenton: État sommaire de la maison de Charenton sous le rapport du service médical et aperçu des réformes qui y sont nécessaires, Antoine-Athanase Royer-Collard, 1811." *Synapse* 58 (1989): 57–66.

———. *Observations et certificats psychiatriques au XIXe siècle*. Rueil-Malmaison: Ciba, 1985.

Jacob, Françoise. "Madness and Politics: French Nineteenth-Century Alienists' Response to Revolution." *History of Psychiatry* 6 (1995): 421–29.

Jean, Thierry. "La folie est-elle une question idéologique?" *Journal Français de Psychiatrie* 19 (2003): 4–8.

Jordanova, Ludmilla. "Medical Mediations: Mind, Body and the Guillotine." *History Workshop* 28 (Autumn 1989): 39–52.

Juchet, Jack. "Jean-Baptiste Pussin, 'médecin des folles.'" *Soins Psychiatrie* 142/143 (August/September 1992): 46–54.

Keller, Richard C. *Colonial Madness: Psychiatry in French North Africa*. Chicago: University of Chicago Press, 2007.

Kromm, Jane. "'Marianne' and the Madwomen." *Art Journal* 46, no. 4 (Winter 1987): 299–304.

Lacan, Jacques. *Écrits*, 2 vols. Paris: Seuil, 1999. Translated by Bruce Fink as *Écrits: The First Complete Edition in English*. New York: W. W. Norton, 2007.

Lantéri-Laura, Georges. *Lecture des perversions: Histoire de leur appropriation médicale*. Paris: Masson, 1979.

Le Brun, Annie. *On n'enchaîne pas les volcans*. Paris: Gallimard, 2006.

———, ed. *Petits et grands théâtres du marquis de Sade*. Paris: Paris Art Center, 1989.

———. *Soudain, un bloc d'abîme, Sade*. Paris: Jean-Jacques Pauvert, 1986.

Lely, Gilbert. *Vie du marquis de Sade*. Rev. ed. Paris: Jean-Jacques Pauvert, 1965.

Lenormand, Frédéric. *La pension Belhomme: Une prison de luxe sous la Terreur*. Paris: Fayard, 2002.

Lenôtre, Georges. *La guillotine et les exécuteurs des arrêts criminels pendant la*

Révolution d'après des documents inédits tirés des Archives de l'État. Paris: Perrin, 1910.

———. *Paris révolutionnaire: Vieilles maisons, vieux papiers*. Paris: Perrin, 1922.

Lever, Maurice. *Donatien Alphonse François, marquis de Sade*. Paris: Fayard, 1991.

Lidsky, Paul. *Les écrivains contre la Commune*. Paris: Maspero, 1970.

Mall, Laurence. "Révolution, traumatisme et non-savoir: La 'longue surprise' dans *Le nouveau Paris* de Mercier." *Études Littéraires* 38, no. 1 (Autumn 2006): 11–23.

Micale, Mark S., and Paul Lerner. *Traumatic Pasts: History, Psychiatry and Trauma in the Modern Age, 1870–1930*. Cambridge: Cambridge University Press, 2001.

Morel, Pierre. *Dictionnaire biographique de la psychiatrie*. Le Plessis-Robinson: Synthélabo/Les Empêcheurs de Penser en Rond, 1996.

Pauvert, Jean-Jacques. *Sade vivant*. 3 vols. Paris: Robert Laffont, 1986–90.

Pigeaud, Jackie. *Aux portes de la psychiatrie: Pinel, l'ancien et le moderne*. Paris: Aubier, 2001.

Pinon, Pierre. *L'hospice de Charenton*. Brussels: P. Mardaga, 1989.

Postel, Jacques. *Éléments pour une histoire de la psychiatrie occidentale*. Paris: Harmattan, 2007.

———. *Genèse de la psychiatrie: Les premiers écrits de Philippe Pinel*. Le Plessis-Robinson: Synthélabo/Les Empêcheurs de Penser en Rond, 1998.

———. "Les premières expériences psychiatriques de Philippe Pinel à la maison de santé Belhomme." *Revue Canadienne de Psychiatrie* 28, no. 7 (November 1983): 571–75.

Postel, Jacques, and Claude Quétel, *Nouvelle histoire de la psychiatrie*. Paris: Dunod, 1994.

Quétel, Claude. *Histoire de la folie, de l'antiquité à nos jours*. Paris: Tallendier, 2009.

———. *Images de la folie*. Paris: Gallimard, 2010.

Quétel, Claude, and Jean-Yves Simon. "L'aliénation alcoolique en France (XIXe siècle et 1ere moitié du XXe siècle)." *Histoire, Économie et Société* 7, no. 4 (1988): 507–33.

Renneville, Marc. *Le langage des crânes: Une histoire de la phrénologie*. Le Plessis-Robinson: Insitut d'Édition Sanofi-Synthélabo/Les Empêcheurs de Penser en Rond, 2000.

———. *La médecine du crime: Essai sur l'émergence d'un regard médical sur la criminalité en France (1785–1885)*. 2 vols. Paris: Presses Universitaires du Septentrion, 2000.

Reverzy, Jean-François. "Sade à Charenton: Une scène primitive de l'aliénisme." *L'Information Psychiatrique* 53, no. 10 (1977): 1169–81.

Riot-Sarcet, Michèle, and Maurizio Gribaudi. 1848, *La révolution oubliée*. Paris: Découverte, 2008.

Roudinesco, Elisabeth. *Théroigne de Méricourt: A Melancholic Woman during the French Revolution*. Translated by Martin Thom. London: Verso, 1991.

Saucerotte, Constant. *Les médecins pendant la Révolution*. Paris: Perrin, 1887.

Sibalis, Michael. "Un aspect de la légende noire de Napoléon: Le mythe de l'en-

fermement des opposants comme fous." *Revue de l'Institut Napoléon* 156, no. 1 (1991): 9–24.
———. "L'enfermement de Théodore Desorgues: Documents inédits." *Annales Historiques de la Révolution Française* 284 (1991): 243–46.
Sironi, Françoise. *Psychologie des violences collectives: Essai de psychologie géopolitique clinique*. Paris: Odile Jacob, 2007.
Sournia, Jean-Charles. *La médecine révolutionnaire, 1789–1799*. Paris: Payot, 1989.
———. "Révolution française et troubles mentaux, 1789–1799." *Vesalius* 3, no. 2 (December 1997): 67–73.
Starobinski, Jean. *Histoire du traitement de la mélancolie des origines à 1900*. Basel: Laboratoires Geigy, 1960.
Swain, Gladys. *Dialogue avec l'insensé*. Paris: Gallimard, 1994.
———. *Le sujet de la folie*. Paris: Calmann-Lévy, 1977.
Szasz, Thomas. "The Sane Slave: An Historical Note on the Use of Medical Diagnosis as Justificatory Rhetoric." *American Journal of Psychotherapy* 25 (1971): 228–39.
Tulard, Jean, ed. *Dictionnaire du Second Empire*. Paris: Fayard, 1995.
———, ed. *Dictionnaire Napoléon*. Paris: Fayard, 1999.
Vasak, Anouchka. "Révolution et aliénation: Aux origines du 'mal du siècle.'" In *Romantisme et Révolution(s): Entretiens de la fondation des Treilles*, ed. Robert Kopp et al. Paris: Gallimard, 2010.
Vincienne, Olivier. "La maison de santé Belhomme: Légende et réalité." *Paris et Île-de-France: Mémoires Publiés par la Fédération des Sociétés Historiques et Archéologiques de Paris et de l'Île-de-France* 36 (1985): 135–208.
Vovelle, Michel. "Notes complémentaires sur le poète Théodore Desorgues, ou Quand les inconnus se font connaître." *Annales Historiques de la Révolution Française* 265 (1986): 341–45.
Weiner, Dora B. "The Apprenticeship of Philippe Pinel: A New Document, 'Observations of Citizen Pussin on the Insane.'" *American Journal of Psychiatry* 136, no. 9 (September 1979): 1128–34.
———. *Comprendre et soigner: Philippe Pinel (1745–1826), la médecine de l'esprit*. Paris: Fayard, 1999.
———. "Philippe Pinel (1745–1826) clerc tonsuré." *Annales Médico-psychologiques* 149, no. 2 (1991), 169–73.
———. "Philippe Pinel et l'abolition des chaînes: Un document retrouvé." *Information Psychiatrique* 56, no. 2 (1980): 245–53.
———. "Un registre inédit de la première clinique psychiatrique à Paris entre 1802 et 1808: Jean Étienne Dominique Esquirol et ses malades." In *XXXIe Congrès International d'Histoire de la Médecine*, 543–50. Bologna: Monduzzi, 1988.
Williams, Roger L. "Revolution and Madness: Blanqui and Trélat." *Journal of the Historical Society* 5, no. 2 (2005): 227–52.

Index

Page numbers followed by the letter *f* refer to figures.